PART I. Educational Television in Perspective: *The Development of Educational Television*, Allen E. Koenig. *A Philosophy of Educational Television*, Martin J. Maloney.

PART II. Educational Stations and Networks: *The Four Faces of Educational Television*, Frederick Breitenfeld, Jr. *The University Station*, Lee Sherman Dreyfus. *The Community Station*, J. Michael Collins. *Problems Peculiar to the Community Station*, John C. Schwarzwalder. *National Educational Television as the Fourth Network*, John F. White. *NET and Affiliate Relationships*, Gerard L. Appy. *The Regional Network*, Donald R. Quayle.

PART III. Instructional Television: *The Development of Instructional Television*, Beverly J. Taylor. *Closed-Circuit Television in Training and Education*, Gary Gumpert.

PART IV. Problems and Issues in Educational Television: *On Earning a Nonprofit*, Kenneth Harwood. *Trends in Station Programming*, Jack G. McBride. *Meaningful Research in ETV*, John M. Kittross. *Rights for Television Teachers*, Allen E. Koenig.

PART V. Education for Educational Television Personnel: *Toward a Better Curriculum in Broadcasting and Film*, Stanley T. Donner. *A Curriculum for Educational Television*, Donel W. Price. *Internship in ETV Management*, James L. Loper. *Training Teachers for Television Utilization*, Charles F. Hunter.

PART VI. The Future of Educational Television: *The Role of Space Communications in ETV*, Russell B. Barber. *Summary and a Look Ahead at ETV*, Ruane B. Hill.

THE FARTHER VISION

The Farther Vision

EDUCATIONAL TELEVISION TODAY

EDITED BY

Allen E. Koenig AND
Ruane B. Hill

The University of Wisconsin Press
Madison, Milwaukee, and London, 1967

Published by
The University of Wisconsin Press
Madison, Milwaukee, and London
U.S.A.: Box 1379, Madison, Wisconsin 53701
U.K.: 26–28 Hallam Street, London, W. 1

Printed in the United States of America by
North Central Publishing Co., St. Paul, Minnesota

Library of Congress Catalog Card Number 67-25946

Contributors

GERARD L. APPY is vice president for network affairs of National Educational Television. He is a graduate of the University of Washington, where he earned a B.A. degree. Following World War II service as a Marine Corps dive bomber pilot, Mr. Appy worked professionally in the legitimate theater, commercial radio, and television. As associate director of the Georgia Center for Continuing Education (1955–65) he managed WGTV. He is a former chairman of the NET Affiliates Committee and member of the NAEB Board of Directors, and was vice president of Educational Television Stations during the first year of that organization's establishment.

RUSSELL B. BARBER is manager of community relations for WCBS-TV in New York City. His higher education includes the B.A. degree from the University of Puget Sound, M.A. degree from Stanford University, and the Ph.D. degree from Northwestern University. Dr. Barber has taught as an instructor in the speech department of Loyola University in Chicago. Currently he is a part-time instructor in the speech departments both of Hunter

College and of New York University. His publications have appeared in the *Journal of Broadcasting* and *Telefilm International Magazine*.

FREDERICK BREITENFELD, JR., is executive director of the Maryland Educational-Cultural Television Commission. He holds four degrees: B.S. and M.Ed. from Tufts University, M.S. and Ph.D. from Syracuse University. Dr. Breitenfeld has held various positions in education. Among his professional activities in broadcasting, he has been associate director of Educational Television Stations, a division of the National Association of Educational Broadcasters (1965–66); project director of the NAEB-ETS Study on the Long-Range Financing of Educational Television Stations (1964–65); director of the Air Force Eastern Test Range Television Office at Cape Kennedy (1963–64); and a producer, writer, and performer for General Electric's Television Demonstrations (1962). His numerous publications have appeared in such periodicals as the *Saturday Evening Post, Adult Leadership, Journal of Broadcasting, NAEB Journal, Television Quarterly*, and the *American School Board Journal*.

J. MICHAEL COLLINS is general manager of WNED-TV in Buffalo, New York. He received a B.S. degree from Canisius College and attended graduate school at Michigan State University. Before assuming his present position, Mr. Collins was assistant station manager, director of development, and promotion manager at WNED. He previously taught in the Buffalo public schools, at Michigan State University, and Mount St. Joseph College. Currently treasurer of the Eastern Educational Network, he is a former president of the New York State Educational Radio and Television Association, and the Public Relations Association of Western New York.

STANLEY T. DONNER is professor and chairman of the department of radio, television, and film, School of Communication, at the University of Texas. He received the B.A. degree from the University of Michigan; M.A. and Ph.D. degrees from Northwestern University. Dr. Donner was formerly associate head of the department of communication at Stanford University. He has received two Fulbright grants — for research in Paris, 1955–56, and as a lecturer, University of London, 1963–64. He is an author in Wilbur Schramm's *Educational Television: The Next Ten Years*, and is editor of *The Future of Commercial Television, 1965–1975*. He has also been the author of a number of journal articles.

LEE SHERMAN DREYFUS is professor of speech and chairman of the division of radio, television, and film at the University of Wisconsin. He received the B.A., M.A., and Ph.D. degrees at the University of Wisconsin. Among his previously held positions were general manager of WDET, Wayne State University; general manager of WHA-TV at the University of Wisconsin; and associate director of instructional television at the same institution. Dr. Dreyfus' publications have appeared in such periodicals as *NAEB Journal, American School Board Journal*, and the *Bulletin of Secondary School Principals*. One of his most noteworthy creative achievements was as producer-director of the "First Intercontinental TV Classroom Exchange — Wisconsin to France" via the Early Bird Satellite on May 31, 1965.

GARY GUMPERT is associate professor of communication arts and sciences at Queens College of the City University of New York. He received the B.S. degree from Temple University, the M.A. degree from Michigan State University, and the Ph.D. degree from Wayne State University. While at Wayne State he served as a producer-director for the university and WTVS-TV. From 1961 until the first part of 1963, Dr. Gumpert was a lecturer at Queens College. From 1963 to 1967 he was director of instructional television development and utilization and assistant professor in the division of radio-television-education at the University of Wisconsin. His publications appear in *NAEB Journal* and *Social Work Education Reporter.*

KENNETH HARWOOD is professor of communications and telecommunications and chairman of the department of telecommunications at the University of Southern California, at the time this book goes to press. As of February 1, 1968, he will be dean of the School of Communications and Theater, Temple University, Philadelphia. He received his B.A., M.A., and Ph.D. degrees from the University of Southern California. Dr. Harwood was chairman of the department of radio and television at the University of Alabama from 1950 to 1954. He is the former president of the National Society for the Study of Communication (1956), the Association for Professional Broadcasting Education (1957–58), and the American Association of University Professors at the University of Southern California (1960). His many publications appear in a variety of periodicals, including the *Journal of Broadcasting.*

RUANE B. HILL is associate professor of speech and director of the Instructional Communications Center at the University of Wisconsin-Milwaukee. He holds the B.A. degree from Beloit College and both the M.A. and Ph.D. degrees from Northwestern University. Dr. Hill previously worked in broadcasting at KFGW, Spokane, Washington; WFGM, Fitchburg, Massachusetts; and WMRC, Milford, Massachusetts. He has taught at Northwestern University, Beloit College, and Syracuse University.

CHARLES F. HUNTER is a joint professor of speech and education and chairman of the department of radio, television, and film at Northwestern University. He holds the B.S. and B.A. degrees from Southeast Missouri State College; the M.A. degree from the University of Wisconsin; and the Ph.D. degree from Cornell University. He previously taught at the University of Missouri and Cornell University. In addition to his duties at Northwestern he has been educational television producer for NBC in Chicago (1952–66), Northwestern University area coordinator for Midwest Program on Airborne Television (1962–64), and director of the Institute for Educational Media Specialists (NDEA, Title XI) at Northwestern (1965, 1967). Dr. Hunter was instrumental in initiating at Northwestern a joint School of Education and Speech M.A. program in educational television.

JOHN M. KITTROSS is associate professor of telecommunications and communications in the University of Southern California. He will join the Temple University School of Communications and Theater as professor of communications in the fall of 1968. He earned his B.A. degree from Antioch College, his M.S. degree from Boston University, and the Ph.D. degree in communications from the University of Illinois. Dr. Kittross has been editor of the *Journal of Broadcasting* since 1960. He has worked in educational broadcasting in a number of capacities at such stations as WNYE, WNYC, WBUR, and WILL-TV. He was also employed in commercial broadcasting, and as a faculty member of the United States Army Psychological Warfare School. His articles and reviews have appeared in *American Psychologist, Journal of Communication, Audio-Visual Communication Review, Journalism Quarterly*, and the *Journal of Broadcasting*.

ALLEN E. KOENIG is assistant professor of speech at Ohio State University and editor of the *Educational Broadcasting Review* (formerly *NAEB Journal*). He received the B.A. degree from the University of Southern California, the M.A. degree from Stanford University, and the Ph.D. degree from Northwestern University. Dr. Koenig previously worked as a news editor at KFAC, Los Angeles (1959–61), and an editorial writer for KPIX-TV in San Francisco (1962). He was director of broadcasting instruction at Eastern Michigan University (1964–65) and assistant professor of speech at the University of Wisconsin-Milwaukee (1965–67). His publications appear in the *Journal of Broadcasting, NAEB Journal,* and *Preaching: A Journal of Homiletics.*

JAMES L. LOPER is general manager for Los Angeles educational television, KCET. He received his B.A. degree from Arizona State University; M.A. degree from the University of Denver; and the Ph.D. degree from the University of Southern California. Dr. Loper was formerly director of educational television and assistant professor of speech at the California State College at Los Angeles (1960–64); from 1953 to 1959 he was assistant director and acting director of the Bureau of Broadcasting at Arizona State University; his commercial broadcasting experience included work as a news editor and announcer for KTAR at Phoenix, Arizona. His publications have appeared in *Western Speech, ETRA News, Journal of Broadcasting, NAEB Journal, Journal of the University Film Producers' Association,* and the *Journal of the Society of Motion Picture and Television Engineers.*

JACK G. McBRIDE is director of television and general manager for the University of Nebraska television station, KUON. He received his B.A. degree from Creighton University and the M.A. degree from Northwestern University. Mr. McBride is also general manager of the developing seven-station Nebraska state-wide educational television network. Previously he was a television producer-director and instructor of speech at Wayne State University and director of radio, television, and drama at Creighton University. His commercial experience was with NBC-TV in Chicago as a production assistant. Mr. McBride's publications have appeared in the *Reading Teacher, Journal of the University Film Producers Association,* and *GPL Education.* He has also been the author of two pamphlets on instructional television and numerous consultant reports both in the United States and abroad.

MARTIN J. MALONEY is professor of speech at Northwestern University. He holds B.A. and M.A. degrees from the University of Kansas, and the Ph.D. degree from Northwestern University. Dr. Maloney is a retired major in the United States Marine Corps Reserve. He has taught at the University of Kansas, St. Mary's College (Leavenworth, Kansas), Cornell University, Iowa State College, Central YMCA Schools, University of Chicago, DePaul University, Mundelein College, and Stanford University. Also, he has written and/or performed in approximately four hundred radio, television, and film programs, for which he has received a number of awards, including citations from the National Conference of Christians and Jews and the Thomas Alva Edison Foundation. He is the author of numerous articles in professional journals and of chapters in textbooks, e.g., *Educational Television: The Next Ten Years* and *An Introduction to Graduate Study in Speech and Theatre.*

DONEL W. PRICE is director of broadcasting services and assistant professor of television administration at the California State College at Los Angeles. He received the B.A. degree from Occidental College and the M.A. degree from the University of Southern California. Currently he is a Ph.D. candidate in communications at Southern California. Mr. Price is past national student president of Alpha Epsilon Rho (national radio and television honorary fraternity) and is currently its national executive secretary. Previously he worked for the *Journal of Broadcasting* as its business manager and was a research associate for the California State Colleges.

DONALD R. QUAYLE is director of the Eastern Educational Network in Cambridge, Massachusetts. He received both the B.S. and M.S. degrees from Utah State University, and is currently working toward the Ph.D. degree from Ohio State University. From October 1960 through July 1962 he was assistant general manager for WGBH in Boston. In July 1962 he became director of radio services for the National Educational Television Radio Center (now NET). From November 1963 to June 1964 he was field services associate for National Educational Television.

JOHN C. SCHWARZWALDER is executive vice president and general manager of the Twin City Area Educational Television Corporation (operator of KTCA-TV and KTCI-TV and colicensee of KWCM-TV) in St. Paul, Minnesota. He received the B.A. degree from Ohio State University; M.Mus. and M.A. degrees from the University of Michigan; and the Ed.D. degree from the University of Houston. Dr. Schwarzwalder, from 1948 to 1956, was professor and chairman of the radio-television department of the University of Houston; from 1945 to 1948, he was cofounder and associate director of the Wall School of Music in Los Angeles. He presently serves as executive vice president of the Minnesota ETV network.

BEVERLY J. TAYLOR is communication analyst in the Educational Broadcasting Branch of the Federal Communications Commission. She received the B.A. degree in telecommunications from the University of Southern California. In addition to her work at the FCC, Miss Taylor is an active member of the American Women in Radio and Television.

JOHN F. WHITE is president of National Educational Television. He acquired the B.A. degree from Lawrence College and the M.A. degree from the University of Chicago. Also, he holds honorary doctorates from Lawrence College, Cornell College, and Hamilton College. Mr. White was previously general manager of WQED, Pittsburgh's educational television outlet (1955–58); director of admissions, dean of students, and dean and director of the development program for the Illinois Institute of Technology (1944–50); and vice president of Western Reserve University (1950–55). In 1962 he was appointed by President Kennedy to the advisory committee of the National Cultural Center. In 1965 he was appointed cochairman of the Cultural and Intellectual Exchange Section of the White House Conference on International Cooperation.

Preface

HISTORICALLY, educational television (ETV) in the United States is over thirty years old. During the past decade interest has quickened and the study of educational television has made conspicuous progress. However, no published work has explored the entire field of ETV. It is the purpose of this book to survey those significant elements that constitute ETV and to put them into perspective.

As defined here, educational television is a medium which disseminates programs devoted to information, instruction, cultural or public affairs, and entertainment. The word *medium* connotes any means employed to transmit an educational program; that is, ETV may be sent either over the air or by closed circuit (wire or cable). Thus, ETV is a broad term encompassing all types of educational programming. ITV (instructional television), on the other hand, is only a part of ETV; it is a specialized service that provides either total or supplementary formal organized instruction.

While commercial television may also include educational programming (particularly in the entertainment category), the concern of this book is operations that concentrate solely on educational broadcasting. Examples are television station WHA of the University of Wisconsin, Madison, which engages in both ETV and ITV programming; KCET, a community-owned Los Angeles TV station, which presents similar programs; the Hagerstown, Maryland, school system, which offers ITV over closed-circuit television; New Trier Township (Winnetka, Illinois), which also programs ITV, but telecasts over a short-range, open-circuit system, called the 2500 megacycle band.

Clearly, educational television may embrace a variety of combinations in planning and use. To prepare this book, we solicited articles from specialists familiar with the many facets of ETV. The six broad divisions of the volume deal with (1) the historical and philosophical foundations of ETV, (2) the problems and operations of "on the air," or open-circuit, TV stations telecasting to both local and national audiences, (3) the development and use of ITV and closed-circuit television, (4) specific problems such as financing, or research, (5) the training considered desirable for either the ETV specialist or the classroom teacher, and (6) the potential of space communication in ETV. The book closes with a summary of the achievements and a look at the future of educational television.

We wish to make grateful acknowledgment to our contributing authors for their cooperation and especially for their continuing efforts, through last minute revisions, to keep their chapters as up to date as possible.

A. E. K.
R. B. H.

June 1967

Contents

CONTRIBUTORS v

PREFACE xv

Part I: Educational Television in Perspective

1 THE DEVELOPMENT OF EDUCATIONAL TELEVISION 3
Allen E. Koenig

2 A PHILOSOPHY OF EDUCATIONAL TELEVISION 11
Martin J. Maloney

Part II: Educational Stations and Networks

3 THE FOUR FACES OF EDUCATIONAL TELEVISION 35
Frederick Breitenfeld, Jr.

4 THE UNIVERSITY STATION 51
Lee Sherman Dreyfus

5 THE COMMUNITY STATION 69
J. Michael Collins

6 PROBLEMS PECULIAR TO THE COMMUNITY STATION 79
John C. Schwarzwalder

7 NATIONAL EDUCATIONAL TELEVISION AS THE
FOURTH NETWORK 87
John F. White

8 NET AND AFFILIATE RELATIONSHIPS 97
Gerard L. Appy

9 THE REGIONAL NETWORK 107
Donald R. Quayle

Part III: Instructional Television

10 THE DEVELOPMENT OF INSTRUCTIONAL TELEVISION 133
Beverly J. Taylor

Contents

11 CLOSED-CIRCUIT TELEVISION IN TRAINING
    AND EDUCATION   155
                                    Gary Gumpert

Part IV: Problems and Issues in Educational Television

12 ON EARNING A NONPROFIT   185
                                    Kenneth Harwood

13 TRENDS IN STATION PROGRAMMING   197
                                    Jack G. McBride

14 MEANINGFUL RESEARCH IN ETV   209
                                    John M. Kittross

15 RIGHTS FOR TELEVISION TEACHERS   247
                                    Allen E. Koenig

Part V: Education for Educational Television Personnel

16 TOWARD A BETTER CURRICULUM IN BROADCASTING
    AND FILM   263
                                    Stanley T. Donner

17 A CURRICULUM FOR EDUCATIONAL TELEVISION   279
                                    Donel W. Price

18 INTERNSHIP IN ETV MANAGEMENT   293
                                    James L. Loper

19 TRAINING TEACHERS FOR TELEVISION UTILIZATION   299
                                    Charles F. Hunter

Part VI: The Future of Educational Television

20 THE ROLE OF SPACE COMMUNICATIONS IN ETV   311
                                    Russell B. Barber

21 SUMMARY AND A LOOK AHEAD AT ETV   337
                                    Ruane B. Hill

    APPENDIX 1: THE FINDINGS OF THE CARNEGIE COMMISSION
    ON EDUCATIONAL TELEVISION   359

    APPENDIX 2: THE PUBLIC BROADCASTING ACT OF 1967   363

    INDEX   367

Part I

EDUCATIONAL TELEVISION IN PERSPECTIVE

The Development of Educational Television

TODAY, many people all over the world are receiving education, information, and culture from educational television (ETV). The United States, Great Britain, France, Yugoslavia, Poland, Soviet Russia, Communist China, Japan, and Colombia are some of the many countries whose populace is viewing ETV.

In Europe, the growth of educational television commenced with the British Broadcasting Company and Radiodiffusion Télévision Française presenting enrichment programs for schools during the early 1950's. In 1958, Italy introduced direct television instruction on a national basis through its *Telescuola* or television school of the air.[1]

The Communist block of nations received ETV for the first time in 1960. Yugoslavia first introduced educational television programming, with Poland starting at about the same time. Since 1962, Soviet television has given a great deal of attention to both its adult and school ETV programming. By 1965, most of the other Eastern European satellites offered regular school broadcasts. In 1962, Communist China began offering university course work in such subjects as chemistry and physics through its Shanghai TV station. Also, its stations in Peking, Tientsin, Canton,

3

and Harbin have offered "television universities" as part of the country's national worker education drive.

Japan has become one of today's world leaders in educational television. It "is the first country in the world that has fully integrated television into its education structure from kindergarten to university-level studies and into the broad field of adult instruction."[2] By 1965, Japan had forty-six ETV stations programming throughout the nation.

Latin America has carried on ambitious ETV programming since the late 1950's. The leader of this movement has been Colombia. This country offers a full range of primary school subjects over a national network during regular school hours. Through the help of the United States Peace Corps, Colombia has become a model ETV country.

Although the growth of educational television has been worldwide, its development is best illustrated by experience in the United States. From May 1953 to May 1967, United States educational television grew from a one-station operation to a complex of over 140 ETV stations reaching a population of 140 million persons. It has been estimated that some fifteen million students receiving elementary, secondary, and higher education, in over two thousand schools, are today obtaining either part or total instruction from television. Since 1963, the Federal Communications Commission (FCC) has received sixty-four applications for 197 channels in the Instructional Television Fixed Service (ITFS, or 2500 megacycle band). Finally, about one thousand closed-circuit TV systems are operating in both public and private education, in service agencies, and in industry.[3]

This tremendous growth of ETV in America did not occur in a matter of a few years. Probably the early experiments with educational radio in the 1920's presented ETV with its first model. That is, education could provide a separate programming service. The actual development of ETV, however, is best traced through its programming, frequency allocations, financing, and networking.

Educational television was introduced as a "second" service for the dissemination of cultural, informational, and educational programming. The first experiments with ETV were probably those that took place at the University of Iowa between 1932 and 1939. Over four hundred programs appeared on Iowa's W9XK, with such subjects as engineering, botany, art, drama, and shorthand being presented. In all, five American colleges and universities pioneered the field of ETV. They were the University of Iowa (Iowa City), Iowa State University (Ames), Kansas State University, the University of Michigan, and American University.[4]

In 1948, the FCC indirectly afforded educators an opportunity to bid for federally assigned frequencies. When the Commission issued its famous "freeze" that year, it stipulated that no new television licenses would be issued until it had re-evaluated how television air waves were to be distributed.

By 1950, educators fully realized the potential of educational television. However, they were not organized as a unified educational body that could influence the FCC's decision on ETV frequencies. In fact, a number of different educational groups prepared petitions for the purpose of reserving ETV channels. Some of these pleas contradicted one another. For example, some educators wanted nonprofit educational television while others wanted noncommercial ETV, and still others wanted both. Thus one group did not want ETV to yield a profit, but would have found commercialism an acceptable means of support. The other group did not want any type of commercials presented over ETV. Finally, in October, both the radio chief for the United States Office of Education and the president of the National Association of Educational Broadcasters (NAEB) brought the educators together by forming an *ad hoc* Joint Committee on Educational Television. This organization later came under the auspices of the American Council on Education.[5] Thereafter, the educators called upon the FCC to reserve a number of television channels for the exclusive use of education. They proposed to operate these channels as both nonprofit and noncommercial undertakings.

The FCC answered the educators' plea in its *Sixth Report and*

Order. Some 242 television channels (80 VHF and 162 UHF) were reserved for the exclusive use of ETV. By 1966, these allocations had been increased to 116 VHF and 516 UHF channels. Under the allocation plan of 1952, KUHT, licensed to both the Houston Board of Education and the University of Houston, became the first station on the air (May 12, 1953). By 1962, there were 62 educationally owned ETV stations operating, and by 1967, over 140. Of these ETV outlets on the air, about one-third are licensed to local or state educational systems, another third to colleges or universities, and a final third to community organizations. Those stations or operations employing closed-circuit television are not licensed by the FCC unless they are responsible for operating Community Antenna Television Systems (CATV).[6]

In 1963, the FCC enlarged the broadcast spectrum by allocating a number of low-powered, super ultra high frequency channels for the use of local education. Instructional Television Fixed Service provides an inexpensive point-to-point school service that is limited to small coverage areas and must be received by pre-tuned multiplex equipment. The new channels do not replace any of the current VHF or UHF channels.

From ETV's early history to the present, its management has looked to a number of sources for its support. Often its financial base has been sorely inadequate. In 1965, the average ETV station's income was only $370,000 a year.[7] Top-rated movies on network television cost more per feature than the total average ETV budget for one year.[8] Recently, a number of different suggestions have been offered for adequately financing ETV. These proposed solutions have included everything from putting on a commercial station telethon for ETV to establishing a special satellite system that would support ETV programming.[9] To date, federal support has been mainly limited to the construction or improvement of ETV facilities. However, the Ford Foundation has given some $120 million to educational television on a nation-wide basis.[10] Even this amount, however, does not permit ETV to operate a regular "live" network. Currently, educational television is supported in the following pattern:

. . . On the average, stations operated by colleges and universities and by school systems obtain about 75% of their income from direct-budgeted support. Stations operated by state agencies receive about 95% of their funds from state appropriations. Community stations, on the other hand, receive about 75% of their support from gifts, grants, and services, the latter primarily for the production of in-school programs. ITFS systems are supported by the local institutional licensee, in some instances with the aid of federal grants.[11]

Networking educational television has been traditionally operated on a delayed basis. Since its modest start in 1954, National Educational Television (NET) has been the primary "network" of informational and cultural programming for ETV. NET supplies tapes and films to more than one hundred ETV stations throughout the United States. Each week, individual affiliates receive five hours of new ETV programming, or a total of 260 hours per year. Separate stations may also draw upon NET's vast film and videotape library for additional programming.[12] In order for an ETV station to become a National Educational Television affiliate, it must meet the following conditions:

1. The station must be committed to a policy of providing a general educational, cultural, and informational service which can be viewed in homes.
2. The station agrees to schedule programs for broadcast in such a way as to allow viewing by the audience for which the program is intended by NET.
3. The station coverage must provide service to a major area and/or population segment not served by any existing NET affiliate. This third condition was established primarily in response to the affiliated stations' desire that their network service not be duplicated by other ETV stations serving the same coverage area.

The remaining conditions for affiliation deal with technical, promotional, and procedural requirements. Prior to 1964, there were affiliation fees based upon population within the station's coverage area and scaled from a minimum of $7,200 to a maximum of $18,700 annually. In 1964, the affiliation fee was replaced by a token annual membership payment of $100.[13]

NET has been mainly supported in past years by the Ford Foundation. In recent years, it has annually received $6 million from the Foundation. This type of support, as mentioned previously, does not ordinarily permit NET to interconnect the entire country with a live network, as do the commercial networks. Fred Friendly, former president of CBS News and now the Edward R. Murrow Professor of Journalism at Columbia University and television consultant to the Ford Foundation, has predicted that 1967 would be the "year in which distance dies" for ETV.[14] Live interconnection and substantial support for a community type of programming will probably be made available in the near future. In January 1967, the Carnegie Commission on Educational Television unveiled its plan for making these goals possible. In March, President Johnson submitted to Congress the "Public Broadcasting Act of 1967," incorporating the Carnegie recommendations and several new proposals. The Senate passed this bill in May, with a few amendments, and the House is expected to act favorably on it. (For a summary of the Carnegie report, see Appendix 1; of the Public Broadcasting Act, Appendix 2.)

Some other notable network operations in ETV include the Eastern Educational Television Network (EEN) and the National Center for School and College Television (NCSCT). During the first part of 1966, EEN was the only "live" interconnected ETV regional network in the country. It distributes both instructional and cultural programming to stations in Maine, New Hampshire, Massachusetts, and Connecticut. NCSCT commenced in 1965 to function as the national distributor of instructional television programming for all levels of education. A number of regional libraries, such as the Great Plains Library of Lincoln, Nebraska, also provide distribution of instructional programming.[15]

Thus, American educational television has achieved its current status through its past experiences in programming, frequency allocations, financing, and networking. The future development of ETV lies in its acceptance as an international resource. The next step in its development should be the world-wide sharing of knowledge and culture. It is hoped that the current satellite capability over both the Atlantic and the Pacific oceans will encourage electronic "people to people" exchanges. This may be the source of educational television's future history.

NOTES

1 Wilson P. Dizard, *Television: A World View* (Syracuse University Press, 1966), p. 210. This book is the source of information in the three paragraphs that follow, also; see pp. 222, 223, 233.

2 *Ibid.*, p. 223.

3 FCC, *Educational Television*, Information Bulletin No. 16-B (Washington, June 1966), p. 1.

4 Richard B. Hull, "A Note on the History Behind ETV," in *Educational Television: The Next Ten Years* (Stanford University: Institute for Communication Research, 1962), p. 334.

5 *Ibid.*, p. 341.

6 I am indebted for the statistics in this paragraph to Hull, in *ETV*, pp. 343, 335; and to FCC, *Educational Television*, pp. 1, 3.

7 FCC, *Educational Television*, p. 8.

8 "Highest Price for Movies?" *Broadcasting*, Aug. 30, 1965, p. 49.

9 See "The Four Plans: ABC, NBC, Ford, Comsat," *Broadcasting*, Aug. 8, 1966, p. 68; also "ETV Stimuli Outlined by Agency President," *Broadcasting*, Oct. 17, 1966, p. 60.

10 "A $16 Million Helping Hand," *Broadcasting*, Oct. 10, 1966, p. 56.

11 FCC, *Educational Television*, p. 7.

12 NET, *A Fact Book* (New York, Jan. 1966), p. 1. This pamphlet is available at NET headquarters, 10 Columbus Circle, New York 10019.

13 Information received in a letter to the author from Gerard L. Appy, of NET, Oct. 26, 1966.

14 Paper read before the national convention of the NAEB, Kansas City, Oct. 24, 1966.

15 FCC, *Educational Television*, p. 12.

A Philosophy of Educational Television

WHAT IS ETV? The question is ambiguous, and it is not our purpose here to consider whether what is broadcast on so-called educational television stations is ETV or community television or something else, or whether ETV should be distinguished from ITV (instructional) or CTV (commercial). Perhaps the most pertinent answer we can propose is one which puts ETV in a historical perspective. ETV is a direct descendant of educational radio, born under a far brighter star than its parent. In the early 1920's, when radio first became a means of public communication in the United States, the notion of using the new instrument for purposes of education occurred to some people, who were usually located in universities. Radio at the time was a popular fad, and educational radio shared the faddish characteristics. The enthusiasm for the idea seems to have derived from the feeling that here was a new wonder of science, which really ought to be tried out. A considerable number of broadcasting licenses went to educational institutions, usually colleges and universities, and most frequently to schools of engineering. The engineers were quite certain that a radio station would be useful to them in teaching radio engineering, and they thought that the programs, an unavoidable by-product, might also serve an educational purpose. The enthusiasm died rather quickly in most institutions, when professors of English and music and languages discovered that it was a good deal of trouble to prepare broadcasts. Educational licenses were given up, and frequently went to commercial broadcasters, who made a great deal of money with them. A hard core of educational radio stations continued to function; some of them are still on the air, and performing a useful service. But in the main the trouble with educational radio was that there was no pressing need for it, and not much money to support its programming.[1]

When television became the new broadcasting medium following World War II, the situation was different — and even more so in the 1950's, following the FCC "freeze" on the issuance of new television licenses. The American educational system was bracketed between the population explosion and the "knowledge explosion," and could no longer meet its responsibilities by conventional means. Moreover, very large sums of money were now available, from private foundations and from government at various levels, to support new educational projects. And as always in the American culture, there was the feeling that television was now the newest wonder of science, and thus must surely solve the educator's problems. It is not surprising that in 1952 the FCC set aside television channels exclusively for educational use, and that funds were forthcoming to build and maintain VHF stations, and later UHF stations and closed-circuit systems.

Behind all this complex activity, here so briefly summarized, lurks the assumption that television is simply a way of extending education more or less economically, of spreading scarce teaching talent thinner. The original thesis among educators seems to have been that the educational experiences provided by TV would be more or less the conventional ones, and that the teaching talent would perform on television much as in the classroom, but perhaps with better preparation. There was little indication that the new medium would make much difference to this process; indeed, a cursory survey of ETV research would suggest that some effort was devoted to proving that television did *not* make much difference. Literally hundreds of studies demonstrate that students can learn French, military courtesy, shorthand and typing, psychology, and so on, about as well by television as they can in the classroom; and that they can, moreover, learn these subjects in various times of day, and at various educational levels, just as they might in the classroom. The phrase, "no significant difference," as used in these studies, after a time becomes a cliché with positive overtones of humor.[2]

Still, the question "What is ETV?" continues to be raised, perhaps out of uneasiness. Behind this question, still unanswered, is concealed the more fundamental one: "What is television? What is the nature of television as a channel of communication?" But even this query is advanced tentatively, and the questioner is usually prepared to retreat if someone responds, "Why do you want to know?" There is some reason for a counterattack. After all, we have had television around, in one public way or another, since the New York World's Fair of 1939, and have been using it assiduously since the late 1940's. Moreover, television has been phenomenally successful in the United States; at the present writing we come closer and closer to 100 percent saturation, and current figures on television viewing suggest that we watch television almost as many hours per day as we sleep. Why then raise a question which seems purely academic?

The answer is: to determine the most effective ways of using television, educationally or otherwise. At present, we use the medium as a work horse, to transmit almost any kind of message which seems commercially or otherwise profitable, with almost no regard for the medium itself: old movies and older classroom lectures, quiz shows and spot coverage of rocket launchings, disasters occurring on camera, brain tumor operations in full color, and recorded music with the album jacket used as a visual. Television performs these miscellaneous functions more or less successfully, and the usual tendency among broadcasters is to ask no questions when affairs go well. But the question, academic or not, remains: If television serves us so well when subjected to this sort of work-horse, knockabout treatment, how much better might it serve us if we knew what we were doing?

ETV: SOME PRACTICAL ADVICE

In an essay entitled "Facts and Fallacies about New Media in Education," Donald Ely has summarized with admirable exactness the position of the American educational system vis-à-vis television:

> We know that over 40 million people are in school in our country and that nearly one-tenth of them are in higher education. How will we handle this flood?
>
> There is an explosion of knowledge. Oppenheimer has said that over 90% of the scientists who have ever lived are alive today. Literature in the field of chemistry doubles every eight and a half years.
>
> Add to these explosions the fact that we continue to report shortages of teachers and classrooms, and we end up with a simple statement of our total dilemma: there are so many, needing to learn so much, in so little time, and with so few teachers.
>
> The option to use or not to use new media in teaching is rapidly disappearing.[3]

Partly because of this situation, and partly because of the American tendency to think in severely pragmatic terms, television has usually been seen as one "practical" solution to a critical situation. As Henry Cassirer writes:

> Television is used in the United States more to compensate for deficiencies than to provide new resources for education which make a contribution to the best of schools. Such an approach has the strength of frank, self-critical examination which prepares the ground for overcoming present handicaps as rapidly and as effectively as is possible with the use of modern techniques. But it also has the limitation of assuming that this is necessarily the most suitable way to remedy the present situation and that the value of television lies in the long run in such emergency relief. Television is not a mere substitute for traditional ways of teaching. It is a medium with its own psychological and emotional appeal, able to transcend barriers of time and place, of disciplines and personalities. But the successful exploration of these contributions is hampered as long as there is a conflict between immediate needs and long-range objectives.[4]

Cassirer's point is well taken. ETV research has concentrated almost wholly on television-as-used (can we teach by television? who learns best by television? how do teachers feel about teaching by television?), to the exclusion of any interest in optimum uses of the medium. The Educational Media Study Panel [5] has raised the question "How can television contribute most to education?" and remarked that

The spectrum of instructional uses of television is not completely known. It is clear that there are some teaching acts it can do superlatively well. It can let a large number of students look into a microscope at the same time, or watch surgical procedures from close at hand. It can let a class watch an activity that would be spoiled by direct observation. But there are also some things it cannot do. It cannot conduct a seminar discussion efficiently. It cannot give specific and direct personal help. These uses and limitations are clear, but, how much longer the list may be is not known. [6]

This modest statement on ETV as a medium is of course welcome, but it is worth noting the much more blunt comment which prefaces it: "Television is a channel for conveying whatever is put into it." Which is to say, apparently, that if television has a logic of its own, it is one which can easily be bypassed.

How-to-do-it advice on planning ETV programs, preparing visuals, script-writing, and performance abounds in many of the standard works on the subject. The advice is universally based on "practical" experience of ETV as it has been used, rather than on any general knowledge of the medium. Thus Donald G. Tarbet's book, *Television and Our Schools*, [7] deals extensively in suggestions of this sort: "Wait to be cued by the floor manager before beginning to talk. . . . If the mike boom is being used, don't look up to see if it is there. The operator is responsible for that . . . . If you are to show a book or material before the camera, hold it at such an angle that the camera may focus on it" (pp. 174–75). Almost the only statement in the book that suggests the existence of principles peculiar to the medium occurs in the final chapter: "Certain courses lend themselves to presentation by television, especially those normally using lectures or demonstrations" (p. 236).

Costello and Gordon, in *Teach with Television*,[8] come somewhat closer to examining the medium and its educational potential; they include a chapter called "The Limits of Television," but open it with a statement which effectively reduces the likelihood of their doing what the title promises: "Television is a *means* of communication. It has neither integrity, brains or feelings. . . . Although many of us are inclined to treat it as if it had an essential moral or intellectual nature of its own, television has no ability *except* to communicate, but if used effectively it can communicate exceptionally well" (p. 24). Their subsequent discussion consists of an analysis of what television "can do" (actually, what it has done), such as staging lectures and demonstrations, panel discussions, and the like, and what it "can't do," such as handling abstract ideas, teaching seminars, and so on.

Further examination of this sort of discussion is hardly necessary here, except to say that it may be useful to the TV practitioner. But obviously, "practical" advice has to be based on practice; it says very little about the potential of ETV.

TV AS LANGUAGE

Edmund Carpenter and Marshall McLuhan, some years ago, suggested a useful metaphor to students of communication, namely, that any channel or medium of communication, whether gesture, telegraph, or printed words on a page, might be treated as a language, having its own vocabulary and grammar and (in the general semanticist's phrase) its own metaphysics, its own set of biases affecting use and response.[9] A communication medium, then, might be studied as a linguist would approach a new spoken tongue, asking, "What is it like? How is it used? What happens when it is used?" Such an inquiry might well lead to conclusions of value on the ultimate question, "How can it be used? What are the communicative limits of the medium?"

While we may not choose to take the "television as language" metaphor with complete literalness, we would hold to it long enough to cite a linguistic maxim which suggests the nature of the problems involved in any such investigation. The maxim is, You can say anything you want to in any language you choose, if you are ingenious enough, and wish to invest enough time and effort. An astrophysicist might, with enough cleverness and trouble, learn to convey his special knowledge in American Indian sign language, or in the tongue of the Australian bushmen. Nor should we make snap judgments about what may seem odd choices of language-media; is not Einstein supposed to have replied to a request that he "explain relativity simply" by saying, "I can't explain it to you, but I can play it on my violin"?

In any case, our tentative attitude toward television at this moment is that while an ingenious manipulator of the medium might use it to say difficult and ordinarily inappropriate things, or while clumsy and insensitive entrepreneurs may realize only a low percentage of its potential, there is nevertheless a certain area of communication in which television works with maximum effectiveness on a relatively low expenditure of cleverness, and this because of its own peculiar nature. We have no objection to the "ingenious manipulator" of television who forces the medium to transcend itself through sheer skill and creative imagination — when, and if, he appears. But the fact is that television is a public medium, dealing daily in vast quantities of information, and in consequence must produce the best results on a small investment of talent and energy.

THE MEDIUM OF TELEVISION: TWO CRITICAL ANALYSES

If we turn to the literature on television as a medium, we find it remarkably scanty. In the late 1940's and early 1950's directors, writers, and performers in the United States were engaged in a running, chiefly private, debate about the nature of television, based largely on rough analogies with other media, and the way stations in the debate were reflected in programming. Stage plays with stage sets appeared on the screen, with the camera a static observer of the action. An excellent radio series, "Dragnet," became a fair television series. A fair radio series, "Gunsmoke," became an excellent television series. Television moved from radio news commentary with occasional visuals to adapt some of the old newsreel techniques. As equipment improved, "filmic" effects became more common, and eventually the "film for television" appeared.

Relatively little thought seems to have been devoted to the problem of adjusting personal styles of writing, direction, and performance to the medium itself, or to the more abstract and transcendent question of how television actually worked. The most noteworthy exception to the former observation was the cluster of program series produced in Chicago in the late 1940's — "Garroway at Large," "Studs' Place," and so on — which are usually remembered as being in the "Chicago style." The latter observation — that there were few critical analyses of the medium — stands intact.

We turn, therefore, to a paper written by the German film critic Rudolph Arnheim, in 1935; [10] and to a comparable effort by the Canadian, Marshall McLuhan, published in 1964.[11] In at least one respect, these papers have a special interest: chronologically, they bracket the history of television to date.

Arnheim, who had interested himself in the study of film and radio for many years before his essay on television was written, in essence says that the new medium will provide a direct, literal extension of human experience, "raw experience," much as if someone had developed a device to produce the X-ray vision of Superman as a commercial venture. Television, he insists, will be without art, almost wholly without craft; it is to be a pure extension of vision. Indeed, it will almost be without language: "The detour via the describing word becomes unnecessary," he writes, "the barrier of foreign languages loses importance. The wide world itself enters our room." [12]

In contrast to television, Arnheim sets radio, and says, "Hearing excels in transmitting speech and music, that is, products of the spirit; it renders little of physical reality."[13] The sounds of life require a commentator or reporter to become understandable.

Thus, to Arnheim, radio is pre-eminently a medium of symbols: of abstractions, and the ideas and feelings they represent. Television, on the other hand, provides instant experience of a visual sort.

Arnheim's bias leads him to see television, so defined, as a troubling development: it will indeed enrich experience, he believes, but at the expense of thought. He even recalls those ubiquitous Laputan philosophers of Jonathan Swift, who carried great packs of objects with them so that they might converse, not with tricky words, but by pointing to things. In the same way, Arnheim thinks, TV tends to make language unnecessary; we can simply look at things.

And this tendency toward a "cult of sensory stimulation" — already present in our culture — is dangerous, since in contemporary society the mere appearances of things teach us little. We do not understand what a war is about by looking at transmissions of a battle, or what politics is about by looking at the faces of presidents, prime ministers, or dictators.

On the face of the respective texts, Arnheim's view of television would seem to be much at odds with that of Marshall McLuhan, as expressed in the latter's book, *Understanding Media*. Where Arnheim argues that "raw experience" is the proper subject matter of television, and that the medium itself amounts to no more than an extra lens for the eye, McLuhan in his well-known phrase, "The medium is the message," maintains that the notion of "content" is irrelevant to the study of media, and that in any case the sensory extension afforded by television is tactile rather than visual.

While it would hardly be either proper or practicable to summarize the full range of McLuhan's theoretical observations here, we may permit ourselves a glance at two or three of those most relevant to our purpose. The picture in television, as is well known, is made up of a series of points of light "painted" on the screen by an electron beam. It is not the same as the picture in film, or in a still photograph, but rather, in its basic components, resembles a halftone engraving. The TV image differs from the halftone in that it is not static but is constantly repainted and recreated. It is evident that an image formed in this way will be more detailed as the number of points of discrimination increases; if I make a *pointilliste* sketch of a flower, and use only ten dots, I will create a highly simplified, abstract image, which may not much resemble a flower at all. If I use ten thousand dots, I can create a much more elaborate representation of the flower because of the greater detail. Television, says McLuhan, presents a screen image of this general type, the detail being variable within a somewhat narrow range.

One of McLuhan's most important observations, which grows out of this technical definition of the medium, really seems to have two aspects. First, he says, a television set, even though it may *look* like a visual instrument, really provides us with little visual information. "The TV image is visually low in data. The TV image is not a still shot. It is not photo in any sense, but a ceaselessly forming contour of things limned by the scanning finger" (*Understanding Media*, p. 313). Second, there is a strong suggestion that, even if the line-definition of television were increased to provide much more data, the essential nature of the image is so peculiar that television could never, regardless of technical changes, become "the same as" film, for example, or even a primarily visual medium at all. McLuhan reminds us: "The TV image is *now* a mosaic mesh of light and dark spots which a movie shot never is, even when the quality of the movie image is very poor" (*ibid.*).

This of course leads to McLuhan's concept of the televison image as sculptural or iconic in its quality, and hence tactile rather than visual in its appeal. But more to our immediate point, he argues that the low-information, mosaic-mesh quality of the image results in a "cool," or highly participative effect. All the omitted information must be filled in, by the viewer; the mosaic must be "felt through," in an intense, but never speedy fashion. This in contrast to a "hot" medium, such as the printed page, which packages a large quantity of data and projects with great speed and intensity.

Regardless of subject matter, McLuhan says, television always achieves what Kenneth Burke calls "a reduction in scope"; it makes small of the overtowering; intimate and even commonplace of the strange; and cool of the hot. But it also provides a highly active, participative experience; the viewer is always, in a real way, the associate producer in television.

All this may seem to confirm an earlier suspicion, that Arnheim and McLuhan are hopelessly at odds, and that insights on which they agree will be trivial, if they exist at all. But this may be a hasty conclusion; the differences may have more to do with values, and less with analysis, than at first seems to be the case. Arnheim sees television as "without art," as dealing in "raw visual experience," as vastly extending the range of that experience at the expense of "thought." He is inclined to disapprove. McLuhan would say that television deals in television — "the medium is the message" — but would agree, I think, that consideration of "art in television" is nearly as pointless as "content in television." As for Arnheim's central point, McLuhan would certainly identify the concern with "thought" and words as essentially a print bias natural enough to a European of Arnheim's age and education, and would probably guess that the earlier writer had reported a valid glimpse of the overwhelming newness of the television medium, his discomfort being caused by the realization, not that television would add too much to the availability of raw experience, but that such a medium, being radically different from radio, film, or print, would produce correspondingly radical changes in the "logics" of habitual viewers. Whether McLuhan approves this brave new world as much as Arnheim disapproves is somewhat difficult to say; he has said of himself that he is a stalwart conservative and detests all innovation; on the other hand, his writings convey a tremendous excitement in the discovery of the nature and direction of change, which might easily be taken for approbation.

TV AS TEACHER

Drawing in part on the foregoing discussion, I propose now to sketch out some of the characteristics of the medium, and indicate their significance in the learning process. In doing so, I shall try to select features which characterize the medium at the present time, which are variable within a fairly narrow range, and which are unlikely to be altered by technical developments in the near future. The first three of the six features discussed below may be found in all mass media, but are especially strongly marked in television; the next two are characteristic of television alone; the final one is a "natural" characteristic of broadcasting, which technical advances have modified considerably.

In general, we may describe television in this fashion: messages are produced through the collaborative effort of a number of technicians, disseminated from a single point of origin, and received (where a transmitter is used) by a random collection of individuals rather than a selected audience. The flow of information is unidirectional; and the entire process of communication is characterized by anonymity; the transmission is instantaneous.

Flow of information

Like all of the mass media, which depend heavily on mechanization for their effect, television exhibits a one-directional pattern of information flow, from the producing agency to the viewer. In a strict sense, there is no feedback in broadcast television; for the term "feedback" usually indicates an immediate response which permits the communicator to correct his effort, and so bring it nearer success. In a face-to-face conversation, for example, the speaker may be interrupted or questioned, or he may be able to guess from the listener's facial expression that he is not making himself clear, and can thus repeat or rephrase what he has to say.

In television, of course, no such situation obtains. *While he is making his statement*, the broadcaster cannot ever be sure that anyone is watching or listening to him. After the fact, of course, he may get some response to what he had to say; but such response, though it may guide him in some future effort, is plainly worthless for the effort just past. Broadcasters have, at one time or another, attempted to obtain guidance by encouraging mail or telephone response; but this is usually too little and too late. Commercial broadcasters rely heavily on audience ratings, more or less to the same end — not that the ratings are very reliable, but that they are regarded as better than nothing. It is also possible to tape or film a program, and pretest it with a representative group; this practice can yield helpful information but it is clumsy and time-consuming. Some educators have set up telephones in conjunction with their closed-circuit systems, and have encouraged students to talk back by this means; but experiments along these lines seem not to have been very successful.[14]

Thus, the unidirectional flow in television appears to be one of the permanent characteristics of the medium — barring, of course, the appearance of George Orwell's set which looks back at the viewer. What significance has this fact for the educator? Principally, we believe, that it raises certain psychological problems for teacher-performers and probably for students, mainly problems of adjustment. The American practice has been to take accomplished teachers, accustomed to classroom situations in which there may be a great deal of feedback, to put them in a television studio in a sort of simulacrum of the classroom, but lacking the essential component of a classroom, namely, a class, and to expect them to carry on as usual. This is likely to be a frustrating experience for the teacher. There is some evidence of student discomfort in the presence of ETV, but whether this stems from the lack of interaction with the teacher is not clear. What is abundantly clear is that students do learn from television — hardly a surprising discovery, since they also learn from books, audio recordings, and films, all of which work in the same pattern.

Television is still a new medium, and educators have not yet learned how to think about themselves in relation to it. The situation is very different with print. A teacher who undertakes to write a textbook has five centuries of accumulated experience to tell him what he is doing; the teacher who undertakes to prepare a televised course has to begin, almost literally, from nowhere. Learning a workable and comfortable stance to take with respect to television is likely to be a continuing project, both for teachers and for students.

Redundancy

It is a maxim of a computerized age that, in any communication system, when feedback is lacking, redundancy must be high. Roughly speaking, redundancy is a measure of the probability that a receiver of a message can anticipate it or correctly fill in the gaps caused by "noise." Obviously, redundancy factors (repetition being one of the most obvious) take up space/time in the message, so that redundancy is inversely proportional to the amount of information a given message-space can convey.

Television at its simplest is rich in factors which make for redundancy: information is carried in words, gestures, facial expression, and intonation. To these may be added, at discretion, music and sound effects, photographs, film clips, demonstration models, and so on, ad infinitum. The performance of commercial broadcasters on this score is brilliant; they communicate very little, but that little with great efficiency.

The principal problem raised for ETV people by the notion of redundancy is that of determining its proportion to the amount of information to be included in a given space. This proportion will vary, depending on the topic, the level of instruction, and the kind of students the instruction is planned for. Producers, writers, and teacher-performers must certainly learn to content themselves with conveying less information in a given time than they might manage in the classroom. On the other hand, it is quite possible to go the way of the commercial broadcaster and present an inconsiderable trifle of information by manipulating a great arsenal of communicative techniques, and thus produce — as commercial television often does — simple boredom.

Anonymity

The television viewer, of any sort of program, may give himself a sudden chill if, as he sits before his set, he asks himself the question, "But who is saying all this to me?" For the simple truth is that, almost always in commercial television and very often in ETV, *nobody* is saying it. Or rather, so many people are responsible for the various bits and pieces of the message that it comes to the same thing.

In much the same way, the performer staring into the red eye of the camera may experience a strong sense of unreality if he asks himself, "Who is listening? Who is viewing what I do?" For the fact is that, as far as he can tell from his position in front of the camera, there may be no one out there at all.

There can be no doubt that television tends to depersonalize and dehumanize communication, not because anyone wills it, but because of its nature as an electronic device. This tendency comes to be of special concern when television enters the sensitive area of education; yet little enough is known about it except in a theoretical way. It is possible to observe that in commercial television, viewers and communicators collaborate eagerly to create personalized message sources, to compensate for the impersonality and anonymity imposed by the medium itself. Thus, we have the "television personality," who is usually a non-actor, non-comedian, non-musician (if he or she has any such talents, they are treated as marginal), whose role is to be plausibly human, friendly, and communicative. Somewhat to the surprise of everyone concerned, television teachers have found themselves converted into "television personalities" among student-viewers.

and apparently for much the same reason. Educational television, though usually much less complex and costly than its commercial counterpart, is also a collaborative enterprise. The teacher on the screen is, as a rule, more nearly the true information source of his program than the Carsons and Cronkites are for theirs, yet he cannot pretend to have worked without advice or collaboration, and there have been instructional programs in which the teacher was simply a performer working from a script written by someone else.

The depersonalizing effect of television — like the non-book, the "music" contrived chiefly by recording engineers, and other examples of mass-produced communication — calls for extensive analysis and investigation. Its by-product, the "teacher-personality," must be expected and may prove useful at certain levels of instruction. After all, we have here created, quite spontaneously, a small group of heroes, not of consumption, sports, or entertainment, but of learning, an area much neglected in the pantheon of American culture.

Screen size

Among professional broadcasters, it is well known that television demands a simpler and more intimate style of statement than does film, and that one reason for this is screen size. Effects which are superb on even the smallest of theater screens become meaningless when reduced to television dimensions.

Moreover, the relative smallness of the television screen seems a more or less permanent characteristic of the medium. Early television sets in the United States had extremely small screens — seven and ten inches. As engineering and production techniques improved, home sets became available with larger and larger screens, and there have been experiments — usually with sports events — in "theater television." However, the tendency in late years has been in the direction of shrinkage. Sets intended for the living room probably average twenty-one inch screens, and with very recent developments in miniaturization, the small portable set with a minute screen has become popular. Television sets scarcely larger than the smallest transistor radio are now available.

If the smaller screen represents the wave of the future, ETV lessons may in future be addressed to the individual, not the class, and we may well have to rethink some of our "practical" ideas about utilization. In any event, the small screen does force a miniaturized, intimate, and simple treatment of its topics. Commercial television writers and directors long ago recognized that television is at its best in the medium shot and close-up, and that the long shots and sweeping panoramic effects which make wonderful film lose most of their meaning when transferred to the TV screen. Most of the "filmic" detail simply disappears on television, and what remains is almost wholly lacking in power to impress or excite.

Marshall McLuhan tells us that television, as a "cool" medium, tends to eliminate excitement, awe, and similar "hot" responses from the repertory of viewers. Or, to borrow Kenneth Burke's phrase, television always subjects its materials to a "reduction in scope." How this works is easy to see. A long shot of the Grand Canyon of the Colorado would be ineffective on television; what we are likely to get, instead, is a shot of one rock with a lizard sunning on it. The great leader on a white horse will probably lose his horse on television; what we see of him may be a lined face, taut with tension. This combination of small picture and close visualization evokes from successful television performers a predictable kind of response: an intimate, frequently informal style; an ability to communicate through small gestures, expressions, and intonations in a medium where large effects are meaningless.

A study of the small screen and the effects appropriate to it is clearly indicated for anyone who works with ETV. The development of a proper teaching style for the medium is extremely important; but this consideration also affects whatever else appears on the screen with the instructor. ETV manuals and textbooks frequently remark that a particular virtue of the medium is that it can give the student an excellent view of experiments, demonstrations, and the like. So it can, but the view ideally is a private one, and on a rather small scale. The medium is likely to filter out whatever is large, complex, or "hot."

Level of visual information

Marshall McLuhan describes the television screen image as "sculptural" and "iconic," a "mosaic mesh." These terms seem accurate enough in theory, although there seems to be rather little evidence that these characteristics really make as much difference to the viewer as McLuhan believes. But he is certainly correct in arguing that the television screen provides little visual information as compared with the film or the still photograph, and that this does make a difference. The television screen image is of considerably higher abstraction than the film screen image; a tremendous amount of detail is left out, and must be supplied imaginatively or felt intuitively.

McLuhan suggests that this feature of television makes it a superior medium for education, because it forces a "cool" response, which is at once intellectual and participative. If he is correct, then it follows that television will work best with certain kinds of subjects and with certain approaches to them. An encyclopedist's approach to an encyclopedist's sort of topic is not for television; a book or a film does indeed provide the ideal package for information. The television approach ought to be creative or, at the least, inductive; and it should present processes rather than things.

There is much to recommend in McLuhan's description of the television screen image as "iconic." We may note, for example, that while cartoons have proved popular both in film and television, the most successful television cartoons are exceedingly abstract in style, from "Crusader Rabbit" through "Huckleberry Hound" to "Rocky and His Friends," whereas the great master of the film cartoon is Walt Disney, whose elaborate "hot" style in such works as "Snow White" and "Pinocchio" seemed admirably adapted to the big screen.

This is not to say that ETV should employ cartoons, which are likely to prove too complicated and costly in production for an educational venture; but it does point to an abstract, "iconic" style for TV visuals of whatever sort.

If these are limitations on the educational uses of television, they are surely not serious ones; on the contrary, such directives for the use of TV point out much the same course as many recent educational experiments. The difference is between an older concept of teaching and learning, which holds that there are "things" to be learned, and a new one, which seems to suggest that there are rather "learning processes" to be engaged in. It is a long way from the multiplication tables, once a "thing" to be memorized, to the "new mathematics," which is conceived and taught almost wholly as process.

Simultaneity

This is a characteristic of the broadcast media which immediately impressed even the most naive of the early commentators. Television seemed especially impressive in this respect. The principal wonder of the new medium appeared to be that one could see an opening night at a New York theater, or a presidential press conference in Washington, while it was actually going on. Film, kinescopes, and videotape changed all that; television began to deal largely in *recent* events which were already part of history, and which frequently had been edited so as to remove the blunders and the occasional boredom of the actual — and also its spontaneity. Only sports events and news of the greatest urgency, such as President Kennedy's assassination, have been spared this treatment.

It may well be that this extensive use of film and videotape is a gross misuse of the medium. Our previous comments have touched on the simplicity and informality which television seems to demand. Painstaking rehearsals, retaping, and editing tend to

elaborate what was simple and to smooth out performances which
should have ease rather than smoothness. It is not an accident
that Jack Paar, when things went with less than maximum efficiency on the old "Tonight" show, used to turn without apology
to the camera, smile, and remark, "I keep telling you this show
isn't rehearsed." There is a useful hint for the educational producer in this remark. Programs should of course be planned
and rehearsed, and, where practical considerations require it,
may be taped. But the producer should remember that television
is not film, and that perhaps the greatest charm of the medium
is that even a taped performance run on closed circuit can rather
easily, as film almost never does, convey the exciting sense that
something is happening — now!

NOTES

1   For documentation see S. E. Frost, Jr., *Education's Own Stations*
    (University of Chicago Press, 1937).
2   Wilbur L. Schramm, "What We Know about Learning from In-
    structional Television," in *Educational Television: The Next Ten
    Years* (Stanford University: Institute for Communication Re-
    search, 1962), pp. 52–76.
3   *In* Alfred de Grazia and David A. Sohn, *Revolution in Teaching:
    New Theory, Technology and Curricula* (New York: Bantam
    Books, 1964), p. 49.
4   Henry R. Cassirer, *Television Teaching Today* (Paris: UNESCO,
    1962), p. 61.
5   Official advisory group to the U.S. Commissioner of Education and
    Office of Education, established in 1960.
6   "A National Policy for Educational Television," *ETV: The Next
    Ten Years*, p. 4.
7   New York: Ronald Press, 1961.
8   New York: Hastings House, 1961.
9   Edmund Carpenter and Marshall McLuhan, "The New Lan-
    guages," *Chicago Review*, I (Spring, 1956), 46–52.
10 "A Forecast of Television," in *Film as Art* (University of California
    Press, 1958), pp. 188–98.

11 See especially "Television: The Timid Giant," in *Understanding Media: The Extensions of Man* (New York: McGraw-Hill, 1964), pp. 308–37.
12 *Film as Art*, p. 194.
13 *Ibid.*, p. 193.
14 Lester Asheim, "A Survey of Informed Opinion on Television's Future Place in Education," in *ETV: The Next Ten Years*, p. 19.

Part II

EDUCATIONAL STATIONS AND NETWORKS

The Four Faces of Educational Television

THIS is the time of educational boom in America. Legislatures as well as industries are paying great attention to schools, colleges, and centers for continuing education. Indeed, education is now a profitable business, especially since most of us have come to loll in the satisfaction that *if it is educational it must be good.*

Educational television, encompassing both classroom instruction and informal programming for general audiences, is beginning to share some of the spotlight. There are now well over 140 ETV stations on the air, and new stations are expected to start broadcasting at the rate of more than one a month in the near future.

New legislation assists ETV, and it will undoubtedly continue to do so. The Educational Television Facilities Act allows federal expenditures — on a matching basis with local money — for activation of new stations or expansion of existing ones. The Elementary and Secondary Education Act includes several possibilities for the use of ETV, in Titles I and III especially. The Higher Education Act makes special mention of television, and permits federal aid for the purchase of equipment. At state levels, many heavy

This article represents the views of the author alone, and is in no way a reflection of official positions taken by any organization.

financial commitments have been made for the development of
stations and networks. Recently, Kentucky, Mississippi, and Maryland, for instance, all approved plans for the establishment of
state-wide ETV networks. Others are now being built and are
operating.

Manufacturers of electronic equipment are aware of ETV's
growth, and several of them are prepared with every prospective
customer to furnish consulting services on the use of television
in education. (One manufacturer has printed a handsome, well-
written booklet titled *1966 Schoolman's Guide to ETV Communications*, which it distributes at no charge.) Clearly educational broadcasting is a market for industry.

But what is educational television? What is it trying to do?

Visits to some ETV stations might give clues as to fundamental
and unanswered questions that continue to haunt educational
telecasters. Consider one station, purely fictional, and its manager:

THE SCHOOL STATION

Howard Bolen is general manager of KXXX, Channel 51, an
ETV station owned and operated by the Windsor County public
school system. Howard is thirty-two, and he is responsible for
a staff of twelve, more than $400,000 in equipment, and an annual
station budget of $84,000. He reports to Dr. Herbert Crenshaw,
the county superintendent of schools, who is really not too keen
on the use of television in education, but who supports it duti-
fully. KXXX serves thirty-five elementary schools, four high
schools, and, presumably, a total community of 280,000 people.

Howard graduated from a state university ten years ago, with
a degree in education. He taught high school history for two years
and then returned to his alma mater, with the aid of a graduate
assistantship, for a master's degree in audiovisual education. Ultimately he took a job as "AV coordinator" with the Windsor County
school system and enjoyed working with Harry P. Strohm, the
driving force behind the establishment of ETV in the county,

and the superintendent until a year ago. Howard is definitely a school man by training and experience.

KXXX is on the air five days each week, and not at all during the summer. It aims its cameras every day at a variety of teachers who come in from county schools to deliver their rehearsed lessons. The station goes dark in the early evening each day, after broadcasting special programs for teachers and a few NET tapes for children and adults at home. There are voices in the community asking for more evening programs and for a more complete community service, but the voices are not loud. Part of the reason is that conversion to UHF among the receivers in the community is still not great.

Thus far, the FCC has chosen not to frown officially at KXXX for so unbalanced a programming schedule, but the county board of education feels that its responsibility is mainly to the schools and it hasn't the money for much beyond that. Teachers and principals like the television service, or so they say at meetings, but use of the medium even in the schools remains moderate and the word "supplementary" is common in descriptions of the service.

Howard knows what is going on across the country, and he has tried desperately to convince Dr. Crenshaw that ETV must be for the entire community. The superintendent has a habit of saying, "Yes, yes, we'll have to look into that, won't we?" Howard never gets much further than that.

If we ask Howard about the mission of educational television, he quotes from Wilbur Schramm and Charles Siepman. He seems to be committed to definite and worthy ideals, but we see clearly that he is speaking theoretically and that on a practical basis he is frustrated. After answering our question about mission, Howard might whisper, "By the way, in your travels from station to station, if you should hear of any good openings involving real community service, would you let me know?" Though promising to do so, we would hope that in time Howard will be able to inject into KXXX a real sense of purpose.

Perhaps no actual school station has so limited an existence as this. The basic question, however, is clear: What part of educational television programming should be for classroom audiences in schools and colleges, and what part should be for other groups?

There are now three means by which schools may distribute instructional television signals to classrooms. (1) They may install closed-circuit television equipment and be totally independent. (2) They may build special low-power multichannel television transmitters to be used solely for formal education. (The FCC has set aside special frequencies for these installations in the 2500–2690 megacycle bands. Ordinary home receivers cannot pick up the signals.) (3) They may operate ETV broadcast channels or make arrangements with existing ETV stations to provide instructional programs to the classrooms. The advantages and shortcomings inherent in these systems vary, as do the costs.

Stations not owned by schools have found that contracts with boards of education for school programming provide income, and most stations produce at least some television for classrooms. The average amount of time devoted to in-school programming, for all ETV stations, is close to 50 percent. Is this an equitable proportion?

The question is not wholly theoretical. The FCC demands that ETV licensees "meet the educational needs" of the communities they serve. This is vague, to be sure, and it leaves up to each licensee the definition of educational needs, but presumably the FCC could challenge an educational broadcaster whose programming is heavily unbalanced either in favor of school programs, or in favor of nonschool fare, depending upon local circumstances. In educational television, the differences between instructional and noninstructional material become important in a number of ways. *What is the relationship between ITV and ETV?* Howard thinks this question is critical to the operation of his station, and it may very well be. At other stations, where there may be no need to make sharp differentiations among types of programming, different issues become important. Howard's colleague, Alan Bennington, knows of at least one:

THE STATE STATION

Alan Bennington is executive director of the State Network, and general manager of the state's flagship ETV station in Capital City. There are eight stations planned for the state, two of which are now on the air. Alan is thirty-eight, and has more than ten years' experience in ETV. He started as a producer-director at a community station, moved to a university station, where he was program director, and then, because he was known by J. Arnold Patterson (through an uncle in the newspaper business), he was offered his present position.

J. Arnold Patterson is chairman of the state ETV Commission, which is a group of eleven citizens appointed by the governor, charged with the responsibility of developing, operating, and maintaining the state ETV system. Mr. Patterson knew the governor in the old days; and when the ETV legislation was passed — and Mr. Patterson was thinking of retiring as state roads commissioner — the governor asked him to take on this new part-time responsibility.

The state ETV bill was passed four years ago. It created the Commission and established a ten-year plan (a total state investment, ultimately, of $6 million), under which the ETV stations will be constructed and activated. The project is set up in five phases, each one of which involves station activation and some interconnection. The present plan calls for an ultimate annual budget of more than $3.5 million for the entire state network when all the stations are on the air, but the operating budgets each year will actually be decided by the legislature. This means that constant contact with legislators — nobody likes to call it "lobbying" — is necessary. J. Arnold Patterson may not know very much about television, education, equipment, or current salary scales, but he *does* know the governor and the legislators. This knowledge has been pivotal in the successful completion during the past few years of phases I and II of the state ETV project. Mr. Patterson, plainly, is a good politician.

Alan is learning rapidly what kind of programming disturbs state legislators. He ran a program a year ago on water pollution in the area, only to learn quickly and harshly that the factory dumping waste into the Capital City River is owned in part by the Speaker of the House. Alan and Mr. Patterson had a long talk at lunch a few days after the program was aired.

The two stations (the newer one is really just a satellite) are on the air ten hours a day, seven days a week, twelve months a year. The state board of education, which was disappointed that it did not get total control of the network when the ETV bill was passed, is responsible for all programming for the schools in the state. The state board develops curricula, hires TV teachers, and administers utilization workshops. The state ETV Commission — the legal licensee — handles all other programming and administration. Most programs for home audiences come from national sources, and no programming deals with local political issues.

The governor mentions the state ETV effort in speeches, and the Capital City Chamber of Commerce has included several sentences about it in their brochure about the wonders of the region. ETV signals will soon cover the entire state, and the network's existence is being made known to more and more people.

Whom should we ask about the social significance of ETV in the state? Mr. Patterson hasn't given it much thought, though he has made several public statements over the years about the "need" for ETV and the "intellectual growth of the children and adults of this great state." He is sincere, and he believes in what he is doing, but his is a world of power, votes, the enactment of bills, the granting of public authority, and the expenditure of tax dollars. His thoughts are seldom what would be called "philosophic."

Alan Bennington would probably be a more appropriate person to ask. He was given his position on the basis of his experience in television production and administration, however, and not because of his beliefs. His application, State Form 1065-B, contained no blank in which he was invited to describe his "philosophy." Instead, the 1065-B asked only for names, dates, jobs held, numbers of people supervised, salaries, and references. Even at best, Alan's answers to our questions would be shaded by his relationship to the legislature, possibly by his recollection of the water pollution disappointment, and by his understanding of the wording in the law that established his very position. Still, Alan does not function without thought, and he tries continually to bring a broad ETV service to as many people in the state as he can.

Stations owned by states and state authorities are only potentially as political as the foregoing. Nevertheless, where the support for an activity comes almost totally from an elected assembly, the activity cannot help but be conditioned by political overtones. Well over three-fourths of the money used by state stations comes directly from public treasuries controlled by legislatures.

Several states have developed educational television stations and some have built extensive interconnection facilities. These system are not indigent, and in fact their budgets are sometimes comparatively generous. In several areas, state governments have established ETV networks to strengthen curricula in the schools and to reach adult populations. State stations remain on the air, on the average, for more hours each day — and more months each year — than do other ETV stations.

A state television network could certainly be a potent political tool, and in the hands of an unscrupulous state agency, reports of current happenings could be severely warped. As a result, most states give total control of television to no existing agencies, and instead create new and broadly representative authorities. The television staffs know that the best way to keep clear of legislative wrath is to broadcast educational programs dealing with noncontroversial subjects. The fare is educational, and certainly meets needs, but where a public issue is politically even warm, state stations are usually not known for fearless programming.

One of these days, Alan is going to ask some serious questions about ETV in his state, and they may not be answered readily. How free and independent can ETV stations be in their programming? Should they stay relatively clear of controversial issues, concentrating instead on problems such as literacy, health training, continuing professional education, school service, and vocational training? *Is it the nature of ETV to be nonpolitical in programming?* Alan will learn to live with these hanging questions, but he'll be comforted in knowing he is not alone. Still, while he worries about the mood of the legislature, his friend Dave Stark, whom he sees occasionally at conventions, has a different set of anxieties:

THE UNIVERSITY STATION

Dave Stark worked as a floor manager at a commercial TV station while he was in high school, and he was able to fill in as cameraman, and once as a director, during the summer months. Since then, he has spent his time in college, in the Air Force, and in graduate school. He has earned a B.A. in speech, an M.S. in television-radio, and a Ph.D. in speech (major area: broadcasting; minor areas: theater and education). While he worked for his doctorate he taught basic speech courses, worked as a producer-director at the university ETV station, and published two articles on educational broadcasting in speech therapy. After being awarded his degree four years ago, he went to a large public university in a neighboring state as an assistant professor. He assisted the administration in the development of the television department, and when the university became an ETV licensee he was chosen as the general manager. The number of his published articles increased, and a year ago he became an associate professor. He is thirty-seven.

Dr. Stark is a very busy man today. He teaches one course, chairs the television department (faculty of three), and manages the ETV station. The station takes most of his time; it has a full-time staff of eighteen people, supplemented by twenty-one students who work part-time in various crew positions. Channel 16 is on the air five days a week, nine months a year, and it is well known both at the university and in the community.

The station is a pet project of the vice president for academic affairs. He has placed the station's operation directly under his own office; so as station manager, Dave reports to the vice president. As a department head, however, he is responsible to the dean of the School of Speech and Dramatic Arts. This interesting scheme looks clean on the university's organization chart, but the actual lines of authority and responsibility sometimes cross.

Dave develops a departmental budget each year, which he submits to the dean. Simultaneously, the vice president receives Dave's proposed budget for the station, which grew to $190,000 last year. The entire university budget is analyzed, some changes are made, and the final submission is to the state legislature. It is fortunate for Dave that he sees the vice president as often as he does. Details of station operation are known to the older man, and the annual budget has never been cut. The broadcasting enterprise has grown steadily since it went on the air.

The station has a contract with the local board of education, and almost 30 percent of the station's programming is specifically for public schools. A few series are aimed at the college students, and the rest of the offerings are for the entire community.

Dave occasionally has trouble getting the full cooperation of the faculty as he develops programs for home audiences. "We're educators, not high-wire acrobats," said the chairman of the sociology department once, "and we cannot sugar-coat basic course content for the sake of 'showbiz.'"

Arguments abound when ETV is on the agenda of the university senate. Dave says that the station should provide good programs for all audiences, but the fact is that most of what is put on the air is strictly for intellectuals. All the discussions in the senate seem to deteriorate sooner or later into general criticisms of commercial television, and how the faculty members have little use for it, so the question of target audiences is seldom really tackled.

One fat little history professor, with tenure, seems to be on Dave's side, but he joins the battle only when it seems like fun. A few months ago, the chairman of the department of fine arts went to great lengths explaining to the assembly that he did not own a television set and that he therefore never watched it. He spoke of it as if it were some kind of evil habit. The history man chose that occasion to speak. He said, "I don't like most of what I see on newsstands, either, but I haven't stopped buying books and reading them." Nothing is resolved, of course. Most of the faculty insist that the station must cater to an elite, providing "alternate" viewing for those who want it. A few, on the other hand, regard the medium as a means for reaching people who are not touched educationally or culturally by other media, and they argue that at least some programs should be aimed at these less enlightened audiences. Dave finds that the station does not get great support from the academic community, except as it participates in programs for intellectual aristocrats.

Meanwhile, Dave's program schedule is full, and he continues to train students in broadcasting skills. "I'll play intellectual handball any time," he says, "but I have students to think about, a station to run, and a new building to design."

Again, the deck is stacked. University stations seldom operate without reasonable faculty support, and this caricature has been presented to accentuate a question that arises frequently: *to whom should ETV appeal?*

There are fundamentally only two camps. One could be called "traditionalist," which supports the assertion that continuing liberal education should be for the elite. In a modern democracy, we translate this to mean that continuing liberal education is for those who want it. "ETV is like a museum or library," advocates maintain, "and it provides alternate television for discriminating viewers." (The inference is that ETV is an alternate to commercial television, therefore establishing what is assuredly an irrelevant comparison.) The traditionalist wants to appeal to community leaders, confident that the blessings of enlightenment will filter through to greater numbers of people.

The "modernist," at the other end of the argument, believes that continuing liberal education should be for all, and therefore that ETV programs should appeal to — and affect — everyone, though not necessarily at the same time. He suggests that education should be for those who *need* it as well as for those who *want* it.

Among adult educators, who are concerned with all media, the same split is apparent in other issues: ideas versus action, humanities versus the social sciences, the inner versus the outer functions of man, the improvement of intellect as happening *with* education versus the same improvement as a *result* of education, the familiar content versus method, and so on. The two camps have also been labeled in a variety of ways, and educators have described them as scientist and humanist, rationalist and developmentalist, rationalist and empiricist, or traditionalist and progressivist. The core of doubt remains, however. *Whom are we trying to educate and why?* To state that we are aiming at all men while we reach only an elite is fraud. Maybe a separate answer must be given for each ETV program, but there should certainly be some defensible relationship between our programs and the audiences we claim to seek.

Dave Stark is a professor, and his problems are largely those of an academician, even in running an ETV station. A few hundred miles away, however, Steve Fenton worries in a different area:

THE COMMUNITY STATION

Steve Fenton is vice president of the Metropolitan ETV Corporation and general manager of WYYY-TV/Channel 9. The station is eight years old, it has a full-time staff of forty-three, and its chief concern is survival. The enterprise, over the years, has been, without a doubt, a nonprofit venture.

Steve started twelve years ago with a degree in marketing and the goal of owning his own wholesale business. He worked as a salesman for a small manufacturing company, and showed such promise that he was made a regional sales manager in three years. "You have the magic of organization and leadership," the company head told him, "and we want to give you every opportunity to grow." Unfortunately, the company was bought and absorbed by a huge syndicate, and Steve preferred not to accept an offer from the new management, which would have involved excessive traveling. Instead, he took on a special assignment for the local YMCA, and spent a year organizing community groups for civil defense training. His success was impressive, and he was then chosen to organize a Community Chest drive, which involved contact with many leaders in the community.

The ETV Corporation was formed a year later, and several important people — clergymen, bankers, industrialists, educators, and commercial broadcasters — became charter members of its board. Steve knew most of them from his experience at the Y and with the Community Chest, and when it was time to take on a full-time chief executive officer, the corporation turned to him.

Steve learned about television in a hurry, as he moved swiftly toward station activation. He was selected by the Junior Chamber of Commerce as one of the area's "ten outstanding young men" last year, though he says modestly that it was "because I know the right people."

Samuel Knapp, president of the Knapp Industries, is chairman of the board, and he and Steve often work together. The entire board meets every three months, at which time the policies, strategies, and tactics developed by Steve and Mr. Knapp are made official, frequently with very little discussion.

Just about everything at WYYY is controlled by the ledger sheet, and very few programs are produced that are not supported by outside agencies in one way or another. Steve is the first (and Samuel Knapp is the second) to defend this procedure as the only way to keep WYYY in business.

A local college provides housing for the station, though present plans call for a new WYYY building in the urban renewal area within four years. The annual budget, beyond donated and rent-free space, is $390,000. Almost half of this amount comes from "participating" school districts in the area, which pay $1.25 per student per year for instructional programs. (Several schools are contemplating withdrawal from the plan in favor of closed circuit or 2500 megacycle installations, however, and this may seriously affect the station's financial base.) A sum of $60,000 a year is realized as a result of individual donations and "subscriptions." Unrestricted grants from local industries and foundations account for 10 percent of the station's budget, programming contracts bring in some money, and other more ingenious schemes result in bits of income. (One of the ad agencies in the city uses WYYY's studio and tape facilities, for a fee, to produce commercials.)

The person at the station who knows the most about educational television is Ron Jamison, the active and talented director of program development. He has been in ETV for ten years and his ability to spot program ideas, including the means to support them, is uncanny. As new series are being contemplated by people sitting around the conference table, Ron's favorite question is, "Who is going to pay for all this?" He always includes a healthy percentage for what he calls "overhead" in every cost analysis, and rightly so. Ron calls himself an ETV realist, though Steve describes him to others as "the only hard-nosed idealist in captivity."

Steve spends a great deal of time in making speeches, organizing new means for sustenance, and approving program ideas. He is seldom in his office, and he seems to be constantly dashing from one part of town to another. His eyes are on the future, and he is determined to make WYYY a solvent and permanent service in the metropolitan area. Mr. Knapp is working with Steve on a plan by which one of the larger local philanthropic foundations will be contributing heavily to the new building.

Ron Jamison is concerned with *short*-term goals, in that he is developing programs for broadcast within one year. He is writing several proposals for industry, foundations, and federal agencies. Steve is concerned with the development of two- and three-year commitments by power groups in the area, while helping Mr. Knapp in his *long*-range planning for the station. The situation at WYYY was perhaps most succinctly described by Ron at a recent staff meeting. Steve asked the members of the staff if any of them would be interested in appearing on a panel at a seminar being given by the television department of a nearby college. The topic was to be "Developing a Philosophy for Broadcasters." Ron threw his hands in the air and mumbled, "Oh, brother!" Then, he turned to Steve, and his voice became almost bitter. "Steve, we're too busy to worry about that kind of thing. After all, who pays for philosophy?"

No educational television station is completely mercenary, of course. Still, American ETV is the only system of broadcasting in the world with no defined means for support. Instead, only *restrictions* describe our educational television stations: (1) they may not broadcast commercials, and (2) they may not operate for profit. For community stations — those owned by private corporations formed specifically to be ETV licensees — these are negative guidelines indeed.

The most successful community stations are similar to each other in character, and many bear strange resemblances to commercial establishments. While there are no stockholders demanding returns on investments, and while the purpose of the stations is not to make money, it is clear that nothing can be done unless it is paid for one way or another. Usually, in fact, an "overhead" or "surplus" figure must be included in a project budget before a station can consider production. Good ideas for ETV series always include plans for raising necessary money, and the best ideas include plans for raising *more* than enough money.

Financing is one of the most fundamental issues today in educational television. *How should educational television stations across the country be supported?* Should the stations be allowed to sell time? Should ETV be pay-TV? Should advertisers on commercial television pay percentages of their budgets for the national ETV service? Or should we let things go as we have, expecting educational stations to get along — somehow?

Steve and Ron make a good team, and their community station will be on the air for a long time. Their main concerns, however, are not educational; they are financial.

There are many basic and unanswered questions in educational television, and four have been asked here. (1) What is the relationship between ITV and ETV? (2) Is it the nature of ETV to be nonpolitical in programming? (3) To whom should ETV appeal? (4) How should ETV stations across the country be supported? Answers to these questions, and others, will change as the years pass. The answers should imply new questions, and the processes of groping, discovering, identifying, and defining will continue.

The University Station

APPROXIMATELY two-thirds of the more than 140 educational television stations in the United States operate on funds provided them from some tax base. This means of course that the remaining one-third are considered to be non-tax supported stations. This is not quite accurate because of the fact that these so-called non-tax supported ETV stations receive a sizable part of their income from tax supported agencies who utilize the services of the stations.

There are some ETV leaders in this country who have expressed strong sentiments concerning the necessity of operating all educational television from a tax supported base. The person most representative of this group is Mr. Loren Stone, manager of station KCTS-TV at the University of Washington in Seattle. He, in fact, feels that it is a mistake for the Federal Communications Commission to license community groups which are not responsible to any educational establishment. He is referring to the community type of station which essentially constitutes the one-third category not supported by public taxes. Stone says, "the educational establishment of the country is based on a publicly supported school system coupled with publicly supported colleges and universities — and augmented by a private school and college system. . . . I do not think we can or will develop a widespread educational television instrument in this country which is 'private' in its concept."[1] Stone compares ETV to the development of libraries and symphonies in this country where the former are generally supported by taxes and the latter by public or community subscription. He points out that there is a vast difference in the number of successful libraries as compared to the relatively small number of successful symphonies in the country and that we cannot afford to have so few successful educational television stations. There are those in the national movement who feel precisely the opposite. Their general position is that an ETV station which is dependent upon a legislature for its existence will avoid any programming which might be found objectionable by the various power centers within that legislature. The result is a station which avoids controversy in public affairs. Whether or not the FCC is wise in providing an opportunity for noneducational institution licenses to exist in ETV, is a question which can only be answered in the future. However, before giving further consideration to these ideas, let us look at the basic philosophy of tax supported education in general.

PHILOSOPHY OF THE AMERICAN UNIVERSITY

In broad terms, American universities see their role as a public one with a goal toward preserving and expanding human knowledge while at the same time transmitting it to the community around them. There is of course the general assumption that the university has the task of preparing the next generation who will lead this nation in its maintenance and development of a free society. A report about the role of American universities in world affairs states,

The university in the United States over the generations has become a distinctively American institution, closely identified with growth and change in American society. . . . In many countries the university as a center of learning combines the function of teaching and scholarship

for the advancement of knowledge. The American university characteristically adds a third form of service to the society that nurtures it —
activities such as professional training, consultation, extension work,
and continued education, serving directly the broader society beyond
the campus.[2]

In addition to these three functions which are so characteristic
of the American university, there is in the state tax supported university an additional concept that education is to be made available for all. In fact, the land-grant colleges not only have a moral
responsibility for this philosophical approach to education but
are also faced with a very clear legal responsibility within the
Act which provided the funds for their establishment. There is
no question that they are both morally and legally obligated to
reach out within the state each serves to provide educational
opportunity and service for all of the citizenry who supply the
taxes needed to operate the institution. Let us now look at television as a tool with unique capabilities for reaching out into the
populace.

A former president of the University of Wisconsin, Charles
Van Hise, put forth a premise which has become the key philosophical basis upon which the University of Wisconsin Extension
operates. President Van Hise took the position that the boundaries of the state were the boundaries of the campus. It would
seem appropriate that this position serve as a guideline for all
state universities and in particular those which were established
as land-grant colleges. In television one readily sees the finest tool
for extending a campus in all of its functions to the citizenry of
an entire state. To fulfill that task, the program content of a state
university ETV station must match those goals which the university has defined for itself in relation to the people whom it
serves. It has been the experience of this writer that many an
ETV operation which is part of a state university system functions quite independently and almost operates as a university unto
itself. In part this is due to the fact that too many top echelon administrators in state universities do not take serious notice of their

ETV operation and do not provide guidelines or policy statements within which their station operators must work. At the same time there have been station managers who have found this lack of top administrative involvement to provide them with an opportunity to build things as they please. No doubt this is very comfortable, but it is highly questionable when one views an ETV station as the complete extension of a given university.

With the above stated view of television, one is then faced with the next question of determining what to provide through this channel to those who support it with their taxes. Here we must look at the traditional posture of universities and American universities in particular. In general, they have not given their supporters what they want. Rather, they provide what the faculty of the university feels the students and the community should have. There has been little question that state universities are reasonably independent entities which provide a soil for free inquiry and free expression of their faculties. This of course is challenged on a continual basis by legislatures as they become aware of what the faculty thinks and says. An ETV station provides the very situation in which what the faculty thinks and says becomes a more public utterance. Thus an ETV station is very apt to find itself in the middle of such clashes between representative government and tax supported universities. Nevertheless, it should be clear that the philosophy of free inquiry and free expression which applies to a university must apply just as clearly to the ETV station which broadcasts the public utterances of the faculty of that university.

The above is not to say that state universities do not determine community needs and try to meet them. On the contrary, the history of state universities in this country makes it very clear that this is one of the functions which they have regularly carried out. In the instance of an ETV station, it is an obligation of the institutional licensee to determine the needs of the community and to attempt to use this allocated channel to meet those needs. In fact, when a university takes on the responsibility and obligation of an ETV channel, it also takes on an obligation to meet the needs of the entire educational community. By this I mean to say that a channel allocated to a state university is in no sense to be used only for the educational purposes described and defined by that particular university. The federal position on this point is quite clear to all concerned. In 1952 when the FCC originally set aside 242 channels for education, it required that whoever licensed one of those channels would provide service for all elements of the educational community within the signal range of the station. It then follows that the ETV station of a state university ought to assess the educational needs of its community, after defining that community. Once this is done, the university can supply its program funds to meet those needs which are most appropriate to the university's goals and purposes. At the same time, it should make its broadcast facilities, skills, and talent available to the remainder of the educational establishments in its community to meet those needs delegated in turn to them. In this manner all of the educational needs of the community can be cooperatively met by all the educational elements within the community.

More often than not, the situation just described is not the case within current practices of state universities and their television operations. It is only fair to say that other elements of the educational family often have not been interested enough to utilize a television station operated by a university or have not been willing to pay a reasonable share of the cost of operating that facility for their own purposes and goals. With that in mind let us now look to the special functions of the university and how they apply to the ETV station licensed to it.

FUNCTIONS OF AN ETV STATION

One might generalize about the purposes of a university and say that any university has three basic functions while serving its public. One function of course is the acquisition of knowledge; another is the preservation of knowledge; and the third would be the transmission of knowledge. This classic kind of description of the university's purposes is applicable when one looks at establishing a philosophy for a university ETV station. There is no question that a television station will give the university a power to increase its influence in the improvement of society, which is one of its purposes within the three basic functions described above. I would then define nine functions of a tax based university ETV station. They are as follows:

(1) Formal education
(2) Informal education
(3) Educational and media research
(4) Community relations
(5) Community service
(6) Public forum
(7) Training laboratory
(8) Recreational service
(9) Alternative service (minority programming)

It is quite obvious that these are not mutually exclusive categories or functions though one can almost use them as such.

In the first category, we see the role of on-campus or extension instruction where a formal structured organized course for credit is provided to students by the station. Category two, informal education, refers to the general adult or continuing education service which one finds in a nonstructured educational program. It is not intended to provide a structured organized course nor is it intended to provide that for which a university normally gives credit. It is, however, intended to be part of the continuing process of education so necessary in modern society.

The next function stated above, educational and media research, is one in which too many state university stations do very little at all. The value of a station as a laboratory for research at the elementary, secondary, and higher education level is obvious to any researcher; however, very little research in the strictest sense has involved the broadcast medium. In fairness to station operators, it must be said that researchers have a tendency to prefer the closed-circuit or clinical situation over which they have more specific control. There has also been very little involvement of ETV stations in developing new techniques for better use of the television medium. In fact, this is one area where universities in this country have contributed almost nothing to industry at large. When one looks at an industry such as the pharmaceutical field, he can see the kind of relationship between university research and development and the commercial industry which serves the American public. However, most if not all of the forms, formats, and techniques used in broadcasting in this country were developed by the commercial broadcasting industry and were not developed or worked out experimentally by university research and university broadcasting facilities. The basic philosophy of a university should require that ETV facilities be used for precisely this purpose.

The next function, community relations, is one in which some ETV stations regularly engage. It is obvious that a university should use its own ETV station to reach out and tell its story to its community. It is in truth almost startling to find that universities which operate ETV stations have in fact made very little use of their own stations to reach those whose taxes provide the base from which they operate. In all probability, this is due to a sensitivity about propagandizing the public or the legislature in order to promote greater funding at the next biennial session. It is true that a public institution should not use funds given to it by a legislature to propagandize or psychologically coerce that legislature into providing further funds. This would most certainly be an abuse, and legislatures are quite sensitive about this kind of thing. However, it is only reasonable that the general public and citizenry can expect from its university that they be informed about what the university is doing by way of instruction, research, and service. There is no question in my mind that this function of a university ETV station should in general be developed and increased among the various stations around the country.

The fifth function listed above is that of community service. Under a function such as this, ETV stations provide general cultural broadcasting as opposed to general informational broadcasting. It is probably true that the presentation of a symphony orchestra or the visualization of a current art exhibit on the campus is not really a form of continuing education. However, this kind of cultural contribution is a form of service to the community and one which a university is particularly well suited to supply. One might also find the programming of a university football game under this function. It is after all a community service to provide an opportunity for that community to see a sporting event which takes place at the university but which for one reason or another all members of the community cannot come to witness.

The sixth function on the list is that of providing a public forum. There is no question that this is a historical and traditional function of universities dating back to our European heritage. It is, however, absolutely clear in a democracy that governmentally supported universities should provide a forum for any and all ideas of men. This function is quite often attacked by sensitive legislatures and extremist political groups within a community. When ETV stations inject themselves into this normal campus function, they have a tendency to become a part of the public controversies. It may be for this reason that one does not regularly see the broadcast of lectures and speeches given by highly controversial figures on university campuses. This is true almost without exception for university owned stations. In fairness to the station management again, they are usually faced with the problem of moving quantities of equipment just to pick up a single lecture or the problem of having enough advance notice to provide for live or tape-recorded facilities for the particular speaker. However, Mr. Ed Bayley, vice president of NET, feels that:

If there is government support for making programs in public affairs, the government is going to want to tell us what programs to make and what to say about the issues. Experience supports this view. . . . stations worry about the legislature, from which they get their funds. In some cases, these stations have refused to run NET programs which dealt with controversial issues or which took a position critical of the government or contrary to the view of the governor. Nor do many of these stations produce local programs on controversial local issues.[3]

Mr. Bayley may be accurate in some of the instances which he has personally observed, but I would suspect that the root of the problem is far deeper than the philosophy or policy of the given ETV station. A university situation in which there is a conservativeness about speaking out or inquiring into any subject or point of view because of sensitivity at the legislative level betokens an academic problem of far greater magnitude than simply the philosophy or operational policies of a television station.

Let me digress just a moment and deal with the specific area of editorializing on ETV stations. This is really part and parcel of the public forum function, and quite often it is brought up as being one of those areas in which university television stations are failing. Essentially, it is a philosophical question and thus properly a part of this article. It is my own feeling that no university should editorialize on an issue if by "to editorialize" is meant to take a particular point of view in a given controversy. If the university is truly a universe of ideas, opinions, and points of view, the station manager would then be faced with the question of deciding who would speak for the university. In the instance of my own university, I cannot conceive of the chancellor, or president, or the president of the Board of Regents presuming to speak for the university as a whole. Certainly if one of these were to do so, there would be some member of the faculty who would immediately object on the basis that his academic opinion was not represented in the editorialized position and that after all his opinion was rightfully and properly a part of the university's opinion.

Thus, a university should not take an editorial point of view on any controversial issue but rather should provide for an exposure of all the ideas relating to that issue and provide a public forum where the various points of view may be openly discussed and exposed to public surveillance. This, rather than providing a public expression of a specific editorial point of view on a specific issue, is really the function of a university in its public forum role. Let me cite the example of a university press. Though the private press of this country does and should properly take editorial positions, one would not expect a university press to take an editorial point of view when deciding what would or would not be published. In general, a university press will establish only the criteria of excellence and significance in determining what it chooses to publish.

Next on the list of functions for a university ETV station is the provision of a training laboratory for those students who are looking for experiential opportunities in the area of television. The management of course is faced with the problem of providing an on-the-air outlet for nonprofessional people. It is reasonable for university station management to expect closed-circuit laboratories of the university to provide the basic training skills for students. When the students are trained, they can properly be used in the broadcast situation. The general rule to be applied here is that the public must not be expected to suffer through the inadequacies and failings of unskilled and untrained students. That is a role and function of professors who have been trained and prepared for this kind of experience. It is, however, true that the more affluent institutions have a tendency to fill every position with full-time personnel and begin to lock out those students who are looking for an opportunity to express themselves creatively and professionally in the television medium.

The eighth function listed above is that of providing recreational services for the community. In a sense this can be looked on as a subcategory under the function of community service; it is that function where a university station provides the broadcast of a motion picture, a football game, or even an educational quiz-type of program. Quite often the commercial broadcasting industry will react negatively to this kind of programming on an educational tax supported station particularly since it begins to cut into the commercial station audience rather heavily. There is nothing within the educational television license or within the prescribed goals of a state university which bars that university from providing some wholesome recreational outlets for the community which it serves. As a matter of fact, motion pictures are provided with great regularity on university campuses without any serious opposition from motion picture distributors in the community. Football games in and of themselves serve almost a passive recreational function for the seventy or eighty thousand people who will come to the campus stadium to watch them. To suggest that the extension of this recreational function beyond the boundaries of the campus by electronic signal is somehow in opposition to the function or purposes of the university is not logical at all.

In part, I suspect that there is a tendency for commercial broadcasters in the community to support the ETV station as long as it does not take a substantial share of the audience. The broadcast of football games and movies attracts a substantial audience to an ETV station. This of course becomes of economic concern to the other stations; and it is only natural that they will begin looking for reasons to object to the popularized programming. As one who has had the experience of programming university stations, I must point out that quite often it is of great value to an ETV station to provide on some occasions the kind of programming which does draw large shares of the mass audience. In this way the station can attract a future audience which it might not normally reach. For example, those who would tune in to a live football telecast would include thousands of people who might normally never utilize the services of the ETV station. During the course of such a sporting event, the station involved can provide "commercials" which will describe some of the other kinds of programming it makes available. In thus seeking to attract new viewers the university has simply reached out to tell its story to those who in effect are paying the bills; and to do this on occasion is hardly breaking down the basic educational purposes of the institution.

Lastly, one sees the function of alternative or minority programming. These are terms which are used rather regularly when describing the purposes of any ETV station. It is probably true that the ETV station is better geared to serve a minority or a small segment of the audience than is the commercial station which owes its existence to attracting a large share of the audience for its sponsors' messages. Therefore, I would agree that minority programming is a function of the ETV station because of its different approach to funding. However, the principle of alternative service has always seemed to me to be a negative approach in that it says in effect that the educational station will do whatever the commercial stations do not do. Since a university is to be an independent educational institution, it doesn't really seem proper that the programming of its station should be determined by the programming of the commercial stations in the area. It also seems to me that the service provided by an institution should be that service which it deems proper and necessary for its community at any given time. That is not to say that the ETV program director should not look to the programming of the commercial stations when he establishes his own program schedule. In this instance, the program director should know what is on the other channels in order to make certain that he has not created an inconvenience for the community. For example, it would be wrong to provide a forum or discussion of a major controversial issue of the community at the same time that one of the commercial stations was providing a program of the same sort. It is not necessary to divide the loyalties of one's viewers or to force a choice between two programs of substantial educational content. This is a part of the competitive economic world which the commercial stations must live in, but it is not a part of the educational world.

In summary, it is a function of a university to retain the best from our heritage, to perpetuate the good in our culture, and produce change toward a better future. Gilbert Seldes, the noted television critic, says that this is a function of ETV which certainly matches the function of a university.

THE PHILOSOPHY OF THE RATING

Let me now mention a few specific philosophical problems related to the state university ETV station. One is the philosophy of the audience rating which is a basis upon which commercial stations must make program decisions. It is apparently inherent in a mass medium such as television that the user should feel the pressure for reaching or building a mass audience. Consequently, audience size and ratings are pursued just as eagerly by most ETV station personnel as they are by commercial station personnel. In general, this practice is to be deplored; but there is no question that if a university is going to put large amounts of money into the operation of a television station it wants a reasonable return of community involvement to justify the expenditure. One extreme is the type of ETV station management which says that it has no concern for who watches and will simply provide a cultural well into which any member of the community may dip his bucket at any given time. Too often this kind of programming philosophy results in what has been referred to as "professors talking to professors." More often than not, it is characterized by some rather dull kinds of presentations which undoubtedly are watched by extremely small numbers of people. There are instances, however, where a small audience is justified despite the expense. For example, on one occasion it seemed to me worthwhile to create an entire series of programs for only 145 members of the community. This was a particular segment of the medical community, whom the series provided with the newest information related to their field. It is obvious here that the university was offering a service to the entire community via those 145 people.

The other extreme of the rating philosophy becomes evident when an ETV station manager sees himself as being in direct competition with the commercial station operators in the community and as needing to draw audiences comparable to the audiences of those stations. This is not a supportable and acceptable point of view. It is at this point that the operators of commercial or private enterprise stations become quite sensitive to the fact that their own tax dollar is being used to compete against them. In this instance the ETV station may lose the support of a very important part of the broadcast community. If an ETV station programs motion pictures, it is the obligation of that station to provide some related programming at some point which will help the viewer to appreciate, evaluate, and understand the motion pictures involved. This has also been true in the educational radio field where stations simply supply hour after hour of classical music for those who appreciate it, but do very little to develop an appreciation or understanding of that music within the general audience. To remedy this failing, the Wayne State University radio station introduced music appreciation courses on a yearlong basis beginning in 1955. Since that time this station has continued to provide that instructional service for its community. Thus, there has been an ever growing audience which can truly appreciate the kind of music being offered to them. The same can be true for cinema.

Quite often it is assumed that universities have no relationship to commercial television stations and can be involved only with ETV stations. This is not the case at all. There is nothing within the Federal Communications Act which precludes a university from owning and operating a commercial station, on a commercial basis. In fact this is being done in several instances within the United States at this time. The first such example would be that of WOI-TV in Ames, Iowa, which is operated by Iowa State University. WHBQ-TV in Memphis, Tennessee, is operated by Harding College; KOMU-TV in Columbia, Missouri, is operated by the University of Missouri; and WHCU-TV in Ithaca, New York, is operated by Cornell University. The position generally taken by such institutions is that the reason for operating a commercial station is to meet high costs of television and at the same time to provide professional training for students of television. The philosophy of the University of Missouri as it operates KOMU-TV in Columbia is provided in the following statement: "The University of Missouri's television goals . . . are to bring a practical education and intellectual and cultural offerings of the campus to citizens by way of television and to provide the best laboratory facilities for TV students."[4]

THE PROGRAM SCHEDULE

Let us now look at the translation of a philosophy of a station into an actual program schedule. Although it is clear that no two stations will be exactly the same, it is clear that the state university owned ETV stations have about them a programming pattern in which one can see the translation of the general philosophy into the specific program schedule. The average program day of a typical university educational television station is described in an unpublished research report by Professor Griffith of the University of Missouri. In this report Griffith describes the typical day of the university station as providing a program which is essentially kindergarten through twelfth grade in the morning period along with some general adult or higher education programs. During the noon hour one would find a continuation of this programming but with a little more tendency toward the general adult or higher education programming. In the afternoon prior to 3:30 P.M., the same kind of programming as is found in the morning would occur; but the 3:30 to 4:00 P.M. period generally will be used for an in-service teacher education function. For the remainder of the later afternoon period, "the station might program Child-Youth, General Adult, In-Service or K-12"[5] while the early evening hours will find programming heavily involving child-youth audiences with some general adult or higher education programming. Beyond 7:30 P.M. until the sign-off period, one finds the general adult program approach. Griffith's survey also included some notions of the justification for programming or, in effect, what was the university's philosophy of operation. He lists the following services in a descending order of importance:

a. Informational and cultural programs to the general public.
b. Units of K-12 (primarily K-6) instruction to schools in the coverage area.
c. Regular university courses for on-campus students and for adults on a credit or non-credit basis.
d. Informational and cultural programs for pre-school and school age children.
e. In-service training for teachers and other professional and non-professional groups.[6]

One can see from this description of a typical programming schedule that most of the functions described previously in this article are carried out. However, it is clear that his survey supports the contention that most state university stations do not utilize their station in the area of community relations or educational and media research. These two functions are characteristically not involved in such a program schedule.

Lastly, let me mention the special issue of providing technical video services to noneducational elements within the community. Most of the financial surveys concerning ETV stations indicate that earning income through services is an integral part of the budgetary support for ETV stations. There is a philosophical question here involving the competition of a tax supported unit with a free enterprise commercial unit. It seems reasonable that services which involve the rental of station studios, video recorders, or mobile units may legitimately be provided on a *quid pro quo* basis as long as those services are not available in that community from a commercial source. If at any time a private concern makes any of these services available for broadcasters and agencies within the area, it becomes a natural restriction upon the tax supported unit. The ETV station must then discontinue providing those services.

In summary, one can say that the underlying assumption or

premise upon which the philosophy of a state supported ETV station rests is that the obligation and responsibility of that institution is to provide teaching, research, and service beyond the borders of its campus. The obligation to educate is not restricted to undergraduate or graduate students but does include all people at all ages wherever they may be. This is not to say that the university does not recognize the special responsibilities and obligations of other specific units of education, but in no sense does it rule out the university's responsibility in any area of education to any group of citizenry anywhere within the state which it serves. This is the basic American premise that education in a democracy is for all. With these principles in mind it is patent that the ETV station is the most effective tool for the extension of the university's services to its community. If an educational television service of quality and significance is ultimately to be made available to every American citizen in every part of the country, it is clear that this will have to be done under the aegis of those educational institutions which are supported by a tax base carrying with it the obligation to meet the goals of a universally available education for all Americans.

NOTES

1 Quoted in Frederick Breitenfeld, Jr., *The Financing of Educational Television Stations* (Washington: NAEB, 1965), pp. 143–44.
2 Harold Boeschenstein *et al.*, *The University and World Affairs* (New York: Ford Foundation, 1960), pp. 9–10.
3 Quoted from a speech by Edwin R. Bayley, vice president of NET, delivered at Lawrence University Alumni College in Appleton, Wisconsin, June 11, 1966. Mimeographed, p. 25.
4 William Kenneth Cumming, *This Is Educational Television* (Ann Arbor: Edwards Brothers, Inc., 1954), p. 52.
5 Barton L. Griffith, "A Survey of the Programming of Twenty-Three ETV Stations Owned and Operated by Institutions of Higher Education" (University of Missouri, 1965; mimeographed), p. 3.
6 *Ibid.*, p. 5.

The Community Station

THE operation of a community educational television station is at the same time one of the most challenging and satisfying professional tasks in the two fields of education and broadcasting. It can also be one of the most sobering and frustrating. The challenge and satisfaction have to do directly with the station's potential value to its community, the fulfillment of which potential can be both difficult and rewarding. The soberness and frustration come from the fact that some of the financial support that makes possible the most rewarding experiences is tenuous, and a decrease in support often makes it impossible to do the type of job which must be done eventually by the community ETV station if it is to succeed.

What then is a community ETV station? Or better still, what should it be?

It would seem that a community ETV station (one held in trust for a community by a board of trustees as contrasted with one operated exclusively by a school system, college, or state authority) should be one of the community's prime resources — a resource in the sense that the local symphony orchestra, the museum, the art gallery, and the daily paper are resources.

It should be the most valuable of all an area's educational-cultural resources purely because, through its electronic capability of instantaneous transmission of information, it can make each of the other resources available to the entire population simultaneously.

But this really is a matter of hardware. The station must do more. It must serve as a resource in its own right — documenting the problems, issues, and accomplishments of its community and its viewers. It must use its power to bring great cultural experiences to those whose previous cultural background has been limited, to uplift the instructional program in the schools, to open the door to the continuing learning process to the undereducated adult.

A community ETV station must mirror its community — the debates of its city council, the medical advances of its hospitals and medical schools, the existence or lack of quality in its art, theater, or musical groups, the daily stories of human existence which point up the problems, the joys, the tragedies of life in this increasingly complex society. Perhaps its most fundamental role is to interpret a man's society to him and, conversely, him to his society. The community station can count itself a success only if it succeeds in this mission. Granted, the mission is broad. But so too, then, are the opportunities for service and consequently the actual programs which become the brick and mortar of these opportunities.

The ETV audience is a sizable one, and one which is growing daily, and yet it is inadequately fed. It often deserves better than it gets from ETV stations. Specifically, a number of stations ignore in their schedules the balance so necessary in daily life. A quick glance at some community stations' program listings might give one the impression he was reading a college catalogue's listing of courses.

Too infrequently are programs designed for large audiences. All too often ETV stations take considerable comfort in the fact that their type of operation allows them to program for minority tastes. This they do — quite well! And often, it seems, to the neglect of a much larger audience which might benefit even more from a larger share of their attention. This is not to imply that these "mass" audiences are completely ignored; they do get a program or series from time to time. Nor can one find any real fault with minority programming. (As a matter of fact, it may be the depth of treatment that this allows which will enable ETV to record its most significant advances. But that is another facet of the community station's responsibility.)

Wilbur Schramm's revelation, based on his ETV survey, that ETV's audience is above average in education, income, and community activity, should be less a source of satisfaction than a matter of concern to all ETV station people.[1] Perhaps it reveals that too much of the schedule is aimed at a rather limited audience.

It may be possible that in this broad land there exists a soul or two who is not enthralled with Dylan Thomas' "Under Milkwood," a fourth repeat of "What's New," or even Julia Child's exotic preparation of sweetbread and brains. The reference here is not to the undereducated or poverty-area resident. The concern rather is with the blue or white collar workers, perhaps even the professional person, who after a difficult working day is not interested in the offerings just mentioned. What is ETV doing for these people? Is there a way to serve them? How can they be motivated to become viewers? The nagging thought persists that ETV has not devoted enough time to trying to find the answers.

Community stations, because of their reliance on the public for support and continuing financial aid, should theoretically be closer to their viewers than stations owned by single agencies with specific interests to serve. If this is the case, a re-examination is in order by the professionals — the station operators — and their boards of trustees. This should extend to recognizing such fundamental concepts as the fact that television viewing, particularly that which appeals to the more general audiences advocated earlier, is a leisure time activity. It is undertaken when the viewer is not occupied with other, more important, tasks.

With this in mind, it is easy to conclude that the ETV station should be available to a viewer when he has free time. And yet, only about one-third of the nation's ETV stations broadcast on *either* Saturday or Sunday, and only half this number carry a seven-day-a-week schedule.[2] Of those who do broadcast on weekends, few indeed are on the air on Saturday or Sunday mornings.

ETV station people are fond of talking about getting out "into the market place" to compete with their commercial colleagues for audiences. It would seem that any real competition would call for meeting them at least during all prime viewing hours. Very often a shortage of funds serves as a handy whipping-boy for this lack of service. But how many less important things are stations doing today at the expense of a Sunday night operation, for example, and the vast audience potential it offers?

And what about programs? Are stations prepared to purchase quality programs from independent producers to serve their audiences? Are they prepared to distribute on a continuing basis the materials which make certain programs of more than passing interest? I have in mind copies of recipes and folk guitar books and Japanese brush painting kits which are so popular with audiences. Are community stations prepared to structure programs which involve the viewer while at the same time offering him materials to make use of the information he's received, after he turns off his set?

Too often these materials are an afterthought and do not affect the design of a series when it is still in the planning stages. And yet ETV has found that its most devoted, loyal, and largest audiences are attracted to programs which allow viewers to participate — whether it be with instructions for a summer vacation trip, bridge lessons, gourmet cooking, building a bookcase, or looking for antique pewter. Station program executives might well spend more of their time creating more programs of this type — and building into them a greater use of supplementary materials.

All ETV stations have a considerable handicap to overcome if they are to reach the great numbers they eventually must to be termed successes. The community stations have been among the leaders thus far in meeting the problem head on, and even among them there is considerable diversity of opinion. The problem, of course, is the built-in reaction many adults have to Education. If educational broadcasters can succeed in removing the capital *E*, in convincing people that they have more to offer than in-school and college credit courses, if they can bring them to their stations just once, they have a chance of converting them to regular viewers.

One of ETV's greatest problems is that it is misunderstood (although some comment that the field is understood too well, and this is the reason for its limited audiences). Some ETV stations have tried to soften the instructional impression which their name seems to convey by calling themselves "community" stations, dropping entirely the label "educational." This too can have its problems when a local commercial station decides it also prefers that description.

In any case, the description must be more than a simple tag, often claimed in promotional copy, but seldom justified. The community ETV station must work hard at serving the various groups and individuals in its region with programs that interest them if it is to merit the name "community television." Perhaps the phrase suggested by the Carnegie Commission on Educational Television — "public television" — is most suited to our needs. This does not mean that instructional television, or formal education, needs to take a back seat in the program planning of such stations. It is, however, only one of the many services of a community station.

One serious problem the community ETV station faces is the necessity to pioneer new uses of television — in consumer education for the disadvantaged, in basic literacy skills which will enable people to move off the welfare rolls, in helping alcoholics, drug users, and the mentally disturbed to understand their problems. The list is endless and yet the community station, by virtue of its need to appeal to wider audiences which will in turn provide greater financial support, often tends to neglect these areas. When they are considered and treated, it is often contingent upon the station's making the series into a project which will be paid for by some government or other interested agency.

It is a difficult thing to walk into the office of a county welfare commissioner and persuade him that televised educational programs can help to lighten his ever increasing welfare load. (The job becomes immensely more difficult when, after selling the benefits of using the medium, it is necessary to convince him that he should pay for what he considers to be an experiment.)

Perhaps the problem is not as acute with university, state, or school board stations, whose operating authority can determine what should be done in these areas and provide the budget for it. The community station, however, often passes up such programs because funding is unavailable and its need for broad public financial support forces it to use its own production funds for programs which appeal to wider audiences.

ETV stations, in some way, must be freed from the necessity of seeking funds for experimental projects from the specialized agencies they are trying to assist. The station should be able to go to the agency with a firm proposal for attacking a specific problem and simply be able to ask for that agency's assistance on content and utilization. Too often the agency head receives the impression that the station is more interested in the money to fund the series than it is in his problem and its solution.

Financing in general, of course, is the most persistent problem faced by any community ETV station. In most stations, financial planning is on a year-to-year, rather than a long-term, basis. Great amounts of staff and volunteer energy and time are consumed in attempts to secure "*this* year's budget." Auctions, benefits, membership campaigns, art sales — all are used to enable the nation's ETV stations to continue operation for another year, hopefully each year at a higher level of support.

And yet the amount under discussion on the whole is ridiculously small. As part of a survey for its report, the Carnegie

Commission on Educational Television found that in 1965–66 all the nation's educational television stations spent slightly more than $57 million on operating and capital costs [3] — less than two-thirds the amount spent by Sears, Roebuck & Company on newspaper advertising alone in 1965. [4]

Community educational television station managers and boards have become so accustomed to justifying and scrambling for meager budgets that they tend to forget their budgets must be considerably larger if they are to have an impact upon their communities. The same Carnegie study quoted previously discloses that 29 percent of all stations operated on budgets under $250,000. How they can provide a realistic and effective service is anybody's guess. A representative school district, with a student population of only 10,000 would normally figure on an outlay of at least $5 million. Should an ETV station be called upon to serve twenty times that number of regular users on a budget only 5 percent as great?

The entire thinking of ETV staff people, their boards of trustees, and the viewers they serve, must undergo a radical change. The station with a $2 million-plus budget cannot serve its community as it should for less than $5 million. The $500,000 budget station must set its sights on a $1 million outlay.

If ETV stations are to fare better than their commercial counterparts do presently in their station-network relationship (many commercial stations simply serving as network distribution agencies, producing a minimum of locally oriented programs), the first priority in any government or foundation assistance to ETV must be the strengthening of the local station. The individual ETV station must have sizable funds to improve its programming, and the discretion to spend them as it determines they can most usefully be spent.

Money to support local operations on a vastly increased scale probably cannot come from increased viewer contributions, or local or state government grants, as suggested by the Carnegie report. These can account for just so much revenue before they begin to level off; indeed in a number of cases, the leveling-off process has already begun. Nor can most stations hope to derive these funds from the amounts earned on production contracts with various federal, state, and local governmental agencies. At present, production money seems to gravitate toward the stations which have previous national production experience and which seem especially well equipped for high quality production. (The Carnegie Commission, in fact, recommended a continuation of this "key" production station principle.) Where then will the funds come from?

Suggestions have been made that ETV stations be allowed limited commercials, that they operate pay TV systems, that annual taxes be imposed upon advertisers based on their ad billings, that excise taxes be placed on all new television sets. All of these confuse the issue, however, and none really meets the problem head on. The question is how is the nation to produce a large amount of money annually for ETV and still insulate that which is to be used for programs from the possible political control which comes through annual legislative appropriations?

Serious consideration should be given to the creation of a large national endowment for ETV, the income of which could be distributed each year, on a population basis, to the nation's ETV stations. Thus, with a single massive effort, the goal of proper financing for ETV could be assured for a number of years. Such an endowment would guarantee stations a basic income, would allow them to plan their operations and services in a much more orderly fashion, and would insure insulation of program funds.

Such an endowment, in order to have the desired impact, would require the cooperation of government, business, industry, and major foundations. It should have a goal of $1 billion. A part of this could come from a one-time appropriation by the federal government of $500 million — less than half the amount spent in the first year under Title I of the Elementary and Secondary Education Act. Another $250 million should be solicited from business and industry nationally. The fourth part — $250 million —

might be made up by the Ford Foundation and other major foundations.

Admittedly this is a substantial sum. But educational television, and those it asks for support, must realize that substantial accomplishments by ETV will call for substantial expenditures.

The current population in the coverage areas of ETV stations approximates 140 million. Income from a $1 billion investment should provide roughly $50 million per year or about 38¢ per person covered by an ETV signal. This amount could be reduced by roughly 13¢ per capita to provide about $18 million annually for a national program service. Such a commitment would leave 25¢ per capita to be distributed among the stations. This per capita aid would have the effect of doubling or tripling many stations' budgets — and surely this amount is not an extravagant one for this country to spend to guarantee a quality cultural/educational television service.

Selecting stations from communities of various sizes, it would provide the following approximate amounts on a yearly basis:

WNDT, New York	$4,285,000
KCET, Los Angeles	2,015,000
WTTW, Chicago	1,825,000
WETA, Washington	1,020,000
WMSB, East Lansing	415,000
WNED, Buffalo	355,000
KCTS, Seattle	235,000
WJCT, Jacksonville	140,000
KUAT, Tucson	65,000

Naturally, modifications could be made in the formula, setting a minimum and a maximum grant for any station, or perhaps a sliding scale for the entire per capita distribution.

In this way, each station could be assured of a sizable budgetary base from which to begin its yearly operations. In addition, this type of expenditure should assure top quality service in most areas of the country and should have the effect of producing more high quality programs capable of being distributed nationally or regionally, resulting in a further upgrading of the program service.

Educational television, community or otherwise, must have the funds it needs to hire the competent people who can create the programs which must be produced. It must be able to hire the on-air talent it needs to give a fresh, colorful face to its programming. Community television perhaps needs more assistance in these areas than its sister stations (which can assign people to the station operation out of instructional budgets), but the whole field suffers for lack of the numbers of talented people, both on camera and off, who can attract the viewers.

ETV in general, and community ETV in particular, needs massive support. It needs imagination, courage, and boldness from its administrators and from its community boards of trustees. If ETV is to succeed, it needs to seize opportunities as they present themselves, or it risks their not passing its way again. Above all, educational television needs fresh and original thinking on old problems of all types — programming, financing, personnel — and the courage to move with boldness and determination when it has resolved on the best course.

NOTES

1 Wilbur L. Schramm *et al.*, *The People Look at Educational Television* (Stanford University Press, 1963).
2 Personal communication from George Schneidewind, assistant director of field services at NET (Dec. 1966).
3 Carnegie Commission on Educational Television, *Public Television: A Program for Action* (New York: Bantam Books, 1967).
4 James W. Button, Sears, Roebuck & Co. vice president, stated that the company spent $93,440,000 in newspaper advertising in 1965 (*Buffalo Evening News*, July 5, 1966).

Problems Peculiar to
The Community Station

SOME time ago an elderly gentleman who was formerly associated with John D. Rockefeller, Sr., told me that the eminent financier always asked promising young men just one question. The question was, "Do you consider yourself a manager or a builder?" The correct answer, in Mr. Rockefeller's view, was, "I am a builder." Mr. Rockefeller would then state, "Builders are worth all you can pay them, managers should be adequately compensated."

The story has relevance to ETV management. Unlike other managerial jobs the ETV manager either builds or he perishes. His is not, and cannot be, the sort of job which is encompassed by well thought-out, time-hallowed rules and regulations. He must be not only a builder but the kind of builder who constantly is forced to improvise not merely his plans, but also his materials. Unless he is able to make a solid, monumental structure out of such improvised materials, such constantly changing plans, and dubiously trained labor, he will hardly succeed. Perhaps there has been nothing quite like the establishment of ETV since the days of the medieval cathedral builders who also depended on local materials and the enthusiasm of the faithful. Their monuments also show very clearly that they were not bound by any rigidly conceived and executed plan. They are not the less impressive for that fact.

There are four major areas which must literally be built up from nothing by the ETV manager if the ETV station he runs is to serve its function. The first area is that of relationships with local educational institutions. The educational institutions must be led to use the station for proper educational purposes and, at the same time, they must be encouraged to support the station.

Next, a strong, cooperative relationship must be established with all sorts of voluntary, civic, and community organizations. The local chapter of the American Heart Association, the Council of Churches, the art galleries, the League of Women Voters, the Chamber of Commerce, the AFL-CIO, and the NAACP — all must feel that in the ETV station they have a friend. All must feel that the station is open to them. All, ideally, should be induced to feel that their support, moral, spiritual, and financial, is something which the nature of their own organization obliges them to give the station.

Third, a workable arrangement with the business community, including the commercial stations, must be achieved. This is not an easy thing to do. In addition to a sort of general mutual suspicion between business and education there are the particular problems caused by the fact that broadcast television is an open medium. Businessmen are not always responsive to the pleas of academic freedom, nor does the academic community invariably sense that it owes a considerable debt to business groups for the very creation of most of the community ETV stations in this country. The manager's job is to build, if possible, a solid bridge between these groups to the betterment of both. Incidentally, his best tool for such a bridge-building job is the understanding of the commercial TV station personnel, who are usually practical men who realize that if an ETV station fails they may very well have a commercial competitor (every bit as commercially bloodthirsty as they themselves are) on the former ETV channel.

Finally, the manager must build a base of solid financial and fund-raising support for his station. This can be done in any one of several ways including public campaign, profits from production contracts, auctions (God help us all), benefits, attachment to United Fund drives of various kinds, and door-to-door campaigns. All of these methods are in some degree unsatisfactory, but some of them at least must be built into the pattern of financial support.

In addition to all this, of course, the manager has the normal problems of getting and keeping a competent staff, matching salaries to budget, overseeing operations, including a great many which he does not thoroughly understand but which he must force to succeed, and a peculiar public relations problem whose peculiarity relates strongly to the fact that most people are unable to decide whether he is a broadcaster or an educator and the same large majority does not consider that a combination of the two is even possible, let alone desirable.

I

The building of a solid relationship with the schools, colleges, and universities of a community is dependent upon three factors. First, the schools and colleges must be convinced that the Educational Television Station can contribute to their *educational* program. (Mere public relations use of an ETV station by a college or school is bound to be a disappointment in the long run to both the school and the station.) Secondly, having decided that the station is educationally worthwhile, the school or college must be induced to pay for the expenses of this service precisely as it would pay for laboratory equipment of visiting professors. Strangely enough, this is one of the chief problems of a station manager, since, for reasons which I do not fully understand, many schools and colleges believe the services of the ETV station should be free to them, even though they would not dream of asking a visiting engineer to contribute free consulting services, or a textbook manufacturer to make his entire warehouse available to them at no cost.

When the worthwhileness of the service is apparent to the institution, and when it has agreed to share the costs of operating the station, one comes to a further difficulty, that of the supervision of academic content. Content of a broadcast program is, by law, the responsibility of the station. Academics by long tradition object to anyone supervising the content of their lectures. The difficulty can be resolved in several ways, but one of the ways is not for both sides to ignore the problem and hope that it will go away. Yet another aspect of this particular problem has to do with the relationship between the ambitions of school administrators in large educational institutions to administer their own broadcast facility versus the natural desire on the part of the manager to make sure that the station's independence is maintained while, at the same time, the program and financial support the educational institution represents will not be diluted.

Less difficult to solve, and more amusing, are the problems which sometimes arise between station personnel intent on what they call "production values" and teachers and lecturers intent on preserving what they call "academic dignity." Fortunately, these latter disputes are not fundamental, although from the amount of attention they sometimes receive one would think they threatened the foundations of the republic.

II

The building of a solid base of community organizations which will support the station can only be done, in my opinion, by the manager of a station. He must personally make speeches before at least fifty organizations a year. He must, if possible, serve on the board of directors of as many of these organizations as he can work into his schedule; he should be an active participant in the cultural, educational, and, yes, the political life of the community. There are few bonds as effective as those forged in the heat of a community campaign for better schools, cleaner politics, improved racial integration, professional civic planning, or a half dozen other major issues of our time. If the manager and his staff all do their parts in this form of endeavor, they will not lack for support from the leaders in these groups when the station needs help. However, I do not believe that this sort of activity will make any great contribution with respect to actual financial or programming results. It can only be said that a station which does not have broad community support will find the going very rough indeed when it is attacked. Whereas a station which does have such support will undoubtedly rise above such attacks.

III

The business community of almost any area is fully aware that by the proper use of tools and machines, the unit cost of the products it turns out or the services it renders can be reduced. Intelligent businessmen realize that quality, no matter what the product or service, can be achieved either by time-consuming and very expensive individual work, or by mass production using the best materials and machines. Such businessmen are fully convinced that the use of television in the service of education can improve the quality of education and lower the unit costs, if not the total costs. No ETV manager of any experience in my acquaintance would deny this.

On the other hand, the teacher is frequently fearful that television will be used in such a way as to make him become a mere adjunct to the educational process like a factory worker tightening bolts on an assembly line. It is the business of the manager to build a relationship between these two schools of thought (both of which are often not completely coherent) in such a way as to point out to the academic that the TV machine is his servant in terms of achieving the high quality of education he desires (or should desire), but also pointing out to him that some of the fruits of the use of the machine should be achieved not only in improvement of the quality of education, but also in lower cost.

There has been an unwillingness on the part of both groups to see the other's point of view, and the manager has the exciting task of attempting to make these apparently divergent viewpoints

become a unity. I do not know of any ETV manager who has yet
succeeded entirely in this endeavor. But I do not know of any who
has made a conscientious effort along this line who has completely
failed. Somehow the manager must convince the educator that
ETV can improve the quality of education even while it cuts unit
costs, and somehow the manager must convince many a business-
man that the improvement of quality comes first and that if it
has been achieved, the cutting of the unit costs can and will
follow. Obviously the manager in this situation is committing a
double heresy — much like certain evangelistic groups in late
Reformation times who were mercilessly hunted down by both
Catholics and Lutherans. Nevertheless the ground on which he
stands is the only solid ground in this morass of ideas, and the
building of a bridge between business and the academic world
is one of the prime tasks of ETV. In addition it's one of the most
interesting functions of the manager's job.

IV

All sorts of voices are being raised today stating that ETV must
have some form of massive infusion of federal funds. Other voices
have been raised pointing out the parlous financial plight of
almost all of the ETV stations. The first statement is based on
incorrect premises and the second upon a misreading of facts.
ETV is *not* in deplorable financial condition, and the figures
usually adduced to support this alleged situation simply do not
include at least two-thirds of what is being spent on educational
television. Of the 140 ETV stations operating today most have
improved and added to their facilities, raised their salary schedules, added staff, and are serving far more people than was the
case when they began; they are also serving their increased audiences better each year. If there is a case for federal funds for ETV
operating expenses it has not yet been made.

All the above does not detract from the fact that money has to
be raised. The prime source of operating money for ETV, it seems
to me, should be the institutions which are served by ETV, and

such institutions should bear the major part of the costs of maintaining the stations. In most cases this is what actually occurs. Large direct tax appropriations are not often secured by community stations. Most of them, however, are paid for the services they render by the public and private educational institutions they serve.

Yet no station wants to exist entirely on payments from these institutions for services rendered, since every station has creative people who have plans of their own, often very good plans, for artistic and cultural programming. The question of where funds to support such programming can come from is a very grave question indeed. I, speaking as one station manager, dislike the idea of conducting auctions and the selling of Kim Novak's used bedsheets. I must admit, however, that this sort of activity appears to raise money which, in turn, has led to the production of some interesting programs by a number of stations. I also do not like the door-to-door, tin cup type of solicitation. Yet, this also seems to have been productive, even though I must say that results seldom last more than a few years. Most desirable, it seems to me, as methods of fund raising are production contracts for foundations, business enterprises, schools, and community organizations. All these groups have need for films, tapes, kinescope recordings, and a number of other audiovisual aids. The station is in a position where it can do such work at a high quality level, having both staff and equipment necessary and this sort of enterprise is related directly to its educational mission.

Also useful in general fund raising is the membership fund drive which entitles those who become members to consideration with respect to the distribution of program schedules, booklets, brochures, and other special materials. Last, but by no means least, are foundation gifts which can be cultivated by the manager but which seldom are received, at least in terms of a large grant, without the active cooperation of the members of the board of trustees or directors of the station.

It goes without saying that either a strong, cooperative board of directors or a weak noninterfering one is essential to the realization of all of these aims and objectives. How a manager can obtain a board with these characteristics, however, is one of the Eleusinian mysteries and beyond the scope of this chapter.

Conclusion

Managers of commercial television stations or other business enterprises are seldom confronted with problems of building bridges between the academic and business community, between community organizations and a production staff, or between fund raisers and donors. These are the "peculiar problems" of the ETV manager. If a manager solves them, or comes close to solving them, he will make his station an indispensable institution in the community. If he makes a major effort to solve them he will probably end up with the respect of the entire community (which will be useful to the ETV station). If he makes no effort to solve these peculiar problems, or if he denies their existence, the station will probably have to obtain the services of a new manager.

National Educational Television As the Fourth Network

IN MAY of 1954, when what is now National Educational Television inaugurated its weekly program service, there were four noncommercial ETV stations in the country, covering areas with fewer than four million persons. In April of 1967 the National Educational Television Network consisted of 112 independent affiliated stations, covering areas with a combined population of almost 130 million.

NET began as the Educational Television and Radio Center, a corporation established in Illinois in 1952, the year the Federal Communications Commission reserved 242 channels in the VHF and UHF bands for noncommercial educational use. In 1953 and early 1954, when the first ETV stations were being activated, this new organization was developing a board of directors, building a staff, and finding for itself a home — in Ann Arbor, Michigan. Created by and, in its earliest years, supported by the Fund for the Advancement of Education (which, in turn, had been created by the Ford Foundation), the Center was conceived as basically an "exchange center," most of whose programming would be produced by the member stations themselves. The Center had no production staff or equipment of its own.

Today the affiliated stations still produce programs under contract for NET, but this programming is only a small part of the whole. Some of the rest is acquired from foreign sources and adapted for American audiences. Most of the rest — or fully half of the 260 hours of new public affairs, cultural, and children's programming that go into the weekly service each year — is produced by NET itself. Now NET production crews traverse the nation and the world. They go into South Vietnam and South Africa and the Soviet Union; they also go into Harlem and Birmingham and Berkeley. NET programming in the mid-1960's, including that produced for NET by the stations themselves, is professional and ambitious. In purpose, scope, substance, and technique, it is undoubtedly, even at this early stage, beyond the visions of some of the men whose enlightened stubbornness brought about the establishment of the Educational Television and Radio Center.

Yet, this programming is not a contradiction to but an evolution from the aims of these men. The evolution was, by necessity, a slow one. Its first phase came to a climax in 1959 when the Center, while leaving its technical and distribution facilities in Ann Arbor, moved its headquarters to New York City and became the National Educational Television and Radio Center. The emphasis now was on programming of high quality, although the extremely limited resources made that a very difficult achievement. This new period also brought the "fourth network" concept as a goal for the future. Then, in 1963, came a second climax. After an extensive study of the problems and potentialities of ETV, the Ford Foundation (which had taken over the basic support of the Center) announced the first of its annual $6 million grants to finance the program service of NET. This, of course, was a substantial increase in the level of support. NET immediately made plans to turn over to other agencies its previous activities in radio, instructional television, and ETV station activation and welfare. Simultaneously, it reorganized and greatly strengthened its program staff. All resources were now concentrated on the one objective: a television program service of substance and quality, to be provided to the American people through the nationwide network of noncommercial ETV stations affiliated with NET.

That network had been steadily expanding. The number of stations climbed to twenty-five in 1957, to fifty in 1961, and to seventy-five in 1963. Two years later it reached and passed one hundred. This was in fact becoming the nation's "fourth network."

Some people in ETV do not like the term "fourth network" and have argued against it. They say it implies — or can seem to imply — inferiority to the three national commercial networks. Partly in deference to this point of view, NET virtually eliminated the phrase from its promotional and publicity materials in 1963. Nevertheless, it refuses to die. Critics, columnists, and editorial writers use it frequently in referring to the National Educational Television Network, and when the editors of *The Farther Vision* asked me to contribute a chapter to this volume, the assigned topic was "The Role of National Educational Television as the Fourth Network."

There is, I think, good reason why the phrase continues to live. If to some people it suggests television's minor leagues, to others it means not that at all but something they eagerly welcome: that is, a national program service different in substance and form from those of the three commercial networks, providing a true viewing choice, and achieving a program quality equal to or higher than that of commercial TV.

Now this is quite all right as far as it goes. I myself and a number of my colleagues at NET have said repeatedly that we have an obligation to be different from the commercial networks. Thus, our programming will provide the viewer with an alternative to the normal commercial fare, and it will often reach out to some of the so-called "minority interests." Certainly also, despite our very modest budgets, we strive for the highest level of quality in that programming — or, to phrase it in another way, for "viewer excitement." But none of these is really the end in itself. Each is either a very desirable secondary goal or a means to the end. And what is that end? What, in other words, is NET's primary function as the nation's "fourth network"? I shall not, at this point at least, attempt to answer that in any neat little sentence or phrase. It would be wiser, I think, to look briefly at what we do and why we do it and where we expect to go from here. The neat little sentence or phrase would then be more meaningful, and perhaps even unnecessary.

I

It is generally agreed that the most urgent educational need in the United States today is for greater awareness and clearer understanding of the complex issues facing us and the people of other nations. I won't labor the obvious. We all know what the world is like; we know what hangs in the balance; and we know that the American citizen, whether he wants to be or not, is deeply involved in the resolution of these issues. We also agree, I assume, that television, with its power to reach and move great numbers of people, has not merely a function here, but an obligation.

NET devotes at least half of its resources and half of its schedule to programs in public affairs. These are programs meant to induce people to think critically about public issues, to provide information to them and instill in them the desire for more information, to provoke in them a new awareness, alertness, and responsibility. It is quite true that in some respects commercial television has done and continues to do an excellent job in public affairs; for instance, its superb coverage of special events has been a highly valuable contribution to public knowledge and understanding. But commercial television, for reasons that go deep into the nature of the industry, cannot do a thorough job — especially in an era whose problems are as numerous and varied, as intricate and interwoven, and as delicate as those that confront us in this last half of the twentieth century.

We at NET believe that, as the programming agency for the nation's independent noncommercial "fourth network," our organization has several particular obligations in the field of public affairs programming: (1) to seek out the submerged issue below the surface problem or condition; (2) to point up and illuminate issues that have been largely neglected elsewhere; (3) to anticipate issues and thus prepare the American people for future challenges and decisions; (4) to trace the evolution of and bring historical perspective to current problems; (5) to relate seemingly unrelated issues and show how the remote problem or condition does now or may someday affect our daily lives; (6) to tackle controversy, not for the sake of controversy but for the sake of the issue, and to handle it with fairness, courage, and responsibility.

The rest of NET's programming — almost half of the total — falls into two categories: cultural programming and programs for children. The needs served by these two are not as immediately compelling as those that our public affairs programs attempt to help meet. Yet, I think it would be difficult to overstate the long-range importance of either.

Our cultural programming includes, on the one hand, performance in drama, music, and the dance by many of the world's most gifted artists, and, on the other, various programs in the arts, the humanities, and the sciences. This programming, as we shall note later, has several functions, but the primary objectives of all of it are the classic goals of the liberal arts ("the arts of free men") and, indeed, of most serious works of art — to help man know the nature of himself, his world, and his fellow man; to give him a deeper understanding of his own and other cultures; to show him what the past was and what the future may be; to help him to think and reason, and to recognize and respond to beauty. These objectives are almost as old as thought itself. The one thing new that NET brings to them is the medium of television.

Our children's programming has always been, for lack of funds, a rather small service, but we hope in time to be able to enlarge it considerably. Covering a very wide range of topics, it is neither "pure education" nor "pure diversion," but a blend of both. To quote the booklet written by the NET staff, *N.E.T. Program Philosophy and Purpose: A Guideline for Staff Planning* (New York, 1964), this programming strives "for the kind of adventure and excitement that will both engage the child and challenge his mind" (p. 12). The purposes, then, are those of the educator, while the means are those of the broadcaster. "Successful programming of this type," the booklet continues, "will have a by-product that is valuable both to the child himself and to the long-range goals of educational television. It will help to develop in the young viewer, while he is young, a lifelong habit of selective viewing. It will teach him, while he is still willing to be taught, the joy of learning through television" (pp. 12–13).

It is clear, I think, that the *primary* objectives of NET in all three program categories are essentially those of the educator. This should surprise no one, for we are, after all, educational broadcasters. Still, NET does have other functions that are important and exciting, and these do sometimes obscure the basic purposes. I will turn to them in a moment, but before I do there are two other points to be made.

The first has to do with the limits and nature of ETV's contribution. Just as in-school television is not meant to be a substitute for the teacher in the classroom, so is NET programming not meant to be a substitute for books, magazines, or newspapers, or, when these are accessible, for the theater or concert hall. There are certain things that television can do far more effectively than any other communications medium, but there are other things it can scarcely do at all. Actually, our programs are intended to serve as a spur. If they are successful, our viewers will read more books, magazines, and newspapers than ever before, and will make more visits to the theater and the concert hall. Incidentally, with the production of some of our programs we print and distribute study guides and reading lists for persons who are stimulated by the program itself to pursue the subject further. We also work with institutions, professional organizations, and civic groups to promote formal or informal group discussions of the material presented in certain programs and series.

The second point has to do with our intended audience. It surely follows, from the objectives I have stated, that we do not think of our audience as consisting mainly of a small group of intellectuals. The learned and the highly creative will be attracted to many of our programs — and we want them to be — but the audience we expect to build, and have in fact begun to build, is much larger and much more diverse. It ranges in age from the very young to the very old, and it includes persons of widely different backgrounds, occupations, and intellectual attainments. Audience research figures indicate that the total ETV audience in the United States more than doubled in the five-year period from 1961 to 1966. The estimate is that more than 20 million persons watched educational television in any given month of 1966. This, indeed, is really only a beginning. That audience will grow considerably more vast, as ETV (and NET) programming gets better and better, and as more and more people come to discover the adventure and the satisfaction of this kind of television.

II

NET, as I have said, does have other functions, and although these must be regarded as secondary, each is highly important in itself and together they add an exciting dimension to ETV and its "fourth network."

First, NET programming, combined with that of the individual ETV station, provides an alternate service, a viewing choice for people who regularly seek from television something more stimulating and substantial than the normal commercial fare. NET dramas, concerts, and ballets help to satisfy the hunger for such performances of a "minority" of millions. Many programs in the humanities and arts and some public affairs programs also appeal to interests that have been largely ignored by commercial TV, and the children's programming of NET and the affiliates themselves is in sharp contrast to the brashness and violence that prevail in the late afternoon on other channels. As all ETV programming continues to improve, this alternate service will in itself become a considerable contribution to the cultural life of our nation.

Second, NET often serves as a testing ground, in talents and techniques, for all of television. Commercial TV generally cannot afford to experiment; we must and we do. Perhaps our most noteworthy endeavor here is our project with the Lincoln Center for the Performing Arts to commission and produce original works for television in various art forms. However, this whole effort pervades our programming; we are constantly searching for new and gifted performers, writers, and directors, for new ideas, and for something else — an elusive something that is best described as "the language of television." The booklet *N.E.T. Program Philosophy and Purpose* says this: "N.E.T. has, indeed, a responsibility to its own medium — the responsibility to help television achieve its highest and best mode of expression" (pp. 6–7). Of course, experimentation means failures, and we have had these and will go on having them. But our failures, though sometimes embarrassing, can be nearly as valuable as our successes, for they tell us all something about this medium of television.

Third, NET programming greatly enhances the schedules of the affiliated stations, helps to build an awareness of these stations in their own communities, and thus serves to increase both their community support and the audience they are able to attract to their local programming. The interdependence of NET and its affiliates is obvious. Flourishing, vigorous, resourceful stations mean a more effective national program service, and a national program service that has quality, substance, and appeal gives strength to the stations. This matter of strengthening the local stations through a national program service was a highly important objective in the founding of the Educational Television and Radio Center. It is still a highly important function of NET.

III

In August of 1966 the Ford Foundation made its now famous domestic satellite proposal, and a new era in educational television had begun. Early in 1967 the Carnegie Commission on Educational Television issued its report, which recommended that the Congress establish a nonprofit, nongovernmental Corporation for Public Television. Soon after, President Johnson sent his proposal for such legislation to the Congress and the Senate began its hearings. Now at last public attention was focused on the needs of ETV at all levels — local, state, regional, and national.

On the national level the three most urgent needs are much greater funds for program production, network interconnection, and conversion to color programming (which, of course, requires conversion to color capability by the individual stations). In January 1967, NET began a series of interconnection demonstrations, to give the American people some idea of the contribution that national interconnection could make. Such interconnection is necessary if only for the negative reason that NET's present system of distribution (by mail, on film or videotape) has become unwieldy and very costly; but there are strong positive reasons too, for it will make possible a much more effective program service. This we intend to prove in 1967 and 1968 with our coverage of special events, our background analyses of breaking events, and our weekly, live experimental series on politics, education, science, and the arts.

Color programming may seem, at first glance, to be a luxury inappropriate to educational television. But unless we convert at least gradually to color, we will lose most of what we have so painfully gained over the years — most of the audience we have slowly built. Perhaps it is true that some types of programming will never be done in color; in time, however, an audience accustomed to color — and the American audience is certainly going to become accustomed to it — will look upon black-and-white television as hardly more than a curiosity. We educational broadcasters do not have to dig very deep into our memories to recall the days when ETV itself was mostly regarded as a curiosity, and we do not care to return to them.

Interconnection, color, and increased program funds will make a vast difference in the effectiveness of the individual ETV stations and of their network, but it will not alter the basic objectives of National Educational Television. Certainly NET has no desire to become a super structure that would dominate American ETV. The probability is, in fact, that when ETV in this country reaches its full development in terms of station activation — perhaps 400 stations — almost half of these will *not* be NET affiliates because their functions will be quite different from those of NET. In that period of full growth, however, NET expects to be able to reach, through its affiliates, from 90 to 95 percent of the American people, and it expects to provide to this public, through these affiliates, a program service that meets the very highest standards of both the educator and the broadcaster. Although the size of that service (that is, the number of new hours of programming per year) will gradually increase, the emphasis will continue to be not on quantity but on superior quality.

Earlier in this chapter I declined to attempt to describe NET's role as the "fourth network" in one neat little sentence or phrase, and I still do, but now I think of two short paragraphs that conclude the text of a small publication of ours entitled *National Education Television — 1965* (New York, 1965):

N.E.T. is a unique development in television; there is no other agency quite like it anywhere in the world. And the contribution it makes to the educational and cultural life of the nation is also, in many ways, unique.

Frequently, and justifiably, television has been described as the most powerful means of communication ever devised by man. N.E.T. was created for one purpose: to take the peculiar magic and the incredible power of this instrument and put them to use in the best interests of man.

Perhaps that says it as succinctly as it can be said.

NET and Affiliate Relationships

A TELEVISION network and its affiliated stations are supposed to go together like love and marriage. Affection and respect are good for openers, but the lasting marriage is based on much more. Each party must have something the other needs, and each must be willing to adjust to change. Once in a while, each has to give up a personal desire for the greater good. Inevitably, there are increasing responsibilities to be shared.

NET-Affiliate relationships have been good or bad, turbulent or tranquil to the degree that there has been balance in station-network acceptance of responsibility. There have been squabbles as in any growing family, but serious imbalance in the give-and-take relationship has been rare and relatively short lived.

A few skeptics have been certain the marriage would never last, and there have been backyard gossips eager to predict and even encourage divorce. Yet somehow, NET and the affiliates have reached a thirteenth anniversary.[1] Far from falling apart, in 1967 the still growing National Educational Television Network appears stronger than ever. The stations and their network are making pictures and sounds that are being seen and heard throughout the land. Together they are now beginning to justify their reason for being and have become bold enough to glance beyond what they are doing today toward what they must be doing tomorrow. If this sounds idealistic, it should be noted that idealism has been the one consistent factor throughout the short, exciting NET-Affiliate history. It has encouraged the doers to override the voices of pessimism. When the delicate balance of NET-Affiliate relationship has been jarred, idealism has unquestionably provided impetus to adjustment. It's a good thing, for in thirteen years there have been some fascinating misunderstandings and growing pains.

At the outset, NET (then ETRC, Educational Television and Radio Center) was an organization divorced from traditional educational ties and procedures. When C. Scott Fletcher insisted that the first board of directors include broad representation of national leadership,[2] he may have made the most important of his contributions to noncommercial television. There were to be distinguished business and professional men involved at the policy level rather than a controlling body dominated entirely by professional educators or educational broadcasters, or both. Most of the early community stations followed this lead, and it set the tone of their operations — the idea that a noncommercial station had as much responsibility to serve the total society as to serve the formal educational establishment. Most of the early university-based operations also accepted this concept. Had this not been the case, the future of noncommercial broadcasting would today hardly be a matter of national concern.

During the early years, there was little open quarreling between the affiliates and ETRC. The few stations[3] were engulfed in the trials of day-to-day existence, and the Center was immersed in the task of providing some kind of service to its affiliates. Communication between them was at a minimum. By 1956 the station managers were virtually unanimous in dissatisfaction with Center program content, technical and production quality, distribution, production contracts, and lack of understanding of station problems. So, the Affiliates Committee was born out of displeasure.[4] Formed in 1956, the Committee first met in 1957, and from that time has been an important influence on NET-Affiliate relationships.

While the stations spoke in one unhappy voice about ETRC's product and procedures, they were *not* unanimous concerning the proper role of the Center. Some felt the comparatively strong centralized organization of the Center would increasingly diminish local autonomy. Leery of a network headquarters which might become too big and powerful, they felt the proper function of the Center should be that of a quality library service, no more. Other station heads called for more Center leadership, more services, and a strong national network concept. This group argued that anything less would rapidly reduce educational television broadcasting to little more than an audiovisual classroom aid. In 1957 and 1958 the latter opinion was held by the majority. How much the Center board of directors was influenced by the station managers is debatable, but at any rate they must have held similar views, for the national approach prevailed. In 1958, John F. White became president. The following year the major offices were moved from Ann Arbor to New York City and the Center became *national* in name and purpose. Through subsequent years the greatest successes and the most serious difficulties in NET-Affiliates relationships have been rooted to the same items that were of concern during the 1954–58 period. How has the marriage worked?

The program product the affiliates now get makes the early effort appear as the dark-gray age. When the stations and NET argue content and production today, the discussions are on a comparatively sophisticated level. Those stations subject to political and social pressures, those with timid leadership, have reservations about public affairs programming that treats controversial issues without equivocation. And, of course, an issue that stirs up pressure groups or the local power structure for one station may be far less provocative elsewhere. Other stations welcome and urge the kind of programming that lights sparks in their community, that prompts reaction from those who agree or disagree on a matter of public concern, and that helps to establish their station as the proper community forum for treatment of ideas that do not inspire consensus.

No longer does the question of the illustrated lecture versus the documentary approach take up hours of station-network meeting time. It is more likely that concern for the level of content and approach, esoteric versus popular, is the subject at hand. Balance and point-of-view problems in the treatment of content are now matters for both heated and thoughtful exchange of opinion between station managers and NET officials. Not too long ago the question of whether an educational quiz show is appropriate programming would have been a more predictable topic.

Not only are the subject and content of NET programs today a far cry from those of several years ago, but the programs are seen by far more people. There are more than twice as many affiliates, and the aggressive affiliate has doubled or tripled its audience. Today the error in judgment or production failure in an NET program occurs far less often than in the past. However, when it does it is of greater import. This is unquestionably progress; and while the NET-Affiliate dialogue is no more heated than in 1960, the subject matter of the exchange is far more consequential.

Affiliate concerns over technical quality diminished rapidly after 1958. The 1959 Ford Foundation grant that NET obtained to furnish its affiliates with videotape recorders was a giant step, and, not surprisingly, a technical honeymoon followed. Also, it is probable that several new stations were induced to join the happy family more by the potential of a free sixty-thousand dollar piece of equipment than by the opportunity to fulfill the responsibility of providing the kind of broad community service implied in their FCC license. Nevertheless, under Howard Town, NET established the largest, best-equipped videotape duplication center in the world and set standards in recording that have led the industry since.

Affiliate approval of NET technical and distribution quality from 1960 on has not been returned in kind by NET. The network has been continually distressed with the technical quality of the average affiliate's production. Some of this concern is directly related to the problem of affiliate production for the network.

Before 1958 it was thought that the Center should obtain much of its programming by purchasing the better efforts of affiliates and contracting with affiliates for the production of mutually planned series. Furthermore, it was understood that stations producing for the Center would gain a measure of financial stability as a result of contract production. The concept was both a success and a failure. It certainly affected station relations.

Undoubtedly, contracts to produce for the Center contributed to the survival of a few stations during the early years. And, in fact, only a few wanted to produce or could produce for national distribution at that time. The producing stations wanted more and bigger contracts. They often questioned the Center decisions on subject selection and worried about producer freedom versus Center influence and control. The Center, on the other hand, felt its money was being unduly siphoned off to general station support at the expense of product quality, considered its control over production far too limited, and often deplored the technical level of the programs delivered.

Difficulties between producers and contractors are to be expected, but they become particularly complex when some of the producers are also users of the product. During the early years, all of the users, nonproducing and producing stations alike, were unhappy with the product. Under John F. White, NET coupled general program expansion with a changing policy on contracts for station production. Today NET spends a sizable amount on contracts with producing affiliates, and has contracts with more affiliates than at any previous time. However, the bulk of this programming comes from a few affiliates with proven capability. NET contracts with stations often carry a sizable financial commitment; and, with rare exception, NET controls and supervises from concept to delivery.

Therefore the relationship problems between NET and a producing affiliate now tend to be conducted separately from the network and its affiliate users. Meanwhile, program heads consistently voice a desire for more affiliates capable and desirous of network production, but point with alarm at evidence that too often the capability does not exist.

One persistent problem between a network and its affiliates will never vanish. Each will never feel that the other "really understands me." Often both will be right. Still, the degree of understanding can be measured in direct proportion to how well the means of communication are working. In spite of startling growth in network action and station numbers, the means for talking together exist. Since 1959, NET has had a station relations (currently called Field Services) department. This arm and the Affiliates Committee are the instruments designed to keep the family "speaking to each other" between meetings of the total group.

There have quite naturally been high and low points, but generally the conversation for eight years has been fascinating. A notable exception was 1964 when a major change in NET financing and responsibility was adopted by NET. This created a temporary situation in which neither NET nor the stations were quite sure whether they were supposed to be speaking to each other or what tone of voice was appropriate. As it turned out, both soon rediscovered their interdependence, and many participants at the affiliates' meetings of 1965 and 1966 were impressed by evidences of genuine group maturity.

If NET sometimes seems arbitrary or unresponsive to the stations, the stations often appear to NET (and even to their own Affiliates Committee) as an enigma. On many issues it is impossible to get a clear reading because station opinion is split. When this happens, NET is obliged to make its own decision or delay action. The Affiliates Committee is hard pressed to represent the stations in split-personality situations and, in fact, the Committee itself is often divided. There have also been some ill-remembered "straw votes" at affiliates' meetings. Viewing an impressive show of hands, NET has on occasion moved quickly to action only to find that many hand-raisers enjoyed second thoughts after returning home. Nevertheless, whenever the affiliates or their Committee have presented a strong and persistent majority opinion, NET has attempted to respond affirmatively. Instances of network refusal to adjust have been rare.

Since 1958, NET has acted vigorously on its belief that it is a network headquarters responsibility to lead its affiliated stations into new technical levels of operation and to encourage better, bolder local programming. In the mid-1960's NET began urging stations to program weekends and to make the necessary financial commitment for color capability. Then, in quick succession, came the August 1966 Ford Foundation satellite proposal, the first NET coast-to-coast demonstrations of interconnection using AT&T long lines, the "Public Television" report of the Carnegie Commission, the Senate and House bills to assist educational broadcasting, the Ford Foundation multimillion dollar grant to establish an experiment called the Public Broadcast Laboratory of NET, and the Senate committee hearings on the proposed legislation. Suddenly, the entire noncommercial television establishment was thrust into a national dialogue. As of spring 1967, NET and the affiliates found themselves subjects of high level attention and objects of curiosity or concern to a host of special interests. Despite considerable confusion, to most it seemed that a dream was about to come true.

Whatever form the Carnegie proposed Public Television Corporation may take, whatever method is finally selected to provide the necessary financing of noncommercial television, whatever the result of bold experiments in interconnected programming, there is no doubt that the basic shape of the ETV structure will be altered. Still, the absolutely vital need for a close producer-distributor-user relationship will remain. How the network and the stations adjust to the give and take that the new era demands will be a key factor in success or failure. And, for a change, there will be a large audience watching the performance.

The system may be more affluent in the years immediately ahead, but some of the problems of 1967 are not financial and will remain. As the number of stations grows, it is increasingly evident that the large metropolitan center community stations share some common goals and concerns not shared by other types of affiliates, such as the small community school-board owned stations. It is not surprising that NET, which must try to serve them all, is speaking out to caution against fractionalization and to proclaim the value of unity versus the weakness of division. Yet the different types of stations make different demands on the network and have differing attitudes toward it. NET is projecting more than 160 affiliates in 1969. If this projection comes to pass, it is certain that family relationships then will be no less complex than they are in 1967.

Individual personalities have been a major factor throughout the short history of NET-Affiliate relationships. Perhaps this will be less so in the future as the numbers of people involved make intimacy difficult. If so, network-station communication will surely suffer a loss of potency. Since 1958, the NET administration has included a number of dedicated, aggressive, outspoken men. The Affiliates Committee has consistently included articulate station managers, often differing greatly in philosophy but determined to work for the greater good. The meetings of the Committee and NET officials have included honest exchange, heated argument, considered judgment, imaginative planning, and incidents of real statesmanship. There have also been some memorable individual statements from the floor at general affiliates' meetings. The personality "mix" has been exciting and of value.

Nevertheless, the basic elements of NET-Affiliate relationships are more lasting than individuals. If the family is to survive and prosper, it will be because the stations need NET for programming and for national leadership and image as much as NET needs affiliates to air its programs and to surround them with local originations worthy of community pride and support.

The network must cope successfully with the facts of station family life: Here are a set of stations varying in age, purpose, ownership, and vitality, led by individuals from differing disciplines. Station management covers a wide spectrum of philosophy, ambition, and ability. For the time being, NET must attempt to serve the owners and managers of stations dedicated to the exposure of ideas, palatable or acrid, as well as those whose greatest concern is fear itself. NET must accept the fact that it is impossible to satisfy most of the stations most of the time and aim to please most of them part of the time. The unacceptable alternative is mediocrity.

The affiliate must face the fact that participation in a vital national network is only partly a matter of airing network programs at the time they are offered or the time for which they are intended. A strong station-originated service to the total community — a service equally as robust as the network offering — is both a responsibility and an insurance policy against domination by any entity, local or national. The unacceptable alternative is mediocrity.

Both NET and its affiliated stations are entering a period when more than ever the give and take must be a mutual exercise. I believe that this can be done. I believe it on the basis of the evidence and because idealism must not be and surely is not dead. That NET and the stations should grow together was a grand concept. That they survived the first few years together was a fortunate miracle. That they have grown together in value and stature is obvious. That their future can be more rewarding for this country than any of the early dreams is evident. Apart, NET and the stations will not achieve it. Together, I believe they can and will. Besides, the first thirteen years have been too exciting not to try for thirteen more.

NOTES

1   First distribution of programs to four affiliates began in 1954. In the spring of 1967, NET listed 112 affiliates.
2   John Walker Powell, *Channels of Learning* (Washington: Public Affairs Press, 1962), p. 78.
3   There were nine stations at the end of 1954 and seventeen at the end of 1956.
4   The Affiliates Committee was formed to represent the stations in matters of NET-Affiliate concern. Six managers, elected by the total managers' group, serve three-year staggered terms. In recent years, a seventh "alternate" member has been elected for a one-year term to fill any Committee vacancy caused by resignation. In practice, the alternate has participated in all Committee meetings.

The Regional Network

THIS is a critical time for educational television. National attention is focusing on the entire noncommercial, educational television movement. ETV is being scrutinized now as never before by important groups and personages to determine, if possible, what the appropriate future might be for ETV in service to the populace and how the movement might be financed.

The strength of noncommercial broadcasting in this country will be judged by the significance and quality of the program service which each station will provide for its many audiences. The capability of the local station to provide the best service possible is directly proportional to the strength of the state, regional, and national organizations which are supportive of the local station's efforts. The local station is the key, the focal point, but it must be supported. There is no one station in the country today that has the financial, personnel, or program resources to do the job alone.

In this chapter I will report on the Eastern Educational Network as an example of what exists, and will project somewhat into the future in an attempt to place the regional network in a proper perspective relative to the total ETV complex.

107

IN THE BEGINNING

In 1959 a small group of people met together in Mittersill, New Hampshire, to explore the possibilities of a cooperative effort to upgrade the quality and the quantity of an educational television service in the northeast United States. Included in the meeting were personnel from the two existing ETV stations in New England, WGBH-TV in Boston and WENH-TV in Durham, New Hampshire. They were joined by people from the state departments of education and by representatives of the Ford Foundation. The meeting probed the concept of regional cooperation and decided to organize a regional network as a corporate entity to foster a sharing of the region's resources among all participants.

An initial grant of $15,000 from the Ford Foundation supported the early organizational work that was necessary. Shortly thereafter the Foundation awarded an additional grant of $45,000 as seed money to get the network started as an operational body. From the beginning it was decided that the members should contribute the funds necessary to support the network by paying dues, but the budgets of the stations were so small and the members so few in number that it was necessary to obtain outside financing to begin.

An agreement of association was signed on December 22, 1960, and the network was incorporated under the laws of the Commonwealth of Massachusetts on February 9, 1961. The purposes of the original incorporators were

To promote education by preparing, producing, reproducing, disseminating, furnishing, relaying and otherwise assisting and cooperating with others in the broadcasting by television and disseminating by other means of historical, literary, musical, scientific, medical, educational, cultural and informational materials and programs and reproductions thereof, and permitting the use of the same by others by sale, gift, lease, license or other means.

Those purposes have served well as guidelines for the network activities over the past seven years and still stand as the best statement of the functions and aims of the Eastern Educational Network.

The first bylaws of the corporation listed as members:

Class A: WGBH Educational Foundation
University of New Hampshire

Class B: WHYY, Incorporated
Western New York Educational Television Association, Incorporated

Class C: The Mohawk-Hudson Council on Educational Television, Incorporated

Class D: University of Vermont
University of Maine
Bates College

Class E: Connecticut State Department of Education
Rhode Island State Department of Education
Vermont State Department of Education

Class F: Canadian Broadcasting Corporation
National Educational Television and Radio Center

The annual membership dues established for 1961 amounted to $1,500 for Class A members, from $150 to $375 for Classes B, C, D, and E members, no dues for Class F. The geographic region originally described included New England, New York, New Jersey, Pennsylvania, Delaware, Maryland, and the District of Columbia.

GROWTH AND STRUCTURE

The only other ETV station on the air within the region described above, at the time EEN was formed, was WQED in Pittsburgh. That station joined the network as a Class B member shortly after the EEN was incorporated. As new stations began operating, they joined the network. The next to join was WETA-TV in Washington, D.C., followed by WCBB in Augusta, Maine; WMHT, Schenectady, New York; WNDT, New York City; WEDH, Hartford, Connecticut; and WMEB-TV in Orono, Maine. A second station had been added in both Pittsburgh and Philadelphia. By October 7, 1963, there were seven Class A members of EEN, each paying annual dues of $3,000, and four Class B members, each paying annual dues of $750. Shortly thereafter the Class B members (stations on the air but not interconnected) requested of the board of trustees that all broadcast stations be considered Class A members and that a real effort be made to exchange programming among all members through the distribution of programs on videotape and film via the United States mails. The request was approved.

There occurred about this time a slight restructuring of the network membership to bring it to what it is today. The region was broadened slightly to include the state of West Virginia. The membership classes were altered to make Class A all broadcast stations; Class B, producing organizations; Class C, developing areas; Class D, state departments of education; and Class E, other networks. Some Class A members operated more than one transmitter, but the decision was made to establish a licensee as a single member regardless of the number of transmitters operated by the licensee.

In 1964, WTTW in Chicago and KQED in San Francisco requested membership in EEN and were refused. However, it was determined that a great deal of unilateral program exchange was taking place between those two stations and EEN members. It was agreed that the network could offer member stations a service by handling this exchange, and the two stations were allowed to subscribe to the network program service if they paid an amount comparable to that paid by Class A members. Later, KCET in Los Angeles was also allowed to become a Program Service Member. These stations participate in the program activity only and do not take part in any of the corporate affairs of the network.

The important thing to remember is that the network is a creature of the members, intended to function solely for the benefit of the participating organizations and the people they serve. The EEN board of trustees is elected from the membership and includes every broadcast station manager and representatives of all other membership classes. They elect a president from their ranks and appoint an executive director who is responsible directly to the president and the board of trustees. As the network grew, some changes were made to allow for greater participation by individual trustees in policymaking procedures. As of November 1964, and still existing, the trustees elected a chairman of the board, a president, two vice presidents, and a treasurer as the five officers of the corporation. Those five, plus two more elected at large, constitute a seven man executive committee having authority to make policy decisions during the interim between meetings of the full board of trustees.

The size of the staff has been increased from one man and a girl to nine full-time employees. As a result of growth in membership plus an increase in dues per member, financial support has improved significantly. The initial budget was $15,000 for planning and organization; it has now become $162,000. The fact that this income is totally derived from payment of membership dues attests to the viability of the self-support principle.

Over and above the regular budget, funds may come from special contracts, grants, and donations for specific projects. In 1961, the EEN entered into a contract with the United States Office of Education, under Title VII of the National Defense Education Act, and established a project known as the Northeastern Regional Instructional Television Library Project (NRITLP). From November 1961 through May 1965, $244,000 were received to conduct this project. An additional contract for $120,000 was obtained covering the period June 1, 1965, through October 31, 1966. At the same time we entered into an agreement with the National Center for School and College Television (NCSCT) to represent their materials in our region; they paid EEN a total of $50,000 during the two-year period ending April 30, 1967.

The Educational Television Facilities Assistance Act has been most helpful in stimulating new station activation and increased facilities for existing stations in the region as well as throughout the rest of the country. The EEN membership now includes twenty-one ETV stations (seventeen licensees), two production

centers, four developing areas, seven state departments of educa-
tion, three other networks, and four program service subscribers.
These stations provide service to over half the population of the
United States who can receive educational television.

PROGRAMMING

The ultimate aim of all activities undertaken by EEN is to serve
the members in such a way as to help them increase the effectiveness of their program service. We function in both the general and
instructional areas.

General programming

There is no single word or phrase to describe this area. The
Carnegie Commission on Educational Television calls it Public
Television, but for my remarks here I will retain the adjective
"general." By "general" programming I am referring to all programming broadcast for an out-of-school audience, or not broadcast for a specific instructional intent. It is not possible to describe all of the programming which has been exchanged over
the past few years. At first, the program exchange was limited
to stations that were physically interconnected. Indeed, interconnection of all stations has been a primary goal for the network
since it began. When it was decided to make all noninterconnected
stations Class A members, an exchange of programming via the
mails began in earnest. Starting with one series of thirteen programs in late 1962, the exchange has grown considerably. As of
this date we are making available to the member stations 700
hours of programming per year, or a little over 13 hours per
week, representing 981 individual program titles. This is the
amount of programming available to the members on videotape
and does not show the increased amount available to stations
in New England as a result of interconnection.

Most of the programming in distribution is contributed freely
by the member stations. In several instances, however, the staff

acquires programming outside of the network. Some series like NBC's "Open Mind" and Metromedia's "Opinion in the Capital" are contributed free. Other series are purchased by the network on behalf of the stations for a negotiated amount which is then prorated among the member stations who are able to participate in the purchase. By doing so we are able to acquire programming for the members at a price considerably less than what they would have to pay individually. This works to the advantage of the syndicator as well, because he can sell to a group of stations by dealing with only one party and usually making only one set of prints available.

In the last year we have been able to establish a modest program acquisition budget which enables us to make an outright purchase of inexpensive but superior program properties which are then distributed to all stations. Another method used to ob-

Station participation in EEN during the fiscal year 1965–66

Nature of participation	Community Station A[1]	Community Station B[2]	University Station[3]	State-owned Network[4]
Programs contributed to EEN	217	41	8	8
Programs ordered from EEN	767	666	557	845
% of evening schedule filled by EEN programs[5]	34%	25%	23%	37%
Approximate number of EEN meetings attended	13	16	11	23
Dues paid	$7,500	$7,500	$7,500	$7,500
Amount spent on program acquisition	$12,965	$5,650	$5,565	$8,096
Amount spent for dubbing	$432	$684	—	—

[1] Major market; station manager is EEN trustee and president.

[2] Major market; station manager is EEN trustee and vice president.

[3] Medium market; new station; station manager is EEN trustee.

[4] Minor market; 3 stations; microwave interconnected from Boston; 54% of total programming is taken off the microwave; station manager is EEN trustee and member of executive committee.

[5] As of May 1966, except for Community Station B, where the figure is for September 1966.

tain programming for member stations is to seek outside funds from business or philanthropic organizations to enable us to purchase a series outright and distribute it free.

The Eastern Educational Network is a mutual network. In addition to membership dues the stations are expected to contribute their best programming, as they can, as well as their personnel, time, and energy in the various meetings, seminars, workshops, and screening sessions. By and large they pay their own expenses to attend these functions. The representative station examples shown in the table on page 113 will illustrate this sense of participation during the fiscal year 1965–66. These examples include general area programs only.

Notice that for the state-owned network a large percentage of programs on the evening schedule are taken off the microwave, and notice that the percentage filled by EEN programs is highest here. This pertains as well to WENH in Durham, New Hampshire, and WCBB in Augusta, Maine. The reason for this, of course, is that the Maine ETV Network microwave system originates at WGBH-TV in Boston and interconnects all of these stations. Programs for the entire system can, and do, originate from either WGBH-TV or WENH-TV. A duplex system exists between WCBB and WMEB allowing for origination for the whole state of Maine from both stations. Interconnection now being installed will complete this duplex capability all the way back to Boston.

When the stations in Maine first went on the air, virtually 100 percent of their programs originated in Boston, enabling them to provide a quality program service from the very beginning. Since that time they have greatly increased the quantity of their local programming. More importantly, they have been able to concentrate their local efforts toward high *quality* programming since they were not burdened with the task of producing everything themselves.

It is important to keep in mind that the program exchange activity, in both the general and the instructional areas, is based on *free* exchange. No charges are made for program rights for series contributed by member stations. Each station is responsible for obtaining all rights and clearances before a program is offered for distribution. When a program or series is contributed, it is evaluated by the network staff for both program merit and technical quality and then accepted or rejected. If it is accepted, an availability announcement is sent out to all stations, and bookings are taken on a first come, first serve basis.

In selecting programs to be distributed, we make every attempt to avoid duplicating what is available to the stations from other sources. The primary national source of programming is, of course, National Educational Television. We maintain close liaison with NET and avoid acquiring elsewhere program materials which they will provide; and we attempt to provide, ourselves, programs that NET is unable to offer because of the number of stations it must serve and their lack of interconnection. We follow a similar policy in relation to the Program Service of Educational Television Stations, a division of the National Association of Educational Broadcasters.

Instructional programming

In November of 1961, the United States Office of Education awarded EEN a contract to establish NRITLP. From that time to the end of October 1966, the instructional activities of the network were supported almost entirely with federal funds. Under the first contract a library was established for kinescope recordings of "samples" of instructional television around the country. This was done in coordination with the National Instructional Television Library, which was funded by the Office of Education and housed at NET in New York. Together with a sample study guide, these kines could be requested by and would be sent to anyone in the region. If, after viewing the program, the person or organization wished to acquire the series, they contacted the producer and made arrangements to do so.

Early in the project it was decided that this procedure would not be effective in bringing about the development of a quality

Instructional Television Service in the Northeast. Better methods of exchange became the object of research, with the first study concentrating on the identification of critical curriculum areas in which television could play a vital part. Another major activity was to bring together educational television and school personnel from within the Northeast to discuss possible techniques for exchange of school broadcasting, the acceptance of programming in various educational communities, and the type of supplementary teaching materials necessary to make a substantial quality offering to the schools of the Northeast. In some cases, unilateral exchange of programming had been taking place, and eight series of programs were being used by more than one station. Arrangement for each of the "uses" was made independently between the producer and the individual station's school-service officer.

The first demonstration of "central coordination" began with the management of the series selected for regional exchange and distribution; 78.5 hours of programming were "managed" through the Project Office. This meant that a schedule to suit each station's requirements was worked out and sent to each station for approval, dubs were made, tapes were labeled, shipping was arranged, orders for guides were filled.

During the first semester of the 1964–65 academic year, in the northeast region, the member stations of the Eastern Educational Network exchanged 1,078 hours of instructional television programming which reached 3,895,745 elementary and secondary school children. The 78.5 hours managed through the Project Office are included in this number.

These courses were being exchanged on a variety of plans. Often a given station was exchanging material with as many as three or four other stations, each exchange being worked out on a different basis. The variety of plans and the complexity of management and the obvious expense in time, efficiency, and money provided additional impetus to implement central coordination of exchange and distribution for the 1965–66 school year. Thirteen instructional television series were selected for distribution to three or more television stations for use during the 1965–66 academic year. This represents 77 hours of programming.

This was a significant development, a coming of age, of the instructional television activity in the Northeast. The needless expenditure of funds, time, and personnel on independently managed distribution plans was ended. The effort and resources could more appropriately be used at each station to raise the quality and increase the use of school programming. The concept that materials must be specifically designed for one single geographic area had been dispelled. The common needs in curriculum of many states can be met with quality instructional television materials regardless of source, as the distribution activities of the network's school service indicate. Now in the second year of serious exchange of ITV program materials, the network is distributing seventeen series representing a total of 348 programs or four hours per week for thirty weeks.

The process of investigation, evaluation, acquisition, and distribution of instructional television programs is far more complicated than it is for the general programming area. It is a process in which the network staff, all school service directors of member stations and their curriculum committees, and some representatives of the participating state departments of education are engaged.

The recent development of Instructional Television Fixed Service (ITFS) and closed-circuit operations has caused concern among many broadcast station operators. EEN has taken the initial steps to effect good working relationships between these groups and our member stations. Possibly of more interest and greater consequence for the open-circuit broadcaster is the recent merging of electronics and educational materials organizations (e.g., Raytheon and D. C. Heath; RCA and Random House). In a few short years these combined organizations will be providing school systems at all levels with well-financed, well-researched, and well-prepared materials to be used in the classroom. They will use new and yet to be developed technological devices encompassing printed, aural, and video techniques which will be available to schools very economically.

Faced with this prospect we feel the instructional programming, as we now know it, will change drastically. We also believe that the financial base for member stations which are largely dependent on school or state systems may also change. We must anticipate this development and plan now for alternative methods of financing.

Program production

EEN is not normally a production agency but there have been some special projects taken on by the network in this area. The most successful was a series of fifteen half-hour programs for teachers of mathematics. Entitled "Sets and Systems," this series was produced by EEN under a contract from the United States Office of Education. It was a cooperative production between EEN and the network affiliate, WETA, Channel 26 in Washington, D.C. The series was very successful and is still being used by member stations and school systems throughout the region and is being distributed nationally by NCSCT.

The first cooperative production effort in the general program area failed due to the lack of central coordination. The next effort, on water pollution problems in New England, was more successful. Plans are now under way for a cooperative effort by the New England stations on mental health problems.

Just recently we have taken on a new project to produce three 30-minute films which will show new approaches to educational problems being made in New England under Title I of the Elementary and Secondary Education Act. These programs will be broadcast throughout New England and made available to all other member stations in the region.

The main problem we have encountered in trying to effect meaningful cooperative production is lack of sufficient funds to support the necessary facilities and personnel. The theory of cooperative production is that two or more stations might participate in the production of a program or series of programs with the network office overseeing and coordinating the entire project. The result should be a high quality program of a type which is needed by all stations in the region and which no one station could produce as economically. We are still testing the theory.

Professional activities related to programming

In an effort to support, more or less indirectly, the program capability of the network and the affiliated stations, we engage in various professional activities. We regularly hold meetings of station managers, program managers, school service directors, business managers, engineering directors, curriculum personnel, and public relations directors. Besides coordinating the affairs of the network, these people are able to exchange ideas and information on matters of common concern relative to the operation of their own stations. We believe this has resulted in a noticeable improvement of the professional capability of all stations.

The nine Northeast state departments of education have established an educational television coordinating committee. We are meeting with this committee regularly to discuss EEN matters and to aid them in their deliberations on matters which may not be of direct concern to EEN.

We have sponsored and conducted several workshops aimed at upgrading the professional ability of personnel in the region. These include a producers' workshop, an art directors' workshop, and, most recently, a workshop for crew members. We are currently planning a workshop for ITV producers. The results of these workshops have been very satisfying, and we will continue to sponsor them.

One of our more important undertakings is to represent our stations on matters pertaining to ETV before government agencies and legislative groups. We have represented them on copyright; CATV, AT&T teletype service and other tariff considerations; the ETV Facilities Assistance Act; and many others. We try to provide information to the members about activities taking place in Washington that are pertinent to their operations. We maintain constant coordination with ETS in these matters and attempt to supplement their efforts with a particular view toward the interests of our members.

INTERCONNECTION

Programming

From the very beginning it has been the intent of the founders and the present members of the Eastern Educational Network to establish physical interconnection of all stations throughout the entire region. The EEN was not intended to operate as a program library. The rather elaborate videotape and film exchange which is now being carried on has grown out of the need for diverse and superior program materials and our inability to effect the interconnection. We feel strongly that interconnection of all ETV stations on a state, regional, and national basis is an absolute necessity if noncommercial broadcasting is to reach its potential as a major cultural and informational institution in this country. Without interconnection the growth of the regional network and the service we can render to member stations will stagnate.

The final result of all our effort, money, and resources will be reflected in the program service which the local station is able to provide. The greatest gap in our program service today results from the inability of the individual station to treat important national and international events and issues while they are happening or while they are in the public consciousness. The commercial networks, by and large, do an adequate job of reporting the hard news. Because of their commercial restrictions, however, they are not able to devote large segments of time to informing the American public about the critical problems of our day. It is, of course, a cliché to restate that we must have an informed citizenry capable of making intelligent decisions which must be made every day if the democratic process is to be preserved and strengthened and given vitality. A cliché becomes such through repeated expression, and we believe the above statement to be true. We also believe it is the responsibility of the ETV broadcaster to *inform*, as accurately and completely as he can, and *stimulate* his audience. He can do this only if he has the necessary resources and support.

Reporting the news is not sufficient. The issues are too complex, the choice too varied, the time for decision-making too short. The problems must be placed in perspective, analyzed, commented upon, and made as clear as possible. This requires a number of kinds of people which no one station can afford. It requires origination of materials from many sources too numerous for any one station to cover. It requires direction and coordination of which no one station is capable. The expense for this kind of effort can only be justified if the results can be made available to many on an immediate or near-immediate basis.

While it is true that interconnection allows for an increase in the *quantity* of programs that can be made available, the primary effect is in the *kind* of programming which is made possible. This kind of programming is obvious in the news and public affairs area. What may not be so obvious is the fact that it is often possible to broadcast a major cultural event (i.e., a live symphony, drama, or opera) if it is done live and carried simultaneously on a one-time only basis. The problems of clearances on such an event, if it is to be recorded for distribution, are often prohibitive.

The psychological effect of a live broadcast — and many more of these would be made possible with interconnection — must not be overlooked. The excitement on the part of a viewer watching something while it is happening is an important ingredient. Moreover, a live broadcast is more likely to get free publicity in the press than is a recorded broadcast that has no timeliness. This means of attracting potential viewers through press notices is important, because one of the most difficult problems the ETV station has, considering the competition for the viewer's attention, is informing audiences about program offerings.

We don't expect that all or even most of the programming

which would be carried on network lines would be of the kind
that could *only* be done via interconnection. We do believe that
the need for programming of the kind we cannot now provide
is justification enough for the interconnection system. Once the
system is established, however, it is by far the most economical
and efficient method of program distribution. Most shipping and
traffic problems, with which we are presently plagued, would be
eliminated. At the same time there would accrue substantial
savings to individual stations in time, money, equipment, and
personnel which could be devoted to doing a better job on their
local programming.

Looking at the present situation which exists in EEN, we are
impressed with the fact that every station has something to contribute. Some contribute more than others, of course, but all
contribute something. Interconnection will increase not only the
quantity, but the quality, of that contribution. When producing a
program every station tries to do the best job, but knowing that
that program will be broadcast by stations throughout the regional network or across the country makes them try harder and
is additional justification to add more of their own resources to
the effort. In many cases it seems that the willingness of people
to participate in an ETV program is directly proportional to the
size and kind of intended audience. This need for an originating
as well as a receiving capability for each station is one reason
why we have always planned for at least a two-way interconnection system. Another reason is the multiplicity of needs of
the member stations.

Included in EEN are community stations, university stations,
and state-owned stations. We have the largest market (New York
City) and probably the smallest market (Calais, Maine) in the
country. The needs of the stations are varied, being very similar
in some instances and very different in others. We must try our
best to meet those needs.

A major reason for interconnection is the need to convert, as
rapidly as possible, to color. Virtually 100 percent of commercial

network prime-time programming in 1967 is in color. Educational television does have to compete for the attention of the viewer. The least expense in converting to color is the transmitter conversion. Most EEN stations' transmitters are now color capable; few have color videotape and film equipment. Interconnection will allow us to convert all stations to at least some color transmission faster than any other method.

The interconnection system would tie the member stations together for a more rapid exchange of television materials, but it could do much more than that. In tying the stations together we are also capable of interconnecting major educational and cultural institutions with which the stations are formally or informally associated. We are proposing a system which can be used as a total communications system. The priority function will be television relay, but eventually we will need to transmit voice, teletype, facsimile, computer data, teleprinting, and a host of other services that will be required by these other institutions. Some of these specialized functions could be handled by the initial system. Our capability will have to be expanded as these further requirements grow.

Facilities and design for interconnection

There are, primarily, two ways of interconnecting television stations. One way is to lease long-line transmission facilities from a common carrier. A second way is to build and operate an independent microwave system. There are advantages and disadvantages to both approaches. Economic and tariff considerations have directed our thinking and effort toward the latter.

National interconnection. — Several plans have been advanced from time to time to effect national interconnection. The primary reason that no plan has yet been implemented is simply lack of money. That is the same reason which explains why EEN has, as yet, not accomplished interconnection.

The relatively recent developments in satellite technology will have a direct bearing on this problem. In a few years, national interconnection will be possible at an economic level which is not now feasible. Meanwhile we are concerned about the interim before long distance transmission via satellite becomes a reality. Our concern is twofold. First and foremost, the need for immediacy in programming becomes more critical each day. Second is the need for some experience with interconnection. Changes in program concepts occur, and there are a host of operational and procedural problems to be solved. We feel these problems can best be met by actually operating prototype or pilot interconnection systems while waiting and planning for total interconnection. The prototype should be large enough and serve enough different kinds of stations to really test the kinds of problems involved and to provide the experience which must be had before a total national system becomes a reality.

Looking ahead to the long-range plans for a national system, we strongly endorse the concept of a multichannel system. The total ETV picture contains many varying elements. There will be, and are, state systems and regional systems. They have need for both instructional and general area programming, and their needs vary greatly within these two large categories. There are community, university, school, and state-owned stations, each kind having, to a greater or lesser degree, different purposes and priorities. Of course we do not intend that a national organization should be all things to all stations, but the national *interconnection facility* cannot provide a multiplicity of program sources on a single channel. Even the time-sharing concept would be inadequate. Let me repeat that the strength of the individual station will have to depend a great deal on the range of choices it has to select from.

At present any station can obtain programming from three national sources. National Educational Television and the Program Service of Educational Television Stations division of NAEB are concerned with the general programming area, while the National Center for School and College Television is solely concerned with instructional television. On a regional basis stations can obtain programming in both categories from the Eastern Educational Television Network, and instructional programming from the Great Plains Regional Instructional Television Library. General programming is supplied to member stations of the Midwest Educational Television Network. Program distribution by all of these organizations is handled, primarily, by shipping videotapes and films by mail.

We feel that there should be multiple national sources for programming in both the general and instructional areas. One of these could result from a consortium of regional networks.

Regional interconnection. — It would require a competent historical sociologist or anthropologist to identify the many similar elements that give any geographic "region" of this country a cohesiveness. Without going deeply into the subject, I may note that there are political, economic, and social considerations in the region covered by EEN which do result in a kind of cohesiveness of attitude and thought patterns which are different from those of other regions of the country. It is no accident that the EEN region does not extend farther south or west. It is not just compass directions that people refer to when they speak of the Northeast, the Southeast, the South, the Midwest, the Plains states, the Southwest, the Northwest, and the Far West. The reference is more often based on political and social attitudes.

We propose that each of these regions should be organized into an incorporated entity concerned with the development of noncommercial broadcasting. Each of the ETV stations in the region should be invited to join the organization and should be expected to meet the necessary costs to make the organization function on their behalf. Since it has worked well in the Northeast from an organizational standpoint, the EEN might well serve as a model for these groups. They would engage in activities similar to what we are doing, but their entire operation would differ from ours according to the specific requirements of their member stations. They should organize and work out their administrative and operational procedures before tackling the problem of interconnection, but it is important for them to become interconnected as soon as practical, because of the need their stations have for live or immediate programming and the necessity of gaining experience with interconnection if they are to participate in the consortium of regional networks.

Interconnection facilities are costly. Long ago a plan for regional interconnection was devised which called for EEN to establish and control an *interstate* interconnection system beginning in Washington and extending through Baltimore, Philadelphia, New York, Hartford, Boston, Durham, Burlington, and terminating in Montreal. Such a system would be able to feed every *intrastate* system in the region. The stations not located on the interstate trunk would receive the network programming through their own intrastate system.

It is, we believe, an inefficient use of a satellite channel if the program being transmitted is for distribution over a relatively small geographical area such as the EEN or, indeed, any of the regions we have named. We therefore propose that all member stations in each region be interconnected in a regional network pattern with a ground based system. Each network headquarters would control the basic regional system which may or may not be via a grouping of state systems. The network headquarters perforce must acquire a master control facility with switching and, at least, film and videotape origination capability. When domestic synchronous satellite transmission is feasible, each regional network headquarters would be equipped with a satellite ground station capable of sending to and receiving from the satellite. Programs would then be received from the satellite and transmitted throughout the regional system to all stations. Conversely, programs taken from the regional network could be transmitted to the satellite and made available to all other regions.

At first this could be handled on one satellite channel with proper scheduling. We would propose that an organization of regional networks would enable the network directors and program directors to meet monthly to solve administrative and programming matters. Eventually we believe it would be entirely practical to have an eight channel satellite handle this requirement exclusively. In that event, the regional networks would beam their entire service to the satellite constantly and could select to receive from the satellite any of the programs being transmitted by other regions. This would be a truly grass roots network since national origination could come, conceivably, from any station in the country.

FINANCIAL SUPPORT

The basic financial support for the regional network now comes, and should continue to come, from the network members through payments of annual dues. It is necessary therefore to consider the individual station as the single most important entity requiring significant financial support. The more money each station has to work with, the more each station can contribute to a central pooling of funds (i.e., the regional network) to strengthen the capability of the network to serve the members. As long as the basic administrative and operational costs for the network are provided by the members, and as long as the trustees' positions are occupied by the members, the network will remain a creature of the stations and other organizations that support it.

At present there are some gaps in the EEN staff structure which need to be filled. The most critical is in the technical area. We need a director of engineering, not only to shape our own plans but also to consult with and advise members. To be somewhat more complete we need to add a director of development and a director of special educational services. At some time we may add educational radio to the regional network and would require funds for professional people to administer and program that division.

These needs are upon us now and will have to be satisfied, in one way or another, in the next two or three years. The cost for salaries and support for this staff would be approximately double our present budget. This means that the member stations' dues will have to increase to approximately $15,000 or $20,000 per year. Their own budgets will have to increase to make this possible.

Quite apart from the basic administrative costs supported by dues are the interconnection operational costs. These, too, should come from member stations but not on an equal proration as in the case of the membership dues. The stations located on the basic interstate trunk should be expected to pay more than other members who get the EEN programming via their own intrastate network. All will have to pay some, and this again will necessitate a percentage increase in their over-all operating budgets.

The practice of many philanthropic organizations to provide "seed" monies to get potentially self-supporting operations going is a good one, and did, in fact, enable EEN to get started. Seed money to establish the various regional networks is desperately needed, *now*. We believe that $100,000 should be made available to these regions as soon as possible. We are convinced that the stations in the regions will support the network once it gets started and the stations can see and receive the benefits of mutual cooperation. We know they are eager to do this because of conversations we have had with individual station managers and the many requests we have had from stations all over the country to join EEN.

SUMMARY

The success of the regional network and the growth of state networks point to many advantages for educational broadcasting. The expansion and improvement in programming is obvious. Less obvious is the possibility these networks offer for providing the climate and room for experimentation and the creation of new program ideas, encouraging the development of new talent and financial resources through offering a larger audience than a single station can command, acting as a counterbalance to the existing national networks, presenting a greater diversity of opinion, acting as buffer against pressures on local stations, allowing for an increase in quantity and quality of local service, and helping to develop local station production, engineering, and audience promotion skills.

We know that the regional network concept works, for it is a reality in the northeastern United States. It works because it fills a real need for the member stations. It works because the stations themselves organized it, control it, and have each made a commitment to it — a commitment which is all important. The financial commitment is obvious. Not so obvious, but very important, is the personal commitment of resources, time, effort, and dedication.

We know also that the regional network must be strengthened and made even more viable. This strength will come through a continuation and growth of support and commitment from the network members. The stations must be able to realize a solid and consistent financial base to support their own activities and those carried out in *their* behalf by *their* network.

Other stations throughout the country must be given the opportunity to form regional networks to serve their particular purposes. If these networks are organized, with independent financing at first, we firmly believe they will continue on a solid self-supporting basis. We are most anxious to see this happen, for the possibilities of interregional program exchange, especially on a live or simultaneous basis, are very exciting and would result in a kind of programming of a high quality which does not now exist but which is desperately needed.

The regional network fits between the national and the state network but has direct relationships with and responsibilities to the individual stations. It can be a most significant element in the total ETV complex of the country and must be nurtured and strengthened if it is to play, as it can, a major role in establishing noncommercial broadcasting as a vital cultural institution in this country.

Part III

INSTRUCTIONAL TELEVISION

The Development of Instructional Television

THE instructional television (ITV) innovations and educational technology of the 1960's have evolved, as it were, through a process of natural, practical, and effective selection. When television was proved workable in 1927 by the Bell Laboratory transmission of a visual image and its associated sound from Washington, D.C., to New York,[1] educators rapidly recognized its potential. The added dimension of sight to the broadcasting medium made television naturally desirable for various types of instruction. As TV receivers became plentiful and stations developed in all parts of the country, educators saw TV as a practical tool to enrich and supplement the teacher-learning process with concomitant gains to both. Today, educators are primarily concerned with the most effective means of utilizing television and educational technology in the learning process.

Some of the earliest TV experiments were conducted by educational institutions. In 1931, the University of Iowa's Department of Electrical Engineering was requested to contribute an exhibit for the university's display at the state fair.[2] The university con-

The views expressed in this chapter are those of the author. No official support or endorsement by the FCC is intended or implied.

structed an elementary closed-circuit television demonstration unit. The Western TV Company of Iowa donated equipment needed by the university to be a leader in electrical communications and a pioneer in ETV.[3] Shortly thereafter, on September 10, 1931, the university applied to the Federal Radio Commission for a construction permit.[4] This was issued January 8, 1932, and the station was licensed May 27, 1932. On January 25, 1933, the new station, W9XK, in Iowa City, joined the facilities of the university's AM radio station, WSUI, to transmit its first formal "sight and sound" broadcast. During the next seven years, W9XK broadcast some 389 ETV programs, including "Elementary Art," "Home Planning," "Introduction to Astronomy," and "First Aid" series.[5] Two other educational institutions — W9XG, Purdue University in Lafayette, Indiana, and W9XAK, Kansas State University in Manhattan, Kansas — were experimenting with similar TV services.

By 1940, a number of TV stations operated by large companies, such as RCA, expressed interest in broadcasting commercial programs as a public service. On April 30, 1941, the FCC adopted rules to permit limited commercial operations, and the first grant for a regular TV operation was issued in June 1941. By November, eight TV stations had made the transition from experimental to commercial authorizations.[6] Pioneer viewers with TV receivers in their homes enthusiastically responded to the increasing availability of programs provided by the commercial enterprise. TV was emerging as the important communications medium of the twentieth century, and David Sarnoff appropriately stated, "Of the whole series of modern inventions that have revolutionized the material aspects of civilizations, this new art is perhaps the most miraculous. . . . TV, I believe, is destined to provide greater knowledge to larger numbers of people." [7]

This "miracle" was on the threshold of such a destiny when the United States entered World War II, bringing normal station expansion to a halt. However, the war emergency produced technical advances and general developments important to postwar application. Educators were also preparing for peacetime activities. There was a substantial increase in the number of schools offering broadcast courses or broadcast training for teachers in summer sessions.[8] One of the first universities to engage in TV training was the University of California at Los Angeles which, in February 1941, offered a short course in TV production and acting as part of the Extension Division curricula. The University of Ohio introduced two courses specifically for radio and pictorial journalism in 1944. In 1945, the General Assembly of the State of Iowa appropriated $525,000 for the University of Iowa to develop a communications center to house journalism, publication, visual education, and radio-TV, in order to provide students with the best training in the communications arts field. In 1947, the University of North Carolina established a communications center which brought together radio-TV, motion pictures, facsimile, and allied fields to achieve more effective use of media in the curricula.[9] Other universities, including Syracuse, Northwestern, and Columbia, were also developing broad communications courses.

The expanding interest in television as an instructional medium influenced educators to such an extent that they began considering the advisability of ETV reservations as early as 1944. When the FCC held hearings in the fall of 1944, "to enable the radio art to take advantage of the important wartime technical advances . . . and to facilitate orderly planning for postwar development," several of the educational witnesses suggested that education might be interested in channels specifically for education.[10] However, educators and individuals testifying at that time [11] were primarily concerned with the allocation of adequate educational FM reservations to meet the eminent needs of state and local plans, and only a small portion of the over-all testimony was devoted to ETV. Therefore, when the FCC issued its final report in the matter it concluded:

With respect to immediate TV development . . . it does not appear that the current educational interest in TV or in the probability of the multiplicity of ETV stations in the near future is sufficient to warrant reserving TV channels. . . . If at any future date, educational institutions believe there is sufficient educational interest in TV and sufficient probability of developing useful ETV services, the matter can be raised anew at that time.[12]

Although educators were not assigned a special band of TV channels they continued to explore various uses of TV. Kansas State University, one of the early pioneers in experimental TV, foresaw the financial burdens on a nonprofit educational institution activating and operating a TV broadcast station and tested the feasibility of providing a low power TV service for a small community at a reasonable cost.[13] In 1946, Kansas State constructed TV station WXBU from war surplus material, operated with a power of 400 watts four hours a day until 1950 when the experimental educational TV operation was terminated. The nation's first ETV broadcast station, WOI, at Iowa State University (Ames), began operation February 21, 1950, and culminated the university's extensive background in educational broadcasting.[14] Initially, WOI operated exclusively as a nonprofit educational station, but its strategic position as the only TV station in central Iowa eventually obligated it to carry commercial programs as a public service to the 70,000 TV set owners in its coverage area.[15] Today, WOI is affiliated with ABC and operates similarly to other commercial stations in the same market. It does offer educational programming and provides a student training outlet through its facilities.[16] Several other educational institutions have since activated similar commercial operation.

While educational institutions experimented with TV and introduced TV training courses into their curriculum, several commercial stations were cooperating with educational and cultural groups to develop ETV programs. As early as 1941, CBS undertook a TV art series in collaboration with the Metropolitan Museum of Art for their New York station, WCBW. In 1945, CBS officials met with members of the New York City Board of Education educational radio station, WNYE, to explore possibilities of a "tele-education" series similar to CBS's radio "School of the Air." CBS cooperated with Dr. Frederick Ernst, associate superintendent of New York City high schools in conducting an informal study of materials best suited to telecasting. The first "tele-lesson" was an explanation to laymen on "Optics and the Action of Lenses." CBS also conducted an "All City R-TV Workshop" for a group of eighty selected high school students for several summers.[17]

Educators saw the advantage of having access to the costly commercial facilities and the benefit of commercial broadcaster's experience; widespread use of commercial TV facilities for training and credit courses was under way by the mid-1940's. The Chicago public schools announced "TV will open startling new methods of instruction" and in 1945 started using TV as an integral part of their educational program through the cooperation of TV station WBKB, Chicago. Ithaca College introduced an ETV course prepared by ABC as part of its regular credit curriculum in the fall of 1946.[18]

One of the first extensive in-school ITV series was inaugurated with one program a week by the Philadelphia public school system in 1947 in cooperation with WPTZ, WFIL, and WCAU. By the early 1950's, the service had increased to thirteen programs a week serving over 60,000 students.[19] Philadelphia schools have continued to be among the leaders in the utilization of ITV. Today, two ETV stations — WUHY, Philadelphia, and WHYY, Wilmington, Delaware — broadcast forty ITV courses per week to some 400,000 public, private, and diocesan school students in Philadelphia and nearby areas.[20] The Nutley, New Jersey, high school introduced TV as a permanent part of its regular school program in the 1947–48 school year when a large screen receiver, TV cable equipment, and closed-circuit facilities were donated by Industry TV, Inc.[21]

In the Midwest, Western Reserve University organized a broadcasting council to explore the possibilities of using TV to teach a very large audience outside the traditional classroom, and in 1950 in cooperation with commercial TV station WEWS, it offered the first broadcast ETV college credit courses: elementary psychology and comparative literature. Even with a tuition of sixteen dollars per credit hour for the three-unit courses, 66 persons enrolled and 472 audited the psychology course; 42 enrolled and 228 audited the literature course. A survey by the station indicated an estimated audience of 58,000. During the next few years, WRU offered courses in geography, child psychology, elementary economics, and music appreciation.[22] Another successful venture into the field of adult education by television was offered by the University of Michigan through WWJ-TV, Detroit.[23] A unique series demonstrating TV as an effective medium for teaching medicine was tested by Creighton University and WOW-TV, Omaha. The series included biological presentations of microscopic life, programs on methods of surgery, and medical symposiums enthusiastically received by the medical community.[24]

An important state-wide ITV undertaking, "Radio House," the Broadcast Voice of the University of Texas, started in 1940 and added TV in 1948. Originally, "Radio House" was an extracurricular project, but by 1950 it had grown into a part of the university's College of Fine Arts. During the 1949–50 school year, it broadcast a total of 1,303 program hours through three Austin commercial TV stations and seventy state commercial stations.[25]

In 1949, the National Education Association and the cooperating boards of education of New York City, Philadelphia, and Baltimore collaborated with NBC to develop a comprehensive series of children's programs, "Stop — Look — and Learn." The series was extended to all NBC stations across the nation and was programmed Monday–Friday after regular school hours as a means of bringing student, teacher, and parent together in joint activity.[26]

Commercial stations — both local and network — have continued to cooperate with or offer time to schools and educational institutions for ITV programs. Two of the most widely distributed educational programs, serving estimated audiences of 300,000, are CBS's "Sunrise Semester" and NBC's "Continental Classroom." "Sunrise Semester" started as a local series in cooperation with New York University, September 23, 1957, with "Literary Heritage" and "Sociology." Several years later, in 1961, CBS introduced a network counterpart, "College of the Air," with courses in biology and American economy. Starting September 22, 1963, only "Sunrise Semester," as the network offering to affiliates across the country, was broadcast. The first network course on "Sunrise Semester" was "Introduction to Ethics." Recent programs have included "Classical Mythology," "Age of Michelangelo," and "Age of Rubens."[27] NBC's "Continental Classroom" began in the fall of 1958 with a course in physics and in the second semester added modern chemistry. Since the first network series, more than 300 colleges and universities have participated in the courses offered by up to 170 NBC stations across the country. Recent programs have included "American Government," and "Contemporary Math."[28]

The mushrooming activity in ETV stimulated education to reexamine its interest in reserving channels for education. This occurred during the initial stage of the FCC's freeze.[29] In Wilbur Schramm's book, *The People Look at Educational Television* (Stanford University Press, 1963), he states, "In some respects it was a blessing to ETV that the Commission froze allocations for two years. This provided time to alert education and civic organizations to the opportunity TV offered" (p. 5).

In 1950, the National Association of Educational Broadcasters and the United States Office of Education's Radio Office convened a meeting of educators from all over the nation to discuss how they could "assure a portion of the TV spectrum adequate to its needs." The official development of ETV began at this meeting with the formation of the Joint Council on Educational Television (JCET), October 16, 1950, sponsored by the American Council on Education, the Association for Education by Radio-TV, the Association of Land Grant Colleges and Universities, the National Association of State Universities, the National Council of Chief State School Officers, the National Education Association, and the National Association of Educational Broadcasters. In its first few months JCET assisted some 833 schools and colleges in fulfilling the FCC request to present statements of intent to utilize educational channels, and it served as the mechanism for making education's wishes known to the Commission.[30]

Throughout the hearings, the high value of TV as an ideal education medium was acclaimed, and JCET and other educational and civic groups supported the concept of reserving TV channels for both instructional and broad cultural community services. Educators were strongly supported by FCC Commissioner Freida Hennock, who lent great impetus to the eventual reservation of 242 channels in April 1952.[31] In a discussion of "Who Should Be Responsible for Education on TV," on ABC's "Town Hall Meeting of the Air" broadcast November 28, 1950, Commissioner Hennock was reported to have said, "ETV can be put to better use as an electronic blackboard rather than an electronic billboard."[32]

The impact of the 242 channels reserved for education challenged ETV to move from theory to a program of action. A major step in this direction was the American Council on Education's sponsorship of the TV Programs Institute held at Pennsylvania State University shortly after the channels were reserved. The focus of the conference was to "gain greater understanding of the role of TV, both through educational and commercial channels, in the total educational process" and "develop a policy that would have direct relationship with the entire educational structure . . . to fulfill its promise of improved educational opportunity for every citizen."[33] A prophetic recommendation of the Institute was to create a National Program Foundation to act as a national and regional production and distribution center for educational films and video recordings. In connection with the recommendation it was stressed that the almost unlimited program resources of the large colleges in major cities combined with some of the unique resources of small schools made cooperative sharing essential for an effective ITV system. It was suggested that the Foundation might be financed by investments of cooperating universities and matched by Foundation grants; that it might acquire rights to video programs of the cooperating universities, for which it would pay the cost of series or program production; and that it might recover the investment by charging other institutions a moderate fee to make use of the program.[34] Although the Foundation, as envisioned by the Institute, didn't come to fruition, the ideas considered were the basis for development of current ITV libraries discussed later in this chapter.

As education moved to a program of action, it was revealed that in April 1950 approximately 350 institutions, school systems, and public service agencies had initiated extensive TV utilization plans and re-evaluated instructional resources.[35] In addition a number of studies were undertaken to determine how TV may best be used to supplement classroom instruction. The Allen B. Dumont Laboratories in cooperation with the Montclair State Teachers College undertook closed-circuit transmission of TV programs to high schools near the college to find practical answers relating to televised instruction.[36]

The Fund for the Advancement of Education (FAE), established by the Ford Foundation on April 19, 1951, was the major contributor in extending and improving quality teaching and funded experiments in the use of TV as a medium of instruction from elementary grades through college level.[37] FAE provided support for numerous ITV studies, including the comprehensive National Program in the Use of TV in Public Schools, a nationwide project involving nearly 40,000 students in more than 200 public rural and major school systems to determine feasibility of teaching classes with fewer teachers while at the same time upgrading the quality of education.[38]

FAE introduced TV on the college level when it made a grant to Pennsylvania State University in 1954 to undertake a systematic inquiry into the effectiveness of teaching by TV. The study compared television instruction with conventional teaching methods. In general, no significant differences in achievement or attitude were found, though in large classes a majority of students chose TV as the preferred method. By 1958, some 3,700 of the university's 14,000 students were registered for one or more of the thirteen courses taught over closed circuit on the campus.[39]

In 1956, FAE made a grant of $500,000 to the Chicago Board of Education and WTTW, Chicago's local ETV station, to undertake a "TV college" curriculum for the Junior College of Chicago. In addition to its successful program leading to an Associate of Arts degree for at-home students, the TV College is involved with teacher training, direct instruction on campus, and teaching gifted high school students.[40]

FAE also supported, along with Electronic Industries Association, a program of the Washington County schools in Maryland to use closed-circuit television (CCTV) as a regular part of their instructional program at all grade levels and in all major curriculum areas. Main studios in Hagerstown, Maryland, send out six lessons simultaneously by cable to more than 800 TV receiving locations throughout the county. Over fifty courses are now presented through the project.[41] Similar CCTV systems are operated by the Anaheim and Santa Ana, California, school districts.

Television has also been widely used by special interest organizations. The military services early found that television can be used to implement and evaluate new methods of instruction, train new instructors, and test new teaching techniques and training methods.[42] The United States Army began using ITV in 1951; Fort Monmouth, New Jersey, and Camp Gordon, Georgia, were the first two military installations in the country to use television in application to basic training. Today, ITV is widely used in military installations and military academies throughout the country. An important military application of TV is for medical teaching requirements. The USAF School of Aerospace Medicine undertakes major experiments with ITV. The Intermedical TV Network in Washington, D.C., uses microwave and cable to tie together six major governmental medical installations (National Naval Medical Center, National Institutes of Health, Walter Reed Army Medical Center, Air Force Base Hospital, Fort George Meade Base Hospital, and Fort Belvoir Base Hospital) for instructional and experimental purposes. Civilian medical groups have also used ITV to provide programming for medical students, researchers, and practitioners. In 1949, the University of Kansas Medical School began utilizing television in its educational program and was soon followed by the University of Michigan and the University of Utah. The Council on Medical Television was organized in 1958 through the Institute for Advancement of Medical Education to coordinate and expand medical television activities throughout the country.[43]

By the end of the 1950's, ITV trends were clearly established and there was no longer any question of whether to use TV, but rather *how* to use TV in education. Robert Hilliard, then of Adelphi College, observed:

Those who feared that television would become an insurmountable mechanical barrier between the teacher and student . . . are generally changing their minds, much like those who had the same doubts about the potential destruction of education by . . . the printed book. . . . It cannot be overemphasized that the purpose of educational television is not to relieve the national teacher shortage. . . . Where television has increased the effectiveness of the classroom teacher, brought an outstanding teacher to more students than could otherwise be reached in a normal classroom situation . . . brought experiences, materials and skills to the students which the regular teacher would not be able to present . . . then this medium has lived up to its potential.[44]

It was for reasons such as these that educators turned their attention to a new dimension of televised instruction, namely developing effective methods of providing quality education in quantity.

One of the most interesting ITV innovations, unique even today, is the Texas Educational Microwave Project (TEMP). The preliminary plans asked whether or not an efficient and practical CCTV system could be developed to serve a large regional area in central Texas encompassing eleven colleges and universities separated by one hundred or more miles. This extensive closed-circuit TV and microwave educational system, operated by the University of Texas, officially began in 1961 as the nation's first TV network of higher educational institutions.[45] College credit courses, averaging ten dollars per credit hour via TV, are produced in the university's CCTV studio in Austin, then microwaved to the participating institutions on business radio frequencies in the 6575–6875 megacycle band presently available for intercity closed-circuit ETV systems.[46] A system similar to the TEMP is being planned at the University of Connecticut for the beginning of the 1967–68 school year. Five microwave towers will connect the university's main campus at Storrs and its four branches for closed-circuit instruction.[47]

Another major innovation in instructional technology came in 1959 when the Ford Foundation lent support to Purdue University to investigate the feasibility of transmitting televised lessons from an airborne transmitter, with a potential coverage of five million students in 13,000 schools within the six-state region of Illinois, Indiana, Kentucky, Michigan, Ohio, and Wisconsin. In 1959, the FCC granted Purdue construction permits to experiment in airborne UHF-TV transmission and instruction. The program, incorporated as the Midwest Program for Airborne Television instruction (KS2XGA and KS2XGD, Lafayette, Indiana), in 1960, became operational on an experimental basis early in 1961. Educators around the country watched with interest the developments of the airborne service. However, when MPATI petitioned the Commission on January 15, 1963,[48] requesting that its operation be authorized on a regular basis and six channels be provided for that purpose, there was considerable concern that a permanent airborne system might limit potential local ground-based ETV development.[49] The petition was denied by the FCC in 1965, with authorization of a phase-out period of five years for the existing systems and recommendation to convert to channels in the 2500 megacycle band. In order to study the feasibility of their use for air-based transmission, MPATI applied for six channels in the 2500 megacycle band in August 1965. The application (BPIF50) was granted by the FCC in 1966.[50]

At the beginning of the 1960's it was evident that anticipated needs of education to fully utilize educational resources and effectively augment the distribution of information to classrooms could not be met with the available broadcast channels or via existing broadcast stations. The Brandeis University studies reported increases of broadcast time devoted to instructional programming.[51] The average amount of in-school programming and college-adult instruction programming broadcast on educational broadcasting stations increased from 34 percent in 1961 to 46 percent in 1966. Furthermore, an important requisite for an effective ITV system is the capability of offering simultaneous instruction to several grade levels in several subjects, not easily possible with broadcast channels. CCTV has multichannel capability; and many schools, colleges and universities, medical and dental schools, and industrial firms continue to develop CCTV facilities. However, the cost of closed-circuit cable systems, whether privately owned or leased from a common carrier, increases with distance and the number of receiving points.

The Adler Electronics experiment in Plainedge, Long Island, paved the way for a new class of instructional service which combines the advantages of a relatively economical by-air type of transmission with multichannel flexibility. This is the Instructional TV Fixed Service, established by the FCC in July 1963 to supplement, not replace, the educational TV broadcast service.[52] The service provides a means whereby instructional and cultural material may be transmitted to one or more selected or "fixed" receiving locations such as schools, colleges, hospitals, clinics, and similar places, for the purposes of formal instruction, in-service training, and similar situations. Educators enthusiastically responded to the service, and within three and a half years over 100 applications for some 300 channels were filed with the FCC; 85 had been granted and 30 systems were in operation by early 1967.

Behind many of today's instructional television systems are regional, state, and national production and distribution libraries. One of the earliest ITV libraries, the Great Plains Regional ITV Library is the outgrowth of a national survey conducted in the late 1950's by the University of Nebraska on behalf of the Office of Education. The survey made a number of recommendations, including, primarily, the establishment of a national instructional library and regional facilities.[53] These were activated through the National Instructional TV Library, recently absorbed into the new National Center for School and College TV (NCSCT), the Northeast Regional ITV Library, and the Great Plains Library. Until recently, only the Great Plains Library provided a significantly wide exchange of tapes. It started in 1962 with one series and offered up to 140 series in 1966.[54] The Northeast Library continues to distribute programs to a limited extent, but is primarily concerned with cooperative production for northeastern ETV stations. The National Center for School and College TV comes closest to original plans for a National Program Foundation. The Center, established in 1965 under the auspices of the Indiana University Foundation, is providing a wide circulation of instructional programs. In early 1967 its plans were to establish a research and dissemination service and initiate a grant service for the production of quality programs.[55] A regional office is located in San Francisco.

Closely related to the activities of the instructional libraries is the National Project for the Improvement of Televised Instruction, established in 1964 through a Ford Foundation grant, and sponsored by NAEB. The primary purpose of the project is to improve the quality and the utilization of televised instruction wherever it constitutes a significant part of the total program in schools and institutions of higher education. To carry out this function, the project provides field consultant services and conducts national seminars throughout the country.

The United States has extended its experience and knowledge of ITV to developing areas throughout the world. In 1962, the Peace Corps initiated a new phase in its international activities by planning an ETV project for Colombia, South America, as part of that country's rural development program. The project went into operation in March 1964, with initial production facilities in Bogota. Peace Corps volunteers are specially trained in TV utilization to work with the project. By the end of 1966, 1,500 television receivers in schools throughout the country were bringing the enlightenment of instructional programming to over 400,000 primary school children and 6,500 teachers.[56] In 1961, the National Association of Educational Broadcasters, in cooperation with the government of American Samoa, conducted a feasibility study of ETV for Samoa and concluded that television would be "the fastest, most effective, and, in the long run, most economical way of bringing the Territory's educational system to reasonable standards."[57] Today, ETV stations broadcast daily lessons to elementary and high school students throughout the islands. A unique feature of the Samoa ETV system is that it provides the core curriculum rather than supplementing the instruction. An independent study team from the International Institute for Educational Planning recently surveyed the Samoa ETV system and concluded that "TV was not being called upon to supplement ongoing work of the classroom teacher, or to help them to do a bit better what they were already doing; it was being asked to share responsibility equally with them, help them do something quite different from rote exercises they had conducted . . . ."[58]

Several federal programs have been especially helpful to instructional TV research and utilization. The National Defense Education Act of 1958 has funded numerous studies related to ITV, particularly under Title III, Financial Assistance for Strengthening Instruction in Science, Math, Modern Foreign Languages, and other critical subjects. Title VI, Language Development, provides contracts to support research in methods of improved instruction in modern foreign languages; and Title VII, New Educational Media, contracts for research in educational uses of TV, radio, motion pictures, and other media. The Higher Education Act of 1965, particularly Title VI, Financial Assistance for the Improvement of Undergraduate Facilities, specifies closed-circuit and instructional TV fixed service. The Elementary and Secondary Educational Act, Title III, Supplementary Educational Center and Services, specifies radio and television programs for classroom and other educational uses. In addition, the Educational TV Facilities Act of 1962 provides matching grants for the construction or expansion of ETV broadcasting facilities. These stations have benefited many classrooms through programming instructional material.

In January 1967, the Carnegie Commission on Educational Television released its report, *Public Television: A Program for Action* (New York: Bantam Books), recommending the establishment of a corporation for public television. This report formed the basis of the proposals for ETV legislation that President Johnson recommended in his message to Congress on February 28, 1967. In addition to the President's recommendation for public television, he also recommended legislation "to authorize a major study of the value and the promise of instructional TV which is being used more and more widely in our classrooms, but whose potential has not been fully developed." The President also recommended the establishment of an experimental program for developing the potential of computers in education.[59]

Other techniques which extend instructional television services to school systems are translators and CATV. Translators, which carry signals into areas not served by primary stations, are operated by many ETV and ITFS stations to boost their signals into outlying areas for community and in-school programming. In addition, many schools operate their own translators to receive ITV programs from distant stations. Community Antenna TV systems carry TV signals on cable to areas which, because of terrain or other reasons, are not able to pick up a particular signal with much clarity, if at all.[60] Several ETV stations, including broadcast and a number of closed-circuit systems such as that at Northern Michigan University, utilize this service to provide educational and instructional programs to schools in other areas.

I have discussed some of the elements that have contributed to the development of instructional television. The impact of ITV is viewed in many ways. The Carnegie Commission report believes "the role played in formal education by instructional television has been, on the whole, a small one, and that nothing which approached the true potential of ITV has been realized in practice," and points out that ITV "must be regarded as an element in the total educational process" (pp. 80, 82).

As education enters the last third of the twentieth century, ITV is evolving into the total educational process as it is absorbed into the "necessary revolution in education."[61] The emerging trends linking electronic technology and publishing houses with teaching machines, audiovisual aids, and programmed instruction will dramatically change present patterns of teaching and learning. The impact of industry's investment in educational systems will alter school structures. P. Kenneth Komoski, director of Educational Products Information Exchange in New York, recently stated: "Given the potential size and educational power inherent in the burgeoning new education industry, it could conceivably become an unprecedented force in American education by contracting directly with local school boards to supply educational service more cheaply and with less bother for the local citizenry than the existing system."[62]

A number of large private corporations such as Litton and RCA have recently acquired publishing firms. McGraw-Hill Book Company awarded a grant to the University of Southern California in early 1967 to expand the university's extensive Automated Cataloguing Project of audiovisual materials into the National Information Center for Educational Media.[63] Xerox, IBM, and Time are making substantial investments in educational technology.[64]

Several years ago Walter Lippmann said that "we must measure not by what it would be easy and convenient to do, but what it is necessary to do in order that the Nation may survive and flourish. We have learned that we are quite rich enough to defend ourselves, whatever the cost. We must now learn that we are quite rich enough to educate ourselves as we need to be educated."[65]

Recent developments demonstrate that we are learning.

NOTES

1   Lenox R. Lohr, *Television Broadcasting* (New York: McGraw-Hill, 1940), p. 19.
2   E. B. Kurtz, *Pioneering in Educational Television: 1932–1939* (Iowa State University Press, 1959), p. 1.
3   *Ibid.*, p. 10.
4   Docket 1409, Before the Federal Radio Commission, Application of the State University of Iowa for Construction Permit (TV): Frequency, 2,000–2,100 kc; Power, 62 w; 3 hours daily.
5   Kurtz, *Pioneering in ETV*, p. 80.
6   FCC, *Seventh Annual Report* (Washington, June 30, 1941), pp. 32–35.
7   Quoted in Lohr, *Television Broadcasting*, p. xiii.
8   Federal Radio Education Committee, *Directory of Colleges and Universities Offering Courses in R-TV* (Washington, 1944–45).
9   The curricular additions discussed here are documented in FREC, *Bulletin*, III, No. 1 (1941), p. 4; VI, No. 8 (1944), p. 1; VII, No. 5 (1945), p. 1; IX, No. 5 (1947), p. 1.
10 FCC Docket 6651, "In the matter of allocation of frequencies to the various classes of nongovernmental service in the radio spectrum from 10 kcs to 30,000,000 kcs" (Hearings conducted Sept.-Oct. 1944), transcript pp. 1183–1644. See especially testimony of John Studebaker, U.S. Commissioner of Education (tr. pp. 1423–47).
11 Witnesses included R. R. Lowdermilk, Office of Education; Harold McCarty, University of Wisconsin; Carl H. Menzer, University of Iowa; and Leopold Stokowski.
12 FCC Docket 6651, "Report of proposed allocation from 25,000 kc/s to 30,000,000 kc/s" (Washington, Jan. 15, 1945), p. 83.
13 FREC, *Bulletin*, XI, No. 3 (1949), p. 1.
14 Richard B. Hull, "A Note on the History Behind ETV," in *Educational Television: The Next Ten Years* (Stanford University: Institute for Communication Research, 1962), p. 334.
15 Carrol V. Newsom, ed., *A Television Policy for Education* (Washington: American Council on Education, 1952), p. 125.
16 FCC station files, WOI-TV, BRCT-75, Renewal of License, granted Jan. 1, 1965.
17 FREC, *Bulletin*, VIII, No. 8 (1946), p. 1.
18 *Ibid.*, VII, No. 6 (1945), p. 2; VIII, No. 8 (1946), p. 2.
19 *Ibid.*, X, No. 7 (1948), p. 2.
20 Philadelphia Public Schools, Division of Radio-TV Education, "A

Statement on Instructional Broadcasting in the Philadelphia Schools" (Feb. 1966), p. 1.

21 FREC, *Bulletin*, ix, No. 7 (1947), p. 1.

22 John F. White, "Western Reserve University Telecourses," in *A Television Policy for Education*, pp. 120–23.

23 *Broadcasting/Telecasting* (Washington: Broadcast Publications, Inc.), Sept. 18, 1950, p. 63.

24 FREC, *Bulletin*, x, No. 5 (1948), p. 1.

25 *Ibid.*, xii, No. 1 (1950), p. 1.

26 *Ibid.*, x, No. 8 (1949), p. 1.

27 CBS, Program Analysis Dept., New York, Oct. 1966.

28 NBC, Program Analysis Dept., New York, Oct. 1966.

29 FCC Docket Nos. 8736 and 8975, "In the matters of amendment of Section 3.606 of the Commission's rules and regulations," Notice of Proposed Rule Making, May 6, 1948. (In general, this order provided that no tendered or pending applications for construction of new TV stations would be acted upon.)

30 Ralph Steetle, "Education's Response to the Challenge of TV," in *A Television Policy for Education*, pp. 26–28.

31 FCC Docket Nos. 8736 and 8975, *Sixth Report and Order*, April 11, 1952.

32 "Who Should Be Responsible for Education on TV?" America's Town Meeting of the Air, Bulletin No. 9 (New York: ABC, Nov. 28, 1950), p. 5.

33 Newsom, in *A Television Policy for Education*, p. v.

34 E. Arthur Hungerford, Jr., "Suggested Plans for Early Action," in *ibid.*, pp. 250–54.

35 See Joint Council on Educational TV study, *Educational TV Resources* (Washington, April 1952), pp. 2–95.

36 *Broadcasting/Telecasting*, Dec. 4, 1950, p. 99.

37 Ford Foundation, *A Ten Year Report of the Fund for the Advancement of Education:1951–1961* (New York, 1961), p. 10.

38 Ford Foundation, *Teaching by Television* (New York, 1959), pp. 46–49.

39 *Ibid.*, pp. 16–23.

40 Renata Von Stoephasius, ed., *Learning by Television* (New York: FAE, Aug. 1966), pp. 55–58.

41 Washington County Closed-Circuit TV Report, Board of Education, Washington County, Maryland.

42 Office of the Chief Signal Officer, Audio-Visual Communications Directorate, *A Report: The Third Armed Forces Television Con-*

ference, October, 1962 (Washington: Department of the Army, 1963).

43 Bernard V. Dryer, M.D., "Lifetime Learning for Physicians: Principles, Practices, Proposals," *Journal of Medical Education*, XXXVII, No. 6, Pt. 2 (June 1962), pp. 61–63.

44 Robert L. Hilliard, "The College Aids the High School Through Television," *High School Journal*, XLI, No. 5 (1958), p. 206.

45 R. F. Schenkkan, "First Year of Operation," unpublished report on the Texas Educational Microwave Project, University of Texas, March 1962.

46 FCC Rules and Regulations, Part 91, Business Radio Service, Section 91.554, "Frequency Availability," footnote 19: "Available only for intercity closed-circuit ETV systems. Such authorizations will be granted on case by case basis and applicants must furnish complete and specific factual data showing wherein, apart from economic consideration, it is not feasible to utilize frequencies above 19,550 Mc/s."

47 Peter Gall, "Branching Out: More Big Universities Open New Campuses to Expand at Low Cost," *Wall Street Journal*, March 22, 1967, p. 1.

48 FCC Docket 15201, "In the matter of amendment of Part 3 of Commission's rules governing TV broadcast stations to authorize use of airborne TV transmitters."

49 *Ibid.* See comments filed by Joint Council on Educational Broadcasting, Association for Maximum Service Telecasters, NAEB.

50 *Ibid., Report and Order,* Aug. 1965.

51 Morse Communication Research Center, and the National Center for School and College Television, "One Week of Educational Television," No. 1 (Waltham, Mass.: Brandeis University, 1961); No. 4 (Bloomington, Ind.: NCSCT, 1966).

52 FCC Docket 14744, "In the matter of amendment of Parts 2 and 4 of the rules to establish a new class of educational television service for the transmission of instructional and cultural material to multiple receiving locations on channels in the 2500–2690 Mc/s frequency band," *Report and Order,* July 1963.

53 Jack McBride, "Sharing ITV on a Statewide Basis and on a Regional Basis," *in* Barton L. Griffith and Donald W. MacLennan, eds., *Improvement of Teaching by Television* (University of Missouri Press, 1964), pp. 187–88.

54 Von Stoephasius, ed., *Learning by Television*, p. 26.

55 *Ibid.*, p. 25.

56 The Peace Corps, *Colombia ETV: A Report* (Washington, 1966), pp. 1–2.

57 Karola Craib, "Educational TV in American Samoa," *Building a New Samoa* (Pago Pago: Office of the Governor, Nov. 23, 1964), p. 5.

58 Quoted by William G. Harley, "Techniques and Cost: I — Technology and Taxes," *Saturday Review*, Jan. 14, 1957, p. 54.

59 Message from the President (H. Doc. 68), communicated to the Senate, 90th Congress, First Session (*Congressional Record*, No. 31, Feb. 28, 1967), pp. S2677–82.

60 FCC, *Educational Television Information Bulletin*, No. 16-B (Washington, June 1966), p. 7.

61 Francis Keppel, *The Necessary Revolution in Education* (New York: Harper and Row, 1966).

62 "Assessing the New Educational Technology," *Automation and Technology*, Hearings before the Subcommittee on Economic Progress, Joint Economic Committee, 89th Congress, First Session, June 6, 10, 13, 1966, p. 203.

63 Personal communication from Glenn McMurray, director of Automated Cataloguing, Film Distribution Center, University of Southern California, Feb. 1967.

64 E. B. Weiss, "The Communications Revolution: Part 2 — The Marriage Between Publishing and Electronics," *Advertising Age* (New York), Nov. 21, 1966, pp. 105–10.

65 Quoted in Keppel, *The Necessary Revolution in Education*, p. 68.

Closed-Circuit Television In Training and Education

ONLY a probable estimate, in the neighborhood of 1,000, can be made as to the number of closed-circuit television (CCTV) installations in the United States, because they are not licensed under the aegis of any central organization or agency.[1] Moreover, it is difficult to determine the scope of a facility or installation, or what elements constitute it. The facility may be limited to one classroom. It might include the entire school system within a state through network interconnection. Some closed-circuit facilities are independent operations, but at times educational stations serve the dual role of providing simultaneous broadcast and closed-circuit services, with the station furnishing production facilities. To a great extent the distinction between educational and instructional television has emerged out of this duality of service. Most closed-circuit systems sharing facilities with educational television stations have been labeled as instructional television systems in contrast to the broadcasting function. The distinction is not accurate since many educational stations serve the instructional needs of the community and school system. Just as instructional television is one function of educational broadcasting, closed-circuit television represents one form of instruc-

155

tional television. This form is broad in scope and covers the areas of training, education, and research. The purpose of this chapter is to examine those unique and particularized functions of closed-circuit television.

DEFINITION AND RATIONALE FOR CLOSED-CIRCUIT TELEVISION

Closed-circuit television is unique because of its design, in which coaxial cable or microwave is utilized to transmit signals or images and/or sound to predetermined receiver or monitor locations. This system is contrasted with the public broadcast of images and/or sound to basically undetermined and nonselective receiver locations. The salient feature of closed-circuit television is the element of control exercised over its reception and hence, it is to be hoped, over its utilization. The *raison d'être* for CCTV has its basis in those advantages accrued by limiting and controlling the signal.

Multichannel flexibility. — Since closed-circuit channels are not licensed by the government, they are more easily obtainable. The limitations for the distribution of closed-circuit signals are generally not the number of channels, but the availability of videotape recorders, studios, receivers, and sundry equipment. Multichannel flexibility means that a facility can provide a variety of learning experiences, in the form of lessons, programs, or stimuli, simultaneously to different and separate groups at various reception points (receiver locations) along the distribution system.

Adjustment for individual differences. — Although the concept of homogeneous groups is relative, nevertheless, greater specificity is achieved through a closed-circuit television approach than with the use of conventional means of broadcasting. Lessons can be tailored according to the needs and requirements of individual classes. The adjustment for individual differences depends, however, upon a knowledge of what elements constitute a learning group.

Selectivity of audience. — A corollary to the adjustment for individual differences includes the point of view that closed-circuit facilities should be able to segment and serve subgroups of a student population. The ability to reach individual classes is the result of the multichannel capability of the system. Although a large number of students can be reached, closed-circuit television should not be considered a mass medium of training and education. For the most part, however, closed-circuit television has been concerned with reaching the largest possible student population, with a criterion for success based on decreasing the cost-per-student figure in comparison with traditional teaching methods. Economy and efficiency must be considered, but the improvement of teaching, as opposed to the mechanical duplication of already existing instruction, should rank high among the goals of closed-circuit television.

Protection of privacy. — Because control of reception can usually be guaranteed, protection of privacy is offered to subject areas where patients or clients serve demonstration roles. This safeguard is particularly important for such disciplines as medicine, psychiatry, and social work. To a certain extent, something *usually* guaranteed is *never* guaranteed. A digression here to describe the two basic types of signals used in closed-circuit television may prove worthwhile, because of the relationship of method of distribution to privacy. The two types are the video frequency signal ("video") and the radio frequency signal in the VHF band ("RF"). In the former only one picture signal, which originates at a camera chain or videotape recorder, can be transmitted through a coaxial cable at any given time. A separate audio cable is required for this system, and the video and audio signals are received on monitors and speakers. In the latter system, the video and audio signals modulate a very high frequency RF carrier. Several signals, on different frequencies, can be transmitted simultaneously through one coaxial cable.[2]

There are economical and operational advantages and disadvantages for each system. The use of the "video" system means that a number of coaxial cables are needed for multichannel capability. Routing and control of monitors can be maintained from a central location and therefore privacy can be guaranteed. An RF system signal can be seen by anyone who tunes in the proper channel on a receiver connected to the coaxial cable distribution system. The number of receivers in a large closed-circuit system suggests that the system can be rather "open." Accidental viewing of confidential material is as probable as it is possible.

Utilization of medium characteristics. — Television is more than a mere channeling device or means of transmission, although it can be used for such purposes. In the spring of 1956 one high school in Wisconsin used CCTV to monitor study halls because of a shortage of teachers available for this purpose. Some institutions have used television as a means of providing an opportunity for overflow crowds to see and hear a speaker they would otherwise have to miss. At times an unobtrusive camera has been placed in the rear of a lecture hall during regularly scheduled class time to transmit the lecture of an outstanding teacher, thereby allowing more students to benefit. But more importantly, the medium has certain intrinsic properties which can affect and enrich the teaching-learning process; for example, the magnifying power of the camera, the ease of juxtaposition, the control of sound and images, and the ability to integrate with relative ease other media.

Freedom from broadcasting restrictions. — There are numerous broadcasting standards to which the public and the broadcaster have been conditioned, some of which are not intrinsic to the medium, but rather are conventions which are the result of practice. People have been conditioned to "shows" as opposed to "lessons." Opening and closing themes, elaborate credits, fast pacing, and a preoccupation with getting "on" and "off" the air on time have become customary practices. There is often showmanship in CCTV, but the emphasis should be on the effect of that quality on the teaching-learning process. More attention can be paid to cause and effect, stimulus and response, to the utilization of motivated showmanship in teaching. Certainly the CCTV educator has a wider latitude in taste and expression than the broadcaster who is constantly on guard against offending the public and who must keep hands off subject matter that is perhaps not appropriate to a home environment.

The legal restrictions stipulated for broadcasting by the Federal Communications Commission in regard to procedure and to technical standards do not apply to closed-circuit television. For instance, hourly station identification is not required in closed-circuit television, and technical standards may vary as long as the air waves are not used. At times, higher standards than those for broadcasting are necessary. The FCC requires a 525 line broadcasting standard in the United States. Some CCTV facilities, particularly in the medical and scientific areas, operate with 800 or 1,000 lines in order to achieve greater resolution of images.

HISTORICAL OVERVIEW

Throughout the history of television the medium has been used with extreme variation. This is also true for closed-circuit television. Generally form has followed function; where failure has occurred it has been the result of a lack of flexibility in adapting form to the needs of function. The diversity of its form and its application makes a complete history of closed-circuit television out of the question here, but it will be useful to sketch out significant developments.

The beginnings of broadcast and close-circuit television are one and the same; later their paths diverged. In first demonstrating the transmission of television over substantial distances, in 1927, the Bell System used wire line for transmission between Washington and New York, and radio link for that between Whippany, New Jersey, and New York.[3] The wire line transmission was closed circuit, as was a great deal of the experimentation at this time when the means for broadcasting were being perfected.

The pioneering work of F. W. Alexanderson for the General Electric Corporation resulted in daily experimental television tests throughout 1928. On September 11, 1928, experimental television station W2XAD and its radio counterpart, WG7, in Schenectady, combined for the production of the first television drama, "The Queen's Messenger."[4]

Development was rapid at this time. H. R. Lubcke, of the Don Lee Broadcasting System, pointed out the state of progress during a discussion following the presentation of a paper at the spring 1935 meeting of the Society of Motion Picture Engineers:

> Our television transmitter, W6XAO, officially went on the air December 23, 1931, and we have been broadcasting television programs since that time. On May 21, 1932, we demonstrated the first television image ever received in an airplane. A self-synchronized cathode-ray receiver was used. . . . Through the courtesy of Pathé News we broadcast scenes of the Los Angeles earthquake soon after it happened; and through Paramount News, the Stanford-U.S.C. football game on Armistice Day two years ago, three hours and forty-five minutes after it was played.[5]

These events are significant in providing a contrast to education's relationship to television. Surprisingly, this alliance occurred very early. In *Pioneering in Educational Television: 1932–1939* (Iowa State University Press, 1959), E. B. Kurtz gives an account of the early efforts in television at the University of Iowa, beginning with the demonstration of closed-circuit television at the university's state fair display in August 1931 (p. 1). The success of this venture so impressed the department of electrical engineering at Iowa that they constructed a small transmitter and receiver, thereby converting the experiment into an open-circuit broadcasting system. On May 27, 1932, the Federal Radio Commission granted an experimental license to the University of Iowa with the call letters W9XK (p. 17). On January 25, 1933, the radio station, WSUI, and the experimental television station, W9XK, consolidated their efforts into their "first formal combined broadcast" (p. 53). The *Daily Iowan* reported the event: "Directed by Professor E. B. Kurtz, head of the department [electrical engineering], the program included a sketch from a university play, a violin solo, a lesson in freehand drawing, and an illustrated lecture. This performance took place on the ground floor of the building, with the radio and television receivers bringing the scenes before the two groups on the top floor" (quoted on p. 68). As in this case, some broadcasting experimentation, although using the air waves, could be considered closed circuit because of the control of reception points and receivers.

At this time Purdue and Kansas State universities also held experimental television licenses. In 1934 the University of Iowa applied to the FCC for a construction permit for a station employing an electronic television scanning system instead of mechanical scanning. The request was granted in 1936 and W9XUI became a reality (p. 147).

The first real test of the new electronic scanning system took place on May 15, 1941, and interestingly enough was a closed-circuit demonstration of a television play directed by a graduate student in dramatic arts. "The title of the play was 'A Cup of Coffee.' It was a rewrite of the short story 'A Coffee Cup Here,' by Walter Hogan. Mr. Abel [the student] also cast the play, studied make-up problems, and conducted the rehearsals. The play was transmitted by closed-circuit to a receiver in an adjoining room, where his Master of Arts degree examining committee observed the show" (pp. 151–52).

A thesis was written as the result of the project: "A Project and Preliminary Investigation of Problems Involved in Producing a Play for Television" (p. 155). The important task of training students in television was demonstrated here as a function of closed-circuit television. More significantly, the work of those universities pioneering in television points out not only their early realization of the educational applications of the new medium, but also the contribution of education to the development of that medium. The early developments of commercial, educational, and closed-circuit television are intertwined rather than separate movements. As broadcasting gathered momentum, however, closed-circuit activities became peripheral to this growth. The same pattern occurred later when educational television stations entered the scene.

By 1936 a transmitter had been installed by the Radio Corpora-

tion of America in the tower of the Empire State Building and
150 receivers distributed to selected viewers.[6] Broadcasting experimentation was becoming commonplace, and a number of
public demonstrations was arranged. The question was where
and when regular public telecasting would begin. In November 1936, regular two-hours-a-day broadcasting was inaugurated
from the Alexandria Palace in London. According to a June 15,
1937, report of the Research Council of Motion Pictures and
Sciences, the British venture constituted "the first and only existing public television service," using as criteria the regular transmissions over a period of seven months, the sale of "not over"
1,000 receivers, and the formation of a broadcasting organization.[7]

Even though the basic thrust was towards commercial broadcasting, education was also involved at times. On May 23, 1938,
New York University Professor C. C. Clark lectured to two hundred students on the principles of electronic television. The lesson
was broadcast by the National Broadcasting Company to students
sitting in the RCA building. Two-way communication between
the professor and the students was arranged. "With each receiver having approximately fourteen students before it, every
student had a front row seat. Through the camera technique used
and the close-up views of the specific parts of the apparatus under
attention at the moment, the students saw more than they actually
would have seen had they been present at the experiment."[8]

Technical refinements and breakthroughs continued to occur.
The principle behind coaxial cable had been known for some
time, but manufacturers had difficulty in producing lengths of
more than several feet. By 1938 this problem was solved.[9] The
application for commercial broadcasting was immediate, but the
later relevance to closed-circuit transmission is obvious now.

With the 1939 New York World's Fair, television was ushered
into the public eye, only to be pushed into the background by
governmental orders and World War II. Television would later
benefit from the growth of the electronic industries induced by
the demands of the war effort. One rather interesting reference

should be noted. During the war, CCTV was used in New York City to train air raid wardens. Two hundred thousand wardens were trained "in their primary duties and responsibilities. A television receiver was installed in every police station in the city. The course was compulsory."[10]

In March 1947, the FCC gave the green light to monochromatic television broadcasting. Applications for stations and construction came swiftly. In September 1948 the FCC imposed a freeze on any new assignments for television stations. The freeze lasted until April 14, 1952, with the issuance of the Commission's *Sixth Report and Order*. The plan provided for the utilization of ultra high frequency in addition to very high frequency channels. The same report also set aside channels for educational noncommercial television stations. By this time television had captured the imagination of the American public, mainly due to the 1948–49 efforts of the Milton Berle Show. There were, at the same time, other forces interested in nonpublic television — medicine, the military, and education.

Medicine

The advantages of closed-circuit television were seen rather early by the medical field. In 1939 surgery was televised at the Israel Zion Hospital in Brooklyn, New York, to seventy-five doctors and interns who viewed the operation in another building.[11] The long-distance view in the amphitheater was replaced by the television close-up. Television was used at Creighton Memorial–St. Joseph's Hospital in Omaha, Nebraska, for surgery observation in 1947. The University of Pennsylvania used the medium for instruction in surgical techniques in 1949, and in September of that year the University of Kansas Medical Center built a permanent closed-circuit installation for daily use of television in medical education.[12] The University of Pennsylvania facility had acquired their own color television equipment by 1950.[13]

The mental health field also began to discover the usefulness of closed-circuit television. In 1952 five television sets were installed in some of the wards of Agnew State Hospital, Agnew, California. It was found that the disturbed patients responded favorably to the commercial television programs. Radio had not had this ameliorating effect upon the patients, who seemed to respond better to the visual impact of television than to the "anonymous messages and disembodied voices" of radio. In August 1954 a closed-circuit system was acquired and used for patient therapy. "Two types of televised therapy programs were used continuously during the study: (a) panel and group discussions, and (b) selected motion pictures. Other therapies employed in conjunction with the above were: music, art, psychodrama, individual therapy, and question and answer programs, all of which were televised to the experimental groups by closed-circuit television." [14]

In 1958, Dr. Raymond W. Waggoner began to present "live" case studies via CCTV in lectures on organic brain syndromes to his psychiatric classes at the University of Michigan. [15] Later, schools of social work began to use television to teach diagnostic evaluation and therapy techniques. With videotape the number of such projects increased so that in 1966 the National Center for School and College Television held a conference assessing current television materials in social work education with the possibility in mind for national distribution of such resources. In New York, two psychoanalysts, Doctors Ian Alger and Peter Hogan, are using home television equipment in their practice. [16] They videotape the first fifteen minutes of each family therapy hour and immediately play back the recording. This becomes the basis for the rest of the session.

Schools of dentistry also began to use television relatively early as a means of instruction. By 1956 the University of Texas Dental School had acquired $75,000 worth of television equipment. [17] In the same year Dr. Michael T. Romano was placed in charge of television facilities at the University of Pennsylvania's Dental School.

By 1958 the Council on Medical Television had been formed.

At the fourth annual meeting of the group, held in Bethesda, Maryland, in 1962, it was reported that closed-circuit television was being utilized by forty-seven medical schools and thirty-one of the forty-eight dental schools.[18] The incorporation of color in the larger medical television facilities enhanced the realism of medical instruction where subtleties of hue were important. The addition of videotape recording made possible standardization, repeatability, and selectivity of resource materials.

Medical television has become a specialized and complex field. Its magnitude is indicated by governmental support of a conference on "Biomedical Communications" held in New York City in April 1966. The conference aim was to examine those ways in which media, personnel, and systems could be used to achieve the objective of medical education, training, and instruction.

Military

With the assistance of the Allen B. Dumont laboratories, television was used for military maneuvers in northern New York State in 1944.[19] In 1949, televised instruction with a two-way radio between students and instructors was used at the Merchant Marine Academy at Kings Point, New York.[20] In the same year the Office of the Chief Signal Officer was assigned the responsibility for the development of military television. For this purpose several mobile television units were purchased and assigned to the Army Pictorial Center at Long Island City, New York. These touring units demonstrated both classroom instructional uses of television and military field uses; but two years of such demonstrations only pointed up the information gap concerning television's effective use, particularly as an educational medium. It was clear that demonstrations alone could not close the gap.[21]

The United States Army therefore established the first military educational facility at Signal School, Fort Monmouth, New Jersey. Numerous military television installations followed suit: Fort Gordon, Georgia, 1952; Fort Eustis, Virginia, 1954; the Ordnance Guided Missile School, Huntsville, Alabama, 1955; Walter

Reed Army Medical Center, Washington, D.C., 1955; Fort Bliss, Texas, 1956; Lowry Air Force Technical Training Center, Denver, Colorado, 1958; the Naval Photographic Center, Anacostia, 1958. Many other military installations and schools were soon equipped with television for a variety of purposes such as management of communications, parade control, and the viewing of rocket engine tests.

Perhaps because of its captive audience, the military had at its disposal a vast controlled resource of subjects, making research into televised instruction both possible and practical. Because of an existing research gap the United States Army asked the Human Resources Research Office (HUMRRO) to study television's capability in regard to military needs, specifically in the area of basic training, where a comparison was sought between conventionally trained military personnel and those trained by television. Could televised instruction do the function normally done by the conventional method? Research conducted at Ford Gordon, Georgia, in 1953, proved that manual skills — in this case the disassembly of a machine gun — could be taught to students who were led in the task by a television instructor. Next HUMRRO went a step beyond this study "to see how far it was possible to go, using television to both improve student achievement and reduce training time in a selected difficult course of instruction in basic electricity. The study provided evidence that both objectives could be achieved, although not without considerable labor." [22] A number of other studies followed thereafter, among them, in 1959, the first comparative color television study. A comparison of achievement was conducted between students who received instruction through color television and students who received instruction through monochromatic television. The results showed no significant differences in achievement.

Color television is still not used by the Army for educational requirements. Dr. Joseph H. Kanner, who has been responsible for much of the military television research, has comments in regard to this policy which go beyond military applications.

Interestingly enough, we are finding that even in the medical television areas the requirements for color television are quite low and more use is made of black and white. As you know, this approach is in contrast with what appears to be a growing movement among television users to acquire color television facilities. In addition to lack of evidence that color enhances student learning, there are the very real considerations of increased initial costs, higher replacement costs and greater skill requirements for color television which should not be glibly overlooked.[23]

With the acquisition of videotape facilities the Army developed a study aimed at the use of television to improve student achievement. As described by Dr. Kanner, a "review-preview" technique was used "in which students were shown at night in a barracks, by television, a review of their previous day's work and a preview of forthcoming events." The results of study indicated that the achievement of students subjected to this "review-preview" technique was far superior to the achievement of conventionally trained students.

The research stemming from military utilization of closed-circuit television must be considered an important contribution in the over-all development of television as a training and educational tool.

Education

Educators were intrigued by broadcasting. Before the FCC freeze on channel allocations in 1948, Iowa State University in Ames, Iowa, obtained a television license. WOI was the first television station owned by an educational institution and operated on commercial channels.[24] There were beginnings of CCTV during 1947–48. These were mainly demonstrations of the medium, some of which occurred at Creighton University in Omaha and at Idaho State College in Pocatello. As yet there was little done in the area of direct instruction. During this period only sporadic interest was expressed by education in the instructional possibilities of closed-circuit television.

In February 1949, Tracy F. Tyler wrote a significant editorial for the *Journal of the Association for Education by Radio,* in which he asked the membership, "How about Wired Television?" [25]

When radio was still an infant, educators joined together with wire circuits all the rooms in a single building. To these circuits were attached microphones, turntables, amplifiers, and loudspeakers. Thus, speech and music, which originated in one room in the school building, could be heard simultaneously in all or as many rooms as were desired.

. . . .

The use of radio to demonstrate master teaching has always suffered because only the auditory aspects of such teaching could be sampled. TV now makes it possible to add the visual. One question only needs to be answered: Is the educational value commensurate with the costs involved?

All colleges and universities which train teachers face the problem of providing ample opportunity for each prospective teacher to observe good teaching. School systems also face the same problem in planning in-service training programs. . . .

Wired television has now reached the stage where it can help solve this problem. A TV camera could be placed so as to command a view of an entire classroom and yet not be visible to the teacher or students. A concentric cable could carry the view to another room in the same building or even to another building. Also, a voice channel could be provided. Thus, the college teacher of methods, whenever he desired, could illustrate his lecture by presenting a normal teaching situation through the use of a TV screen and a loudspeaker.

This is only one area in the educational field, but an extremely important one, where wired TV offers assistance. Others might include the televising of an operation for medical students, with the camera in as good a position to observe as is the surgeon himself; a televised demonstration of the operation of tools and machines for shop students; a televised projection of microscopic studies or of telescopic images for group observation; and the remote observation of hazardous processes in chemical or physical laboratories.

Whether the consequent CCTV activity was partially the result of Professor Tyler's editorial is difficult to determine, but things did begin happening. In 1950 plans were announced for a closed-circuit system for Stephens College, Columbia, Missouri. The facility was to have a dual purpose: "In addition to providing instruction and practical experience for students in television programming and production, television will be integrated into the total instructional program at the College, transforming many classroom procedures and improving present instructional methods."[26] The training of students in broadcasting and closed-circuit instruction became an effective and economical combination. The students gained experience in television production as they served as crew members for the facility. This trend was established early in contrast to the emerging professionally staffed educational television stations.

The early 1950's represent a period of experimentation, introspection, and variation in the use of closed-circuit television. This is the period for organization and unique individual efforts.

In the summer of 1951 a course in "Citizenship" was experimentally taught via closed-circuit television at Syracuse University. At Cornell University television was restricted to one classroom equipped with two 21-inch receivers so that students could witness magnified physics experiments. "The method gave students a good view of normally invisible particles suspended in a fluid ('Brownian Movement') making it unnecessary for the students to line up at microscopes."[27]

By 1953 the "television freeze" was over and the University of Houston's KUHT became the first educational television station operating on a noncommercial license. By 1967 there would be approximately 140 educational television stations.

Some universities and colleges entered closed-circuit activity during the time of the freeze to prepare and train staff for the institutions' possible entrance into educational broadcasting. In 1951 Michigan State University set up a CCTV installation for use in experimental programming training of a television staff, and laboratory training for students. In 1954 Michigan State's WKAR-TV was on the air. The University of Wisconsin regents authorized a "closed-circuit television laboratory for teaching and research in the new medium" in 1952.[28] With this period for preparation WHA-TV began broadcasting in 1954. In most situations where stations emerged out of closed-circuit installations, the latter were de-emphasized in the initial broadcasting years, but ultimately emerged with specialized functions in training and education. In a sense, the thrust of education into broadcasting defined the purposes of closed-circuit television. Prior to this time the educator was ambivalent as to function and method. Education was ready to begin a full-scale testing of televised instruction by 1955, and received help from outside funding sources.

In 1954, Pennsylvania State University submitted a proposal to the Fund for the Advancement of Education in which the university offered to undertake a program of demonstration and research in closed-circuit television instruction. The grant was awarded with the condition that no changes be made in teaching procedures; television "was simply being introduced into a normal classroom." [29] The first three courses were taught in the spring of 1955 by closed circuit — two in psychology and one in chemistry. The lack of adaptation for the medium is fairly significant. Television, in this case was being used purely as a means of transmitting a photographed class lecture. This may certainly be one of the important functions of the medium. During the summer of 1955, when Pennsylvania State University and the Fund for the Advancement of Education were negotiating the objectives for the project's second year, the university expressed some important reactions to their experience in a letter sent to Alvin C. Eurich of the Fund:

> We have answered to a limited extent your basic question: "Can you teach regular college and university courses by closed-circuit television for a full semester?" The answer is yes, for the three courses we have televised. . . . However, we hasten to add that this should not be done routinely. Television projection of good (conventional) instruction, in brief, should require that the potentialities of television be fully used, and that the limitations be overcome. This basic operational principle, of which we are strongly convinced, requires the adaptation of courses and instruction to the characteristics of closed-circuit television and the adaptation of television to the demands of courses, instructors and students in the interest of improved effectiveness of teaching. . . .[30]

The Pennsylvania State University project and research efforts, under the leadership of Professors C. R. Carpenter and L. P. Greenhill, provided the stimulus for a national increase in the use of televised instruction. Eventually the financial aid from the Fund for the Advancement of Education was discontinued and CCTV became a normally funded facet of the university.

In February of 1955, sixty educational leaders met in East Lansing, Michigan, at a conference concerned with credit courses taught by open-circuit television. Out of this conference emerged the recommendation for a future meeting dedicated to closed-circuit television. This meeting was held in Iowa City, Iowa, on February 26–28, 1956. Representatives of the University of Iowa, Pennsylvania State University, New York University, Miami University, Stephens College, Case Institute of Technology, University of Texas, State Teachers College, Montclair, New Jersey, and the University of Houston were among those who made progress reports on their institutions' use of CCTV. Of special interest was a comment made by John C. Schwarzwalder, representing the University of Houston. He pointed out that his institution was considering the use of closed circuit as a complement to the open-circuit VHF channel for teaching because of the premium of time.[31] Apparently the demands for televised instruction were beginning to be heard.

E. DeAlton Partridge, of the State Teachers College, Montclair, New Jersey (now president of the Near East Foundation), reported on the use of television at the elementary school level,[32] describing a one-day experimental project initiated in April 1952 with the aid of the Dumont Television Corporation. On April 30 eight lessons were transmitted to public schools in the towns of Bloomfield and Montclair. The lessons were broadcast on UHF channel 54, one of two UHF channels licensed to Dumont by the FCC for experimental use. At that time home sets were not yet adapted for UHF reception and only the thirteen schools involved were able to receive the lessons. Previous to April 30 the college had experimented with television on a closed-circuit basis. During May and June of 1951 the Dumont Laboratories had loaned the college complete color equipment for the purpose of experimentation.[33] Dr. Partridge termed the experiment quite successful (speaking of it in a telephone conversation in December 1966), but it was discontinued as the result of the New Jersey state administration's insistence that the television should not come between the student and teacher. This project must be considered significant, since the initial work in instruction by CCTV had been fairly limited to higher education; this early utilization for elementary and secondary school instruction represented a new important direction and called for careful analysis and research. The "Hagerstown" project served this purpose.

The Washington County (Maryland) Closed-Circuit Television Project began in 1956, sponsored by the Electronic Industries Association and the Fund for the Advancement of Education, assisted by the Chesapeake and Potomac Telephone Company. The 1956 network utilized three simultaneous channels interconnecting eight elementary schools in Hagerstown, Maryland. By 1961, forty-four schools (kindergarten through twelfth grade) were included in the circuit. The use of television at Hagerstown allowed for some particular benefits, among which were included the enrichment of the elementary school program through the addition of courses in art, music, conversational French, and remedial reading; the introduction of advanced courses for gifted high school pupils; the organization of a teacher in-service educational program; and the rescheduling of the school program in order to allow teachers more time for planning and individual conferences with small groups.[34] In 1966 over 84,000 students were receiving some instruction via television.[35]

The Chelsea Closed-Circuit Television Project represents another dimension in the development of this means of instruction and training. Beginning in 1957, the project attempted to use CCTV for direct teaching, school enrichment, teacher training, language instruction, and improvement of community integration within a specific ghetto in New York City. With the aid of a grant from the Fund for the Advancement of Education, this unique project created a CCTV system coincident with the needs and problems of the Spanish-American community by interconnecting schools, homes, and health and social services, via television. A number of new specialized functions for which CCTV was useful emerged out of the Chelsea Television Project. Closed circuit proved useful (1) as a distinct in-school system within a large city, where special problems of home environment tend to be recognized in their distinct distribution; (2) as a city-wide school system specifically used for teacher-training, examinations, and administration; (3) as an unlicensed ETV station where local conditions require a community antenna and there is no ETV reservation; (4) for education directed to institutions other than schools and colleges, e.g., prisons, youth homes, hospitals; (5) as a means of meeting the challenge of the small urban area containing a high concentration of people with hard core educational or cultural problems; (6) as an instrument for the development of community leadership; (7) as a form of psychotherapy.[36]

A 1958 survey conducted by a subcommittee of the American Association of Colleges for Teacher Education reported the relative commitment of institutions of higher education to CCTV.

361 institutions responded to the survey (88%)
252 were not using or planning to use CCTV (70%)
22 were studying possible use of CCTV (6%)
50 were planning to use CCTV (14%)
37 were utilizing CCTV (10%)[37]

Although the survey indicates an increase in CCTV utilization, many institutions were still wary of the medium and its effects upon students and faculty. At times the resistance to the experimental use of televised instruction was more emotional than logical. To a certain extent, the failures of commercial television had been generalized to extend to both educational and instructional television. Often these attitudes were the result of inadequate personnel, insufficient funds, and a lack of quality on the part of CCTV output. At times the administrators' expectation that the new medium would decrease instructional costs was misguided and hence not met.

In September 1958 the regents of the State University of New

York initiated the Cortland County Closed-Circuit Television Project in eight elementary and secondary schools which were connected via coaxial cable. The two-channel system included a talk-back system for student response.[38] The initial optimism for the project gave way to some discontent and community resistance. Although it is not certain what caused the enthusiasm to disintegrate, perhaps one factor may have been a $50,000 annual cost for cable charges out of a $97,000 total figure for the 1958–59 school year.[39] Some members of the community maintained that "rather than making education superior, ETV is making it inferior." The group felt that "ETV is something which should be experimented with in a school system that has everything else and has the time and place for it."[40] The project continued to sputter along until April 11, 1963, when the Cortland board of education voted to discontinue TV. The failure of the project may have stemmed from a problem in public relations, but the medium became the scapegoat.

Videotape: aid to education

Before 1956 one of the problems which surrounded the efficient utilization of closed-circuit television was the lack of an adequate and economical recording capability. Some larger installations did have kinescope recorders at their disposal, but obtaining final prints was slow and results were inferior to film. The lack of an adequate recording capability affected every potential user of television. In 1953 Bing Crosby Enterprises displayed a prototype of a videotape recorder, a nonfilmic device which used tape similar to audio tape; but the model was not yet perfected for production and distribution. The Ampex Corporation demonstrated the first production model of a videotape recorder at the Chicago convention of the National Association of Broadcasters in 1956. In November, the Columbia Broadcasting System in Hollywood began using the videotape recorder for network delayed broadcasts because of the time differential between the East and West coasts.[41] The first ETV station to use videotape was WGBH, Boston, in June 1958.[42] In 1959 the University of Texas became the first university to utilize videotape recording for closed-circuit instruction.[43]

The advent of tape must be considered an important breakthrough for televised instruction. Here was a means for recording and immediate playback with the impact of a live transmission. In addition, videotape was erasable and reusable. With the ability to pre-record lessons, quality control became possible. A lesson could be evaluated, analyzed, tested, and produced again, if needed, before being used in the classroom. Videotape allowed for the repeatable playback of lessons. Although the capital investment for videotape recorders was high, the economics favored the educator. Lessons could be produced once, but used for several years, thereby reducing some instructional costs. The use of videotape also allowed for the exchange of lessons between institutions possessing videotape facilities. Because of this capability a number of distribution agencies have been created, such as the Great Plains Instructional Television Library in Lincoln, Nebraska, and the National Center for School and College Television in Bloomington, Indiana. The use of videotape for training, self-criticism, and improvement became apparent. Schools of education and speech departments were among the first to grasp videotape as a training and teaching tool.

The recent development of portable videotape recorders (also referred to as helical scan or slant track recorders) now has given playback and recording capabilities to those institutions unable to invest in such studio facilities because of the high costs of equipment. The most important effect of the development of the portable television recorder is a return of control to the classroom teacher who, because of the operational simplicity of such recorders, is able to integrate the video resource materials into the lesson structure at his own pace. It should be pointed out that each recorder serves particular functions and needs. A relatively inexpensive recorder and system may not be suitable for disciplines in which high resolution is required. This is true of the total facility as well. Each should be planned in accordance with specific needs. It is neither economical nor desirable to invest in expensive, perhaps broadcast quality, equipment if simplicity is desired and high resolution is not necessary. The converse is also true. A low investment in nonbroadcast equipment (even here there is considerable variance in choice and cost) may not meet the flexibility and quality required.

Scope and utilization of CCTV

The growth of CCTV has accelerated with the advent of the videotape recorder. The primary users can be basically categorized into the areas of military, medical-mental health, education, and industrial-management. It is important to point out several significant directions of growth CCTV has followed in terms of scope and utilization.

Closed circuit was defined as a system in which coaxial cable or microwave is utilized to transmit signals of images and/or sound to predetermined receiver or monitor locations. Therefore, any closed-circuit facility comprises three parts: a signal source, a means of distributing the signal, and reception points for the signal.

Scope of utilization depends upon the complexity of the distribution system used. Television can be restricted to intra-room use for magnification purposes or can be extended to an inter-room basis for multiple room reception of lessons. The same may be true of intra- or inter-building, or intra- or inter-institutional use. For example, South Carolina established the first state-wide closed-circuit television network in 1960. This multichannel network uses microwave to interconnect city with city and coaxial cable to interconnect schools within each city. On the university and college level, the Texas Educational Microwave Project (TEMP) connects eleven central Texas schools. In this way each school's faculty resources can be shared. The concept of interconnection extends to both national and international utilization.

On May 31, 1965, French language class students at the West Bend, Wisconsin, high school had a two-way closed circuit television conversation with an English language class at Lycée Henry IV in Paris, via the Early Bird Satellite.[44] The scope, magnitude, and possibilities of CCTV instruction have indeed become limited only by a lack of imagination.

The functions of closed-circuit television in training and education have, I hope, emerged in this survey of its historical development. These functions can be broken down into training, instruction, therapy, communications-administration, observation, and research. Of these, perhaps not enough has been said of CCTV as a research tool. One example in this area has been the work of Professor Karl U. Smith at the University of Wisconsin, much of whose psychological research in perception and motion has depended upon the use of closed-circuit television. Professor Smith comments on the value of television for experimental purposes:

The future of television as a laboratory instrument seems assured, for it gives unmatched experimental control over all aspects of the visual feedback of motion.

.   .   .   .

Video systems provide a means of electronic variation of all the psychological dimensions of visual stimuli. Accordingly, many new innovations in the visual sciences of psychology and perception of color, space, and form are made possible by closed-circuit camera-monitor chains, videotape techniques, and three dimensional television.[45]

In regard to form and instruction, CCTV has been used as the total method of teaching, in a complementary fashion in which television is integrated into the classroom lesson structure, and in a supplementary manner where students view the material outside the classroom on their own time for the purpose of review, preview, or enrichment. In addition, television has been used for the nonstructured purpose of teacher observation and for the "mirror" television function in which the student views himself for the purpose of self-improvement.

CCTV AND THE FUTURE

The future of closed-circuit television is dependent upon its integration, with other media, into the training and teaching structure of American education. This means coordination between the development of media technology (hardware) and the goals of the teaching-learning process through a systems design approach to education.

The future will witness a multimedia approach supporting educational needs and the attempt to simulate tutorial teaching through the use of media. Dial access retrieval, programmed instruction, and video-tutorial laboratories will become commonplace. The traditional image of the library will change to include both print and nonprint forms which the student can use at his own rate and pace. The communication satellite will bring national and international resources into the classroom.

The transition

Even with the tremendous proliferation of closed-circuit television facilities, televised instruction has remained outside the educational mainstream. The reluctance of American educators to utilize the medium has sometimes reflected emotional prejudices, but it is also true that the output of CCTV installations has not been of uniformly high quality.

Edwin G. Cohen, director of the National Center for School and College Television, has coined the term "GIGO (garbage in, garbage out)" as a warning to users and producers of instructional television.[46] "GIGO" suggests that television can be a dangerously efficient medium for distributing poor teaching poorly produced to a considerable number of students. The responsibility for the present mediocre state of televised instruction rests both with producers of instructional material and with the authorities on content. The producers' lack of knowledge about the teaching-learning process has been matched by the teachers' distrust of outside advice on content. Often the teacher who has participated in the development of teaching materials has done this without any release time for the task. Sometimes the least experienced producers and directors have been assigned to instructional television projects. The emphasis has been on quantity, not quality.

The production of effectively structured television lessons is both time-consuming and difficult. It means the collaboration of television and teaching personnel. The development, production, and utilization of televised instructional material will, ideally, reflect and affect the entire teaching milieu. Half-hearted attempts may result in demonstrations, but not necessarily meaningful instruction. The problem is succinctly stated by C. R. Carpenter and R. N. Willis:

> . . . The assumption is widespread that TV can be added to educational systems without markedly changing standard traditional requirements for funds, buildings, faculties, and personnel.
> In this connection a principle can be stated: *When a new significant development is properly introduced into a system, its introduction significantly changes many or most of the other parts of the system.*[47]

Education is always at a crossroad or at the threshold of a new era. The future of closed-circuit television in training and education is somewhere between these two clichés. The technology of television has come a long way since the early efforts to transmit sight and sound. In a sense, the development of electronic media has far outstripped man's knowledge and ingenuity in terms of his utilization of those media. The basic objectives of individuals involved in closed-circuit or open-circuit instructional television must be to narrow the gap between technical virtuosity and effective teaching and training.

NOTES

1 Judith Murphy and Ronald Gross, *Learning by Television* (New York: Fund for the Advancement of Education, Aug. 1966), p. 23, state: "There are probably close to 1,000 closed-circuit installations serving educational purposes, including 275 systems that

are substantial in scope and size. Surveys indicate that slightly over half the educational systems are in colleges and universities, about one-fourth in the lower schools, and the rest in medical institutions and military installations."

2 See *Design for ETV: Planning for Schools with Television* (New York: Educational Facilities Laboratories, 1960), p. 25.

3 L. R. Lankes, "Historical Sketch of Television's Progress," *Journal of the Society of Motion Picture Engineers* (hereafter cited as *JSMPE*), LI (Sept. 1948), 226.

4 Erik Barnouw, *A Tower of Babel: A History of Broadcasting in the United States* (New York: Oxford University Press, 1966), p. 231.

5 H. R. Lubcke, "The Theatrical Possibilities of Television," *JSMPE*, xxv (July 1935), 48–49.

6 Scientific Committee of the Research Council of the Academy of Motion Picture Arts and Sciences, "Television," *JSMPE*, xxvii (July 1936), 75.

7 "Television from the Standpoint of the Motion Picture Producing Industry," *JSMPE*, xxix (Aug. 1937), 144.

8 Noran E. Kersta, "Television in Education," *Film and Radio Discussion Guide*, xi (Nov. 1944), 18.

9 Ronald L. Ives, "Pictures Through a Pipe," *Science News Letter*, March 12, 1938, p. 170.

10 Kersta, in *Film and Radio Discussion Guide*, xi, 18.

11 George P. Adair, "What Television Offers Education," *Journal of the Association for Education by Radio* (hereafter cited as *JAER*), vi (Feb. 1947), 84.

12 William Kenneth Cumming, *This Is Educational Television* (Ann Arbor: Edwards Brothers, Inc., 1954), p. 84.

13 "TV Viewers See Surgery," *JAER*, xi (April 1952), 40.

14 Gaither Lee Martin and Charles H. R. Over, "Therapy by Television," *Audio-Visual Communication Review*, iv (Spring, 1956), 122.

15 Donald J. Holmes, M.D., "Closed Circuit Television in Teaching Psychiatry," *University of Michigan Medical Bulletin*, xxvii (Nov.-Dec. 1961), 330.

16 Peter D. Hogan and Ian E. Alger, "Use of Videotape Recording in Family Therapy," paper presented at the 43rd Annual Meeting of the American Orthopsychiatric Association, April 16, 1966, in San Francisco.

17 "Informal reports from Experimental Centers," *Teaching by*

Closed-Circuit Television (Washington: American Council on Education, 1956), p. 23.

18 S. A. DiSanto, "New Techniques in Closed-Circuit Television for Dental Teaching," *Journal of the Society of Motion Picture and Television Engineers*, LXXIV (Sept. 1964), 770.

19 "Television Goes Military," *Newsweek*, Sept. 16, 1946, p. 54.

20 "Who? What? Where? When?" *JAER*, VIII (March 1949), inside cover.

21 Letter from Joseph H. Kanner, Special Assistant, Pictorial and Audio-Visual Division, Tactical Systems Directorate, Office of the Chief of Communications-Electronics, Department of the Army, Washington, D.C., Nov. 4, 1966.

22 *Ibid.*

23 *Ibid.*, May 6, 1966.

24 Cumming, *This Is Educational Television*, p. 1.

25 Tracy F. Tyler, "How about Wired Television?" *JAER*, VIII (Feb. 1949), 61.

26 "Broadcast by Colleges: TV at Stephens College," *JAER*, IX (April 1950), 96.

27 Cumming, *This Is Educational Television*, p. 82.

28 "Events of Significance: Wisconsin Takes First TV Steps," *JAER*, XII (Oct. 1952), 8.

29 John C. Adams, C. R. Carpenter, Dorothy R. Smith, eds., *College Teaching by Television* (Washington: American Council on Education, 1958), p. 3.

30 *Instructional Television Research: An Investigation of Closed-Circuit Television for Teaching University Courses. Report Number Two: The Academic Years 1955–1957 and 1956–1957* (University Park: Pennsylvania State University, 1958), p. 2.

31 "Informal Reports," in *Teaching by Closed-Circuit Television*, p. 21.

32 *Ibid.*, p. 22.

33 Lawrence H. Conrad, *Educational Television Moves Forward: A Report of a Full School Day of Ultra-High Frequency Classroom Television Programs in the Public Schools of Bloomfield and Montclair, N.J. on April 30, 1952* (Montclair State Teachers College Television in Education Project, March 1953), pp. 14, 15.

34 Robert Lesher, "The Hagerstown Story," in Lee S. Dreyfus and Wallace M. Bradley, eds., *Televised Instruction* (Wayne State University Press, 1962), pp. 109, 110.

35   Lawrence E. McKune, ed., *Compendium of Televised Education,*
     Vol. xiii (Michigan State University Press, 1966), p. ii.

36   Lawrence Creshkoff, "The Chelsea Closed-Circuit Television Proj-
     ect," *NAEB Journal,* xviii (Dec. 1958), 26.

37   "NAEB Research Fact Sheets. Series III: Bibliography. (12)
     Closed-Circuit Television in A.A.C.T.E. Member Institutions,"
     NAEB Journal, xviii (Nov. 1958), 10.

38   *ITV: Instructional Television,* brochure published by Regents
     Closed-Circuit Television Project (Cortland, N.Y.).

39   Rocco Palladino, "Cost of Television Teaching Is Figured from
     Various Angles in This Installment on ETV," *Cortland Standard,*
     March 27, 1961, p. 3.

40   Rocco Palladino, "ETV or Not ETV: Group Tells Reporter That
     Survey Should Be Conducted by Trained Social Scientist," *Cort-
     land Standard,* March 29, 1961, p. 3.

41   Howard A. Chinn, "Status of Video Tape in Broadcasting," *Jour-
     nal of the Society of Motion Picture and Television Engineers,*
     lxvi (Aug. 1957), 453.

42   Richard A. Enger, ed., *Teaching with Videotape* (St. Paul, Minn.:
     3M Company), p. 3.

43   Hugh A. Greene, "Videotapes Aid German Instruction: Closed-
     circuit and Tapes Replace Weekly Session at University of Texas,"
     NAEB Journal, xviii (Oct. 1959), 15.

44   Lee S. Dreyfus and Gary Gumpert, "Students Visit Via Satellite,"
     NAEB Journal, xxv (May–June 1966), 6–13.

45   Karl U. Smith and William M. Smith, *Perception and Motion:
     An Analysis of Space-Structured Behavior* (Philadelphia: W. B.
     Saunders Company, 1962), pp. 15, 149.

46   Murphy and Gross, *Learning by Television,* p. 47.

47   C. R. Carpenter and R. N. Willis, "Barriers to the Use of ETV
     and ITV," *NAEB Journal,* xxiv (Nov.–Dec. 1965), 28.

Part IV

PROBLEMS AND ISSUES IN EDUCATIONAL TELEVISION

On Earning a Nonprofit

YOU might at first think of a nonprofit as a wraithlike being. Perhaps you see it doomed for a certain term to walk the night of insolvency, and for the day constrained to forgo fortune. Not so. A nonprofit is no less than a wholly corporeal gain or asset turned to the good of a community. Transmuted from crass to noble, the profit become nonprofit may be banked, spent, or borrowed upon. It may be risked for gain or lost for ill.

Like a profit, a nonprofit is almost always earned. Windfall profits and windfall nonprofits are rare. If you run a church, a club, a school, a government, a hospital, or a noncommercial television station you are likely to be helping to earn a nonprofit. You provide something worthwhile, and someone pays you for it.

Taxes, fines, fees, gifts, and return from investment are your main kinds of revenue if you run a government. Your revenue probably is from the same kinds of sources, excepting taxes and fines, if you run a private nonprofit enterprise. But then you have some exemption from tax. And if you run a firm that is organized for profit, your main revenue is in the forms of fees and

Copyright © 1966 by Kenneth Harwood. By permission of the editors of this book, the *Journal of Broadcasting* published this article in its Winter 1966–67 issue (Vol. XI, No. 1).

return from investment. You have very little, if any, exemption from tax.

Nonprofit enterprise, both governmental and nongovernmental, shares with profit-seeking enterprise not only the problems of getting revenue, but also those of allocating limited resources to the different functions of the firm, minimizing costs, and distributing the benefits that are created by the firm. Both enterprise for profit and enterprise for nonprofit face the problems of providing for their futures.

What makes the difference between the nonprofit firm and its counterpart for profit? It is simply a difference of emphasis.

The nonprofit firm emphasizes the defense and development of people among its several goals, while the profit-seeking firm holds the making of profits chief among its goals. At the same time the best profit-seeking firm is interested in culture, health, education, and welfare, as is the nonprofit firm; and the best nonprofit firm is interested in a favorable balance of revenue over cost, as is the firm for profit. In the long run it is nearly impossible to operate a profit-making firm without providing something worthwhile to a large number of people; and it is as nearly impossible in the long run to operate a nonprofit firm without earning substantial nonprofits.

REVENUE

The nongovernmental nonsectarian nonprofit institution now becomes the subject of discussion. A good example of that subject is the noncommercial community television station. Much of what ensues also applies to governmental nonprofit units such as municipal noncommercial television stations, as well as to sectarian nonprofit institutions.

To be sure, churches provide the fullest history of well-tested ways of getting money for nonprofit causes.[1] Appeals to join the organization and pay regular sums in recognition of membership are new to neither churches nor community stations. The seeking of bequests is long since common to both, too, as is the soliciting of irregular and occasional gifts during the lifetime of the giver. Private benefactions to noncommercial television have ranged from the candy-money of children to the millions of dollars of the major charitable foundations and the thousands of annual membership donations of families. Full development of private giving remains to be accomplished by noncommercial television units.

For many years various churches in the United States have conducted the Every Member Visit in which every member of a local church is visited by a trained worker who describes the aims of the church and obtains a commitment of money from the member; the commitment is based upon a minimum standard of giving. When appeals by mail or by telephone are substituted for the personal visit, revenue usually declines.[2] Well-organized direct personal yearly solicitation of large numbers of people on behalf of noncommercial television stations is rare, except where a station is a regular beneficiary of a campaign by a united community fund or a community chest.

Professional fund-raising counsel has been engaged by churches for some years, often for the purpose of raising money for capital investment in church buildings. Similar engagements are sometimes made by noncommercial television stations. Inquiries concerning such counsel are served by the American Association of Fund-Raising Counsel, 500 Fifth Avenue, New York, New York.

A local church traditionally has access both to advice and to other aids for fund-raising through a central office of its denomination. Permanent and intensive professional assistance in local fund-raising has yet to be organized for and by the noncommercial television stations in the United States.

Various insurance plans and annuities are more or less standard revenue-producing devices of religious organizations, but not yet of noncommercial television stations. For example, a church group may form a trust fund from which the church may borrow. In guarantee to repay its borrowings the church takes an endowment insurance policy on the life of each person who puts money in the trust fund and undertakes to pay the premiums from the annual budget of the church for a period of, say, twenty years. Some seven-tenths of what is put in the trust fund by an individual may be counted as a gift. Any dividend from the endowment policy may accrue to the church and not to the person who is insured.

Payment to enhance the reputation of the individual giver is a very old kind of church revenue which remains to be developed for noncommercial television. Corporate supporters of particular television programs receive mention on the air, but individuals usually do not. If the names of individual donors to a charitable organization may be published with good effect, the opportunities before a noncommercial television station should be large.

The sale of religious souvenirs has some counterpart in the auctions, fairs, bazaars, and thrift shops that are operated on behalf of noncommercial television stations.

Benefit amusements of many kinds long have been used to raise monies for churches, noncommercial television stations, and other nonprofit organizations. Dances, parties, dinners, excursions, showings of motion pictures, golf tournaments, and similar events are common sources of revenue.

Lottery is an ancient source of support of churches. Lawful options include benefiting from lotteries which are permitted by law and campaigning to authorize lotteries for the support of non-commercial television where lotteries are not lawful. In many places state-supervised betting on horse races is lawful, and char-itable donation of winnings from certain races customary.

The glebe or land-grant by government to an established church was a mark of early settlements in North America. Its adaption during the last century to the support of the land-grant universi-ties in the United States has not been developed for noncommer-cial television. The western part of the country contains large tracts of public lands which, although not especially productive, might be developed to the benefit of noncommercial broadcasters.

Indeed the regular suggestion of different ways in which government may support noncommercial television appears to be a frequent recreation of the many and a thriving business of the few. Taxing of commercial broadcast licensees, operating a jointly commercial and noncommercial satellite-relayed common carrier communication system, placing an excise tax on television receivers, and appropriating the toll revenues of the Panama Canal have been proposed, to state but a few examples.

In fact both direct and indirect governmental grants and gifts to noncommercial television broadcasting have been varied and numerous. They have supported purchase of transmitters and studio equipment, purchase of receiving equipment for use in schools, and the development, production, recording, testing, evaluation, and distribution of educational programs. States, municipalities, and private organizations have been encouraged to give by matching federal monies and in other ways. Governmental action is likely to remain a large and growing source of revenue for noncommercial broadcasting.

Because most rents, dividends, interest, annuities, and royalties are not taxable income to a nonprofit charitable entity, they are in part equivalent to the governmental land-grants of yesteryear. Tax law opens a variety of opportunities to imaginative financial management, as well as potential pitfalls. The best legal advice is essential to success in such matters.

Today private owners take some tax advantage through "bootstrap" acquisition of their property by nonprofit organizations, and the nonprofit organizations may benefit through acquiring revenue-producing properties without investment of their other funds.[3] A business is transferred to a charitable foundation, for example, with the down payment represented by a tax-deductible gift of as much as 5 percent of the current annual income of the business, the remainder of the price being payable from the later earnings of the business. The seller may reclaim the business if regular payments are not made by the buyer. The business is operated by a new corporation in which the seller and the foundation participate, the stock of this corporation perhaps being held by employees of the business. The foundation leases the business property for five years, in return for rent which represents most of the profits of the business. The seller may be paid a salary by the new corporation to manage the activities of the business. The seller takes payments which are taxed as capital gains, the seller escapes taxation on the income of the new operating corporation, and the new corporation takes its rental payments as business deductions from taxable income. Rental income probably is tax-free to the foundation. A noncommercial community television station could benefit from such income through a foundation or directly.

Encouragement of private gifts to noncommercial television stations has been given by the Federal Communications Commission as an indirect form of glebe. Several million dollars worth of gifts in cash and in kind has been donated by the commercial broadcasting companies to which licenses are issued and reissued by the Commission. Similar encouragements could be stimulated in the future.

A singular encouragement of private gifts to noncommercial television has been provided by the FCC in choosing a special profit-seeking corporation to be interim licensee of a major radio station while the Commission sought to select a regular commercial licensee from among some twenty applicants. The speciality of the profit-seeking corporation lay in the owning of the whole of its capital stock by a nonprofit charitable foundation from which the Commission had the pledge that the largest part of the profits coming from the corporation to the foundation would be given by the foundation to a noncommercial television station. During the first two years of the arrangement the commercial broadcast licensee provided some hundreds of thousands of dollars through the foundation. This relationship between commercial broadcast licensee, foundation, and noncommercial licensee might be applied more widely than it has been.

Establishment as an official instrument of government, with consequent support from tax monies, characterized the church of early colonial America. Possibility of such a relationship looms before the governing board of each noncommercial community television station, if the possibility has not been converted to at least partial reality through provision of tax monies in recognition of some services of the station.

This sketchy survey of some historic founts of nonprofit revenue should freshen and whet the minds of the ingenious. Of course, it is only suggestive.

REVENUE AND INCENTIVE

Perpetuity being a very long time, few mortals make much of it. Yet almost all corporations are founded for that term, and almost all noncommercial community television stations are incorporated, albeit not for profit. Perpetuity is deemed to be longer than ten years or a hundred; it is much longer than the current fiscal year.

To hear the talk in the governing board of an ordinary local nonprofit nongovernmental nonsectarian charitable organization, you might conclude that perpetuity will last until next Tuesday, and maybe with special luck until two weeks from Tuesday. That is how far into the future it may be given to foresee payment of bills due or coming due. No prudent man would undertake obligations beyond those for which payment is in prospect. And people are called to be trustees because they are prudent.

Corporate decline and death follow hard upon that kind of prudence, thus bringing perpetuity a little closer to now than it would have been. The surest way to asphyxiate a firm, be it for profit or for nonprofit, is to keep it from changing with the changing combinations and permutations of human wants and needs. A firm that does not change withers and ossifies. The common way down hill is to keep on doing exactly what has been done because it is not prudent to make commitments beyond immediately visible revenue, and because there is neither time nor reason for long contract or planned growth. Two weeks from Tuesday becomes a self-fulfilling prophecy.

Reserves against depreciation and depletion are ignored or minimized. Gain-stimulating long-term borrowing is laughed aside. Forecasting and budgeting of revenues and costs are slighted. Potentially gainful long-term investment is bypassed because the term is not seen to be long. Managerial enthusiasm lags because the future is short and dead-ended. Professional staffs and maintenance crews alike sense the lack of tomorrow and leave in spirit, if not in fact. The board itself flags; new members are few, and they are less distinguished than their earlier fellows. The spiral of decline is complete. Very little less than radical reform will reverse it, if that.

Should the firm be saved, if salvation is possible? Not necessarily. If it is dissolved, its members and its remaining functions probably will be taken up by other and better-guided firms. It should be saved only if the members are willing and able to begin and continue long-term change.

Which kinds of incentives should be provided, assuming that the firm is worth saving and that it is possible to save the firm? A proper combination of earthly glory and material reward might be best. Penury serves well neither the nonprofit firm nor the others. Appeals to be loyal to the dear old firm are of little avail when people transfer easily from one firm to the next, and first-rate people almost always transfer easily.

The selling or fund-raising function is common to all firms. Someone arranges to get the revenue. What kind of incentive should he be given? Too often in the nonprofit firm the chief operating officer is seen and rewarded by the trustees as a getter of revenue, and not as a general manager of both revenue and cost. Especially when the scale of rewarding the officer is as materially modest as it is likely to be in a nonprofit organization, he tends to be rewarded in part by the number of people he manages in the firm, and costs mushroom as the staff grows. One cure is to reward the chief operating officer with money according to neither revenues of the firm nor the number of persons he oversees, but according to a favorable and improving ratio of benefits to costs. The external criterion is the benefit-cost ratio in a similar organization, and the internal one the benefit-cost ratio of the same organization in a like recent period. The list of benefits may be quantified through numerical weights which are assigned and periodically reassigned by the trustees, and the costs may be quantified in dollars. This technique requires the trustees and the operating officers to assess regularly both the relative importance of the several goals of the firm and the extent to which each goal is being achieved at optimum cost.

Reward of nonprofit fund-raising according to a single benefit-cost ratio may be self-destructive. Funds from nongovernmental sources are least costly to raise for buildings and most costly to raise for current operations, with funds for equipment falling between the extremes. Under a single standard of reward the tendency is to solicit funds for buildings or for equipment because total revenue per time unit is maximized and cost per dollar raised is minimized. Compensation of those who produce programs and operate the noncommercial station tends to be neglected. The long-run result of the single benefit-cost ratio in fund-raising is to have a very good plant for the production of inconsequential broadcasts which attract declining interest to the station from potential donors. Fund-raisers should be compensated according to the difficulty of raising money for each different purpose. Major hurdles for the trustees and the chief operating officer to pass are their own recognition of the inherent differences between costs of raising funds for different purposes and their determination to reward the achieving of the best balance of purposes.

Programming and engineering departments of the noncommercial community television station, as well as fund-raising and general administration, should answer to favorable and improving benefit-cost ratios in assignment of compensation to them, if the whole organization is to survive. The major caution is that the ratios normally differ according to function or purpose within departments as well as between them.

A large incentive to all departments is prospect of a good future for the firm. It is an essential incentive to the trustees and the chief officers, for they more than others are public figures who gain or lose widespread reputation daily, according to the prospects of the firm. Two valuable and sometimes slighted financial techniques for insuring that future in nonprofit firms are diversification of revenue and growth of an investment portfolio from a yearly balance of revenue over cost.

Any firm depending upon one or two main sources of revenue is vulnerable to sudden and irremediable reduction in one or both. Need to undertake the large, painful, and sometimes terminal readjustments resulting from such reduction is minimized as the number of sources increases. Perhaps a reasonable goal would be to have at least three or four main sources of revenue.

Ideally the nongovernmental nonsectarian nonprofit firm should hold a portfolio of investments from which the yearly return would meet all yearly costs, including those of depreciation and depletion, wages and salaries, interest, and rent.[4] Net proceeds of fund-raising would be added to the portfolio, and operations would be enlarged only as additional returns from investments were in hand. No fee would be charged those who take the services of the firm. Few existing nonprofit organizations are able to attain that position, and fewer still are bequeathed it by their prudent predecessors. The demands of today seldom seem less pressing than the needs of the future.

Yet there is a reasonable minimum goal of the nonprofit firm which, for one reason or another, operates this year from this year's fees and this year's net of fund-raising. The goal is merely that there be a balance of revenue over cost for the purpose of providing an investment fund from which capital may be drawn on a rainy day. Such a fund permits trustees and operating officers to maintain essential services for a time until the sun shines again;

it represents a minimal responsibility to those who depend upon the organization for valuable service.

Having come full circle we notice that, although a profit-seeking firm would call the balance of revenue over cost a profit, the non-profit firm calls it an investment fund against times when the balance is of cost over revenue. And however dainty we may be about naming positive balances, a negative balance is a loss to the nonprofit firm as well as to its profit-seeking counterpart. What, then, is a nonprofit? As was said near the start, it is any gain or asset put to community good instead of individual use. What could be simpler?

NOTES

1 Luther P. Powell, *Money and the Church* (New York: Association Press, 1962), contains an excellent survey to which the present one is indebted.
2 T. K. Thompson, *Handbook of Stewardship Procedures* (Englewood Cliffs, N.J.: Prentice-Hall, Inc., 1964), p. 15.
3 Marion R. Fremont-Smith, *Foundations and Government* (New York: Russell Sage Foundation, 1965), pp. 167–69.
4 Professor John E. Elliott, of the economics department, University of Southern California, made helpful comments upon the substance of this paragraph and the next two.

CHAPTER *13* JACK G. McBRIDE

Trends in Station Programming

TODAY, after one and a half decades of educational television, an examination of American use of the medium reveals at least two trends which serve as harbingers for the improvement of future ETV and ITV programming — the expanded use of TV libraries and of nonlocally produced programs, and the pooling of resources for the cooperative production of programs. These developments promise to have an increasing influence on ETV program schedules of the future, but they have been slow in evolving and the process has been elaborate and somewhat painful.

To appreciate the changing situation, one must examine the sources of programming available to the schedulers of our ETV distribution systems. During the decade of the 1950's, the prime source and the principal focus of programming, both in-school and cultural, was local production. Nearby resources were assembled in freshly equipped studios, and local productions made the biggest community impact in the ETV station schedule. Commercial properties, both free and rental, helped compose the early ETV program schedule. "The Big Picture" and "Industry on Parade" filled more than one program slot as schedulers attempted to satisfy the voracious appetite of their ETV transmitters. Thanks to a sympathetic local commercial station, an occasional commercial network public affairs program was made available to the local ETV outlet. The only systematic mode of program procurement and distribution in the first decade of American ETV was provided by the National Educational Television and Radio Center, organized from the outset by farsighted individuals to service and improve ETV programming. The attention of NETRC (now NET) was, as it is now, directed principally to a general educational and cultural service.

Particularly did instructional programming emphasize local production. As educational institutions activated television systems and began using the medium, there appeared almost uniform insistence on original production; for the problems being addressed by television were considered by each educational entity as peculiar to that specialized environment. Only the local educator could appreciate his problems and needs; only the local ITV practitioner could assemble the specialized means to see these unique problems alleviated.

Teachers and supervisors were hypercritical of the program efforts of their counterparts and mistakenly believed that they themselves could mount far better instructional television productions. As a result, programs of all types were manufactured in volume. Program quality, however, suffered in direct proportion to quantity.

As the programming treadmill continued its course, educational administrators and ETV directors came to recognize the need for improvement of both ETV and ITV programs. Pressures on staff and facilities mounted. Kinescope recording systems appeared at more and more ETV installations. Delayed broadcasting was initiated. Repeat broadcasts were scheduled. A sophistication process slowly set in. ITV programmers became aware that other ETV stations were experiencing the same problems, were producing programs of strikingly similar content and approach, and were recording certain of these programs for re-use. And the idea dawned: possibly, just possibly, the neighbor's program could be borrowed and screened; it might not be too different from the local effort. After all, how many ways are there to teach second grade arithmetic? Slowly, a sporadic exchange developed between stations which either traded programs *quid pro quo* or engaged in a direct rental arrangement. And acceptance, albeit reluctant, of nonlocally produced programs came to ETV. School administrators arrived at the realization that through use of recorded programming, program schedules could be economically expanded, and limited personnel, facilities, and budgets could noticeably be relieved. Using nonlocally produced programming reduced the demand for local production, and allowed the concentration of more time and dollars for fewer productions. The quality of the local ETV endeavor could thus be substantially improved. As a result, recorded programming exchange increased, and instructional television schedules benefited from outside production acquisitions.

With the noninstructional ETV service, recognition of the necessity of recorded programming has always been present. Minus the restrictions of formal instruction, from the outset programmers have relied on acquisition programming. But the local-live versus recorded syndrome in American instructional television can almost be charted.

Videotape made as much of an impact on educational broadcasting as it did with the commercial industry. With the advent of video recorders and the early placement of these units by the Ford Foundation through NET, the quality of educational recordings was significantly improved, the cost decreased, and local taping facilitated. As a result, recorded programming exchange again increased. ETV station postage and express budgets took a dramatic dip into the red. However, as the 1950's drew to a close, with the notable exception of NET, ETV program exchange was still disorganized, sporadic, inefficient, and unformalized.

In the early 1960's, several events transpired to speed the exchange process. With United States Office of Education funding through the National Defense Education Act, the University of

Nebraska undertook a national study, published in 1961 by the university press, on the *Use and Distribution of Recorded Televised Instruction* (by W. C. Meierhenry and Jack McBride). From this came the conclusion that a considerable body of recorded instruction existed at ETV centers throughout the United States, that educators were increasingly interested in employing quality recorded instruction to improve local programming, and that systemized exchange and distribution was a necessity. As a result, the National Instructional Television Library, the Northeastern Regional Instructional Television Library and the Great Plains Regional Instructional Television Library were activated on a demonstration basis to address the problem.

Concurrently, here and there neighboring ETV stations managed to interconnect, thus permitting the immediate exchange of programs. Attention turned to the development of regional networks; the Eastern Educational Network and Midwestern Educational Television materialized. The Midwest Program for Airborne Television Instruction (MPATI) was activated and began production of a substantial body of recorded courses available both within their service area and to nonconstituents. Additional commercial properties were marketed. These varied elements combined to override the objections of the last ETV isolationists. Acquisition programming filled an increasing portion of the total educational television endeavor. As a direct concomitant, the quality of local program schedules showed long overdue signs of improvement.

With the availability of increased quantities of recorded programming, with increasing interconnection, and with the development of organized systems of distribution and exchange, dependence upon recorded programming grew to the point that by 1964–65 the local-live/recorded syndrome had come full circle. ETV stations were being activated and initially programmed largely, if not solely, with recorded materials.

Today, increasing attention is devoted to nonlocal programming, as librarying and distribution efforts expand at state, regional, and national levels. NET has increased the quantity of its program offerings and has achieved yearly improvement of its program quality. At the continued urging of ETV managers, the Educational Television Stations Division of the National Association of Educational Broadcasters successfully activated a general program service and began stocking a new videotape bank. Program submissions and orders the first year have far exceeded original projections. The National Instructional Television Library has been succeeded by a new National Center for School and College Television, at Indiana University, and is building toward national distribution, toward the reproduction of existing courses, and toward service as an ITV clearing house and research center.

The Great Plains Instructional Television Library mirrors this acquisition programming development and serves as an excellent illustrator of its progress. Following activation at the University of Nebraska as a demonstration project in 1962, Great Plains during its first operational year was responsible for two course exchanges. As the accompanying table illustrates, course rentals grew to thirty the second year and sixty in 1964–65. By the close

Course rentals from the Great Plains Instructional Television Library

School year	Course uses	Lesson units	% of use increase
1962–63	2	30	—
1963–64	30	752	2,500%
1964–65	60	1,654	220%
1965–66	131	3,900	235%
1966–67	259	7,770	199%

of the 1965–66 academic year, Great Plains had distributed throughout the United States 3,900 instructional units representing 131 course uses. As the 1966–67 school year began and Office of Education demonstration funds terminated, the Great Plains Library transferred status to a permanent educational service agency housed at the University of Nebraska and directed by a policy board of distinguished educational administrators whose chairman is the superintendent of the Denver schools. Every demonstration objective had been met: the development of successful procedures for course acquisition, evaluation, duplication, and distribution; sustained and enlarged operations; and fiscal independence through self-generated rental revenues. With the achievement of independent status, the Library had developed into the largest instructional television program distributor in the world. Over 7,000 lesson units were booked from a catalogue of 47 carefully evaluated courses, and Great Plains had been selected as the national distributor of 31 additional courses from the Chicago City TV College.

The trend from total reliance on local originations and towards increased use of recorded programming has developed because of two basic forces: the constant pressure to expand ETV service, and the continuing pressure to see it improved. Though it has survived a somewhat precarious period of infancy, American ETV is still in its adolescence. Each month there is increasing demand for the variety of tailored services educational television is capable of rendering. With a growing schools-television service, with an enlarging general cultural and community service, and with the expansion of in-service and other specialized programming for the various professions, the broadcast day is rapidly being devoured. Then, too, the classroom student and the viewer show increasing signs of impatience. Consciously or unconsciously, they compare ETV with commercial television. Viewers are accustomed to network quality and will not sit still for the amateurish, poorly planned and produced programs too frequently bearing the educational imprimatur.

Because of these pressures, and for the same reasons that American education began general consolidation and the sharing of educational resources, educational television began investigating the potentials of cooperative production. From various quarters there developed an awareness of the strength in pooling unique and specialized resources. Administrators came to realize that by combining inadequate individual production budgets they could have more realistic sums of money available for attracting talent and mounting better productions. It became clear that cooperative planning of programs could improve quality and would result in increased program use. The Eastern Educational Network, spurred on by Northeastern Regional ITV Library funds from the Office of Education, undertook cooperative production as its major demonstration. Committees representing all constituents planned programs which were produced at central locations, with content and talent approved by the steering committees. Midwestern Educational Television undertook a variation of the same theme. Under the auspices of an executive producer, member stations developed individual programs for a given series (called "A Look at the Land") which tapped the resources of an entire region. Using a similar approach, the Great Plains Library produced a widely used series on ITV utilization. NET developed "Regional Reports" and "Local Issues" as vehicles to take advantage of local resources and present points of view from various sections of the country. ETV interests in such states as Florida, Ohio, and Oregon cooperatively developed programming for use over multiple systems serving viewers within their borders.

Educational broadcasting compacts have served as the largest single influence upon the development of cooperative production. These television councils are a unique development in American education. For several years the Southwestern Indiana Educational Television Council, the Central Michigan Educational Broadcasting Council, the Nebraska Council for Educational Television, and their counterparts in every section of the country have proved that individual elementary-secondary school systems, with independent schedules and diverse methods of operations, can pool resources, can resolve differences, meld similarities, and can jointly devise educational program content useful to the total membership. The MPATI experiment proved that instructional programming could be designated, produced, and utilized on a multistate basis.

Not all of these cooperatives have been restricted to the lower educational levels. The Television Subgroup of the Committee on

Institutional Cooperation of the Big Ten Universities and the University of Chicago have for several years addressed themselves to the problems and potentials of cooperative production at the collegiate level. With Office of Education funding, the Southern Regional Education Board is currently cooperatively developing instructional segments in six content areas for use by institutions throughout the sixteen-state service area. The Council on Higher Educational Institutions in New York City is deep within an investigation of cooperative production to service the forty-six colleges and universities composing its membership. All twenty-four colleges and universities, public and private, in Nebraska have joined together to form the first state-wide collegiate compact, the Nebraska Educational Television Council for Higher Education, Inc., designed to share instruction over a seven-station state network. The Texas Educational Microwave Project and the Oregon State Higher Education System pioneered in the sharing of college instruction through television.

Though problems seem to increase in proportion to the level at which instruction is jointly used, the potential inherent in cooperative production serves to motivate continual attention. American educational television is undergoing extensive analysis and evaluation from both within and without the structure. From these depth investigations, from such exercises as the NAEB's Washington long-range financing conferences, from private foundations' evaluations, and from studies conducted for the Carnegie Commission on Educational Television and the Ford Foundation, several factors emerge clearly. American educational television will continue to be plagued by insufficient funding for an indefinite period. The pressures from all sides for more and better programs will continue without abatement. Since virtually every major metropolitan area is now serviced by an ETV signal, the major future broadcast ETV development will occur in the least populated areas. Here, local talents and other production resources will always have restrictions and limitations placed upon them; hence the smaller stations will always require importation of outside programming. Motivated by the Educational Television Facilities Act and by stirrings from within, an increasing number of states will activate state-wide networks. Alabama, Maine, South Carolina, Oregon, Georgia, and Nebraska already have state-wide systems in various stages of advanced development. Maryland, Kentucky, Vermont, Wyoming, South Dakota, and a number of other states have networks on the drawing boards. Increasing attention will be devoted to interconnection of ETV channels across state borders. All of these factors point clearly toward increased cooperative production, and the increased stockpiling and use of recorded materials.

As educational television looks to the future, its program directors will need a wide variety of sources from which to obtain programs. The ETV programmer, having analyzed his audiences' needs from every point of view, will want to pick and choose from local, area, state, regional, and national sources, commercial as well as nonprofit, and will need to be supported with sufficient funds to permit such selection. The ITV or ETV programmer will acquire and schedule programs for his distribution system (or systems) from:

(1) Local productions

(2) Area programs, educational broadcasting compact courses, cooperative productions

(3) State agencies' originations, network programs, and department of education productions

(4) Regional availabilities: networks, libraries, production centers

(5) National nonprofit agencies' banks of materials and professional in-service programs

(6) Commercial properties from commercial television stations, production agencies, publishers, etc.

(7) International agencies

Rapid technological advances in television recording and transmission will drastically affect ETV programming of the future, as will color, interconnection, and satellites. Tomorrow's educational programmer will receive his programs from permanent satellites via ground-based relays, from state, regional, and national interconnection facilities, and from state, regional, and national program banks. The "cluster concept" may well emerge; i.e., groups or clusters of local ETV systems, representing a variety of licensees and distribution systems, will be served their programming by state networks which in turn are fed by regional operations who receive much of their programming from national agencies. NET could in a relatively short period of time deal only with state network systems, and ultimately only with subregional or regional centers. Certainly, as ETV progresses, the stress on major programming agencies will be towards increased specialization and quality productions. These motivations will foster additional program distributions for both ETV and ITV. The educational television programmer will have maximum flexibility. He will be able to transmit programs directly from the network feed, will be able to record and delay broadcast network programs or order recorded programs into the shop for future use. Network lines, both intrastate and interstate, will be used in off-times to feed programming for delayed use.

NET's 1967 long-lines interconnection tests linking over half of its affiliates have presented dramatic evidence of the national ETV interconnection potential. The Public Broadcast Laboratory plan, funded by a special Ford Foundation grant to NET, will offer both regular Sunday night live programming and an eight hour per day, six day per week national interconnection. As activated, this long-lines reservation will enable NET additionally to distribute flexible service programs during scheduled periods, and could ultimately replace the current videotape transshipment process. Current plans call for use of the long-lines for previews, for program promotion, and for in-service counseling. Certain periods will be made available as well for use by the ETS Program Service and other programming organizations.

The satellite concept of interconnection, whether that of the Ford Foundation, Comsat, or AT&T, offers even greater programming flexibility. State networks are already planning towards use of the midnight-to-dawn swing shift to distribute programming to school systems and colleges for subsequent use on individual distribution systems, whether they be broadcast, closed circuit, or point-to-point. The heart of the ETV station of the future will be a master electronic control and switching center capable of receiving and distributing a multiplicity of audio and video signals to and from a variety of sources. And the local television recording center will be a close second in terms of importance.

The ETV programmer, who will assume increasing importance, can, by taking advantage of the rapid-paced trends and adapting them to his local needs, project a bright and exciting future for American educational television.

Meaningful Research in ETV

INTRODUCTION

"I finally have an idea for my thesis!"

"Oh?"

"I want to study whether TV can be used to teach boating safety!"

"Why?"

"Well, I work for the State Water Recreation Board."

"So?"

"Well, nobody in the department has ever written a thesis that tries to find out whether television can work as well as live instruction in the boating safety field."

"What would be the significance or implications of your study?"

"Gee, well — we would find out if we could get the budget to use TV."

"Nothing else? Why bother with all this fuss? Just use existing data on ETV effectiveness. There are cases that go all the way back to air-raid warden training in the 1940's, the Army and the Penn State studies . . ."

"But this would be the *first time* that a *state water recreation board has used TV!*"

To follow this dialogue any longer would be needlessly cruel. Few professors, despite current opinion, *like* to turn down a student's idea for a thesis topic. The fact that this not-quite-hypothetical student hasn't the slightest idea of the purposes, characteristics, and standards of graduate research is beside the point. What is important to *all* of us — teachers, researchers, ETV specialists, administrators, librarians, editors, and students — is that the proposed topic is senseless makework. The pages of *AV Communication Review* and the *NAEB Journal*, tons of mimeograph paper, and a gaggle of journals in the field of education are full of similar "research." The waste in time, manpower, and money is frightful. The number of degrees, promotions, budgets, and kudos that have been awarded is frightening.

A defense of these so-called researches is that they are what the various school systems and other educational agencies and institutions want and use. Unfortunately, the weight of evidence denies this. In 1955, Carpenter underscored his warning that "plans for and the development of research activities have been at best a very minor consideration in the rise of educational television."[1] MacLean pointed out that "the educational administrator, with pressures either to buy or not to buy new media systems — pressures much stronger than any tentative, preliminary research findings — goes his merry way."[2] A. A. Lumsdaine commented in 1963 that researchers in the new media field

often do not deserve serious consideration by the practitioner because of deficiencies in their conception or execution which have rendered their conclusions meaningless or misleading. But this is beside the point at the moment, for even sound research products have not generally met with enthusiastic adoption and widespread implementation. However, even this may sometimes be smarter than we think. Sensing the uselessness or absurdity of some conclusions enunciated by researchers and lacking a technical basis for discriminating good from poor research, he is sometimes not to be blamed for resisting *all* research implications for the conduct of his trade.[3]

More recently, McIntyre reminded us that papers by more sophisticated researchers "by and large leave the TV practitioner bewildered as to their meaning for him."[4]

WHY ETV RESEARCH HASN'T BEEN MEANINGFUL

There are three interlocking reasons why ETV (a term that subsumes "ITV") research has led to so few "practical" results. First, ETV practitioners or their purse-holding supervisors might be unable, through lack of training, ability, or inclination, to ferret out and interpret the meanings of ETV researches. Second, those who are conducting the research might be similarly lacking in training, ability, or inclination to conduct meaningful research. Third, there might be something wrong with the entire concept of ETV research as practiced thus far.

With respect to the first reason, it would be silly to label all teachers, all administrators, and all ETV specialists as incompetent. Nevertheless, much of the blame for failure to adopt the few existing experimentally derived principles of instruction by television does rest here. It is far easier to listen to the attractive blandishments of equipment manufacturers, gaze with envy at what another institution may be doing, "shoot for the moon" at budget-making time, and then settle for what one can get. The failure of many practitioners fully to understand, and hence *rationally* to adopt or reject the results of research, however well or badly done, hardly inspires confidence in the quality of the education most specialists expose themselves to in addition to their professional or vocational training. Certainly, the distinction between a "demonstration" and an "experiment" eludes most educationists.[5]

The second reason echoes the first. Many of these same complaints might be levied against the researchers, despite their excuse that they must do most of their research in their spare time, after a full day of administering, teaching, or producing ETV programs.[6] Adkins wrote that "the truth is that broadcast researchers generally have been backward in formulating and promoting substantial research plans and in establishing a reputation as qualified and serious investigators. . . . Radio-television students, and faculty members too, are often guilty of distributing checklists and questionnaires which would make a trained researcher shudder."[7] The former president and executive director of the NAEB, Harry Skornia, laments that "many of the so-called research reports are products of workers with no research training or standards. They do not stand up under any valid research criteria." Skornia adds his "own view of several thousand studies [which present] a disheartening picture. There are too few significant studies. The lack of a tradition of solid learning research in the schools for the last hundred years has left us unprepared. There should be hundreds of professional researchers, with proper training and disciplines. There are hardly any qualified to do both communications and educational research."[8] Lumsdaine emphasizes that "it is important to insure that research effort produces studies which are, by and large, technically as good as current knowledge permits. This goal in no way precludes the exercise of ingenuity in trying out new approaches, but it does suggest the need for better training of, and communication among, research workers" (*Handbook*, p. 670).

Skornia echoes Kanner and Carpenter when he proposes that "there must be the development and training of a generation of research workers, and more communication among them. We need a truly national educational research center and program . . . ."[9] Such a center or centers would turn out most major ETV research, much as the present communication research centers at Illinois, Stanford, Michigan State, Wisconsin, Boston, and other universities produce a quantity of valuable research that is far out of proportion to the number of researchers involved. There might be benefits in locating these new centers in larger cities, to avoid continuing the practice of generalizing from experimentation conducted upon undergraduate students living in mass-communication-poor isolated prairie communities. Additional centers for the study of communication and education would lead to less "incest" in the selection of research personnel, and would act as a safeguard against the possible development of rigid "schools" such as those that plagued psychiatry. However, there are also possible drawbacks to this idea. If the recent Cartter report for the American Council on Education is valid, the concentration of *research* into a few institutions will have the effect of slowly draining the ability of all other institutions to provide outstanding *teaching* in that field.[10] It would be a dull and inefficient world indeed if *all* the research were left to a few mighty institutions.[11]

Instead of upgrading a few select institutions, by far the greater social and professional benefit would come from upgrading *each and every ETV specialist's ability to plan, conduct, and evaluate research.* I suggest that the best way to upgrade the research abilities of the educational media specialist would be by college curriculum revisions that would provide for mandatory enrollment by would-be ETV specialists in research-oriented courses in the social sciences. These courses would be offered outside the professional schools. They would require the carrying out of researches involving a variety of methods (experimental, descriptive, etc.), techniques (inferential and descriptive statistics, content analysis, etc.), and subject matter (social psychology, political science, etc.), meeting proper standards of validity and reliability. Also, as Adkins delicately puts it, since "the ability to develop a significant piece of research and the ability to write interesting articles are not always present to the same degree in one person,"[12] some practice in the lucid reporting and interpretation of research results should be required.

The third reason why educational television research has had little practical effect is the *kinds* of research that are performed. The confusion between experimentation and demonstration, both of which have their place, has been mentioned before. More basic is our "shotgun" approach to research in this field. We collect data for their own sake, not for their utility in testing hypotheses or answering questions. In a psychology article nonetheless appropriate for ETV research, Gordon W. Allport pointed out that "empirical testing is . . . an important aspect of heuristic realism, but it is an empiricism restrained throughout by rational considerations. Galloping empiricism, which is our present occupational disease, dashes forth like a headless horseman. It has no rational objective; uses no rational method other than mathematical; reaches no rational conclusion. It lets the discordant data sing for themselves."[13] Furthermore, to quote Lumsdaine (*Handbook*, p. 666), we flounder in "a morass of ambiguity and inconsistency which has led some, including the writer, to wonder whether it is worth doing experiments until some basis for achieving comparable sensitivity from experiment to experiment is achieved. . . . in the absence of suitable, uniformly applicable criteria of experimental sensitivity, it is nearly impossible to know just how bad [the situation in experimental instructional media research] is." In brief, we must learn to ask and answer *questions* — and not just squirrel information away into a convenient filing cabinet or bookshelf.

TITLE VII RESEARCH

Until 1959, the primary excuse for the inadequate standards of much ETV research was poverty. It was frequently argued that the costs of television programming prohibited the unsupported researcher from adequately studying the problems he believed most important. This argument was supported by the history of research in the field. Paul F. Lazarsfeld, who produced many of the early volumes on radio research, would have found his accomplishments more difficult to achieve had not the Columbia University Office of Radio Research been supported by the Rockefeller Foundation. The Ford Foundation, partly through the Fund for the Advancement of Education, financed much educational television research and programming during ETV's formative years. But it was not until the passage of the National Defense Education Act of 1958 (Public Law 85-864) that more than ample funds for research were made available. No longer could "insufficient funds" be an acceptable excuse for "inadequate research."

Title VII of this act authorized the expenditure of funds to support research, experimentation, and dissemination of information about the uses of television, radio, motion pictures, and related media of communication that might prove useful to educational agencies and institutions. Several million dollars were distributed by the United States Office of Education in furtherance of these aims, primarily through contracts with academic researchers. More than a thousand projects were initiated, and several hundred reports of these projects are now available.[14] Title VII projects had to be initiated voluntarily by the prospective researcher, and could not be assigned by any priority scheme devised by the Office of Education. Allen, early in 1960, commented that under these ground rules, "it is not surprising to find almost half of the approved grants comparing the instructional effectiveness of the various media with conventional approaches to instruction. Nor is it surprising to note that about one-third of the grants have been made for the study of televised teaching."[15] Criteria for the awarding of these grants included examination of their relevance to the purposes of Title VII, the educational significance of the problem(s) to be studied, the adequacy of research procedures, the qualifications of key personnel and adequacy of available facilities, and economic efficiency.[16] There was an "open season" on almost any ETV research problem that could be conjured in the mind of a potential "principal investigator."

How well was this money used? Twyford commented that "at times, television research is an afterthought to be endured, or is just an opportunity to get additional funds."[17] Malcolm MacLean, then acting director of the Communications Research Center at Michigan State University, spoke for many observers when he published a scathing review and criticism of a number of early Title VII reports in 1962. His introduction was milder, but left no doubt as to his opinions:

Spread out on the desk beside me are several pounds of Title VII research reports, representing many thousands of research dollars. They bring to mind the picture of social science researchers, new media producers, subject matter specialists, and educational administrators scurrying to develop proposals before the next deadline, the discussions of production problems and research designs, the hopeful waiting after the proposal is in, the excitement as the grant is received, *etc.*

Somehow, the research report seldom seems to be half as intriguing as those ideas which set the project in motion. The researcher finds that he gets no significant differences where he was reasonably sure that he would. The new media producer finds that the questions he thought the project would clarify for him are left almost as muddled as before. He suspects that there must be something wrong with research which does not prove that the thing he produced worked better than some traditional method. The subject matter specialist may revert to his usual lecturing; he finds it easier, and after all the research evaluation didn't indicate that the use of new techniques would help much. The educational administrator, with pressures either to buy or not to buy new media systems — pressures much stronger than any tentative, preliminary research findings — goes his merry way. And what about those poor guys sitting up on top of Title VII? They may well be wondering what went wrong, why a project which seemed to hold such great promise now looks like a straggly old dog.

I wonder if others who read and do research in the areas of communication and education have come to this conclusion: Frequently, the best designed, most carefully thought out and conducted, the most useful research seems to be that done by one investigator, possibly with help from a graduate student, on a budget of $500 to $1000. There seem to be some things about the research team and the $50,000 or $500,000 budget that stifle common research sense.

.   .   .   .

I don't think that statistics and design are the chief problems by any means. The problems are really much broader, and are all mixed up with scientific and human values. They are summed up in a question which I hate to hear asked of my own research findings, but which I think needs to be asked of all studies of problems in education and communication: So what?

.   .   .   .

I have taken this opportunity to raise some serious questions about the philosophy and direction of our research. I have said that we seem to be wasting much fine research talent on trivial matters. We frequently use high prestige methods where they are not appropriate to our level of knowledge or theory. We control unimportant factors and leave important ones uncontrolled and undefined. We have learned statistics (sometimes), but have not learned to think and behave as scientists. We become so encumbered by elaborate manipulations and by unwieldy organization of research that we find little time to ask where we are going and why.[18]

It would be sad indeed if this judgment were all that could be said for Title VII research. Few times in history has such financial support been available to researchers outside the physical sciences and engineering. There are unassessable benefits, to be sure: increases in the number of research-conscious specialists and administrators; a great mass of data that might be valuable to a future generation of analysts; a number of still-unfinished studies that might contain important findings and conclusions; needed financial support for many graduate students; increased communication among researchers in this field; and, allied to all of these, the probability that the experience of Title VII aided the researchers themselves in their intellectual and professional growth. However, should such a windfall ever again fall into our laps, it might be constructive to ask what might have happened to Title VII if we had followed the course of action of the (British) Television Research Committee, which "decided that it would have to proceed slowly, clarifying by its own studies both the significance of the terms of reference and its own ultimate objectives, identifying the problem areas amenable to social scientific research, assessing the social relevance of the specific questions that could be formulated within these areas, seeing what methods, skills and resources were available and could be used in attempts to answer these questions, and then finally establishing its research priorities."[19] Furthermore, in the words of Kenneth Harwood, "If there should be available some increases in Federal research funds, the increase should be used to support individual researchers and not institutions. While individual researchers tend to create worthwhile research, institutions tend to create administrative hierarchies of questionable value."[20]

"NO SIGNIFICANT DIFFERENCE"

The larger number of studies financed under Title VII investigated the relative effectiveness of teaching over television systems as compared to conventional classroom instruction. What were the findings from these studies? To our initial surprise and later disappointment we found over and over again that there were "no significant differences" (NSD) between televised and conventional instruction. Schramm assembled 393 cases in which instructional television had been compared to other classroom teaching. In 255 cases, or 65 percent, there were no significant differences between the two modes of instruction. In 82 cases, or 21 percent, students learned significantly more; in 56 cases, or 14 percent, students learned significantly less from television. In 32 additional cases where open-circuit television instruction broadcast to the home was compared to classroom instruction, 21 exhibited NSD, 10 cases showed a significant advantage for television, and the remaining case showed a significant advantage for conventional instruction. Schramm found that there were significant differences in test results when the 425 studies were analyzed by kind of subject matter taught, and when the 393 in-school studies were compared by grade level. Although he offered some speculations as to the reasons for these differences, little additional analysis has been performed on these findings.[21]

Although Schramm states that these studies have "what seemed to be adequate design, controls, and statistics,"[22] there is some question of this. Stickell analyzed some 31 studies that made 250 comparisons between ETV and conventional instruction. He judged each comparison on the criteria of comparability of control and experimental subjects, assignment procedures, comparability of instructions, tenability of statistical assumptions, and adequacy of other controls. Only 10 of these 250 comparisons were fully interpretable on the basis of these minimal criteria! Another 23 were partially interpretable, and 217 that did not meet two or more of the criteria were uninterpretable. There were no significant differences found in all 10 interpretable, and in 20 of the 23 partially interpretable comparisons.[23]

When considering the question of "meaningful research," there are at least three ways of looking at these NSD findings. First, we should try to isolate the factors in the learning situation that might cause these results. Williams, for example, suggests that the attitudes, ability, and personality of the classroom teacher may be the most important missing variable.[24] Schramm has speculated as to whether the Hawthorne effect (increased effort from the students due to being in the limelight as part of an experiment) or a novelty effect may have been important factors for NSD findings in a closely allied field.[25] Also, there is little agreement as to what constitutes "conventional classroom teaching," and there are so many uncontrolled variables in the classroom situation that it is of little value to compare the two modes of teaching. Skornia claims that

class-to-class and school differences are now so great as to invalidate much of the research at hand. Re-tests should be considered before results are published. A single experiment rarely proves anything. Materials, teachers, and other environmental factors must be objectively recorded, so comparability means something. Studies will need to restrict themselves to measurement of factors that can be controlled and really measured so differences will be genuinely significant and generalizable.[26]

Second, we may be asking the wrong questions, and analyzing the wrong factors. Forsythe, in a review of educational radio research, points out that "a discussion of relevant research in educational [broadcasting] is meaningless unless it is placed within a larger frame of reference and related to functions that we ascribe to the medium."[27]

Third, our measuring instruments and techniques may be too imprecise or invalid for adequate determination of whether or not differences exist. This point is often overlooked because of deference to the subject matter "television teacher," who, we assume, knows how to construct a measuring instrument that will adequately index whether or not the students learned anything.

Regardless of the reasons for NSD findings, many researchers have relied upon *interpretations* of the findings to arrive at more palatable conclusions. For example, an NSD finding may cause the researcher to rejoice in print with paraphrases of "See, we are as good as classroom instruction, and we can reach more students in the same amount of time!" More recently, a petulant questioning of the research design and techniques has been substituted, as the ETV specialist finds it disturbing to believe that televised instruction is not *superior* to conventional methods because of the time, money, and attention that have been lavished on the television lesson. Sometimes this unhappiness can only be classed as "sour grapes." But, frequently enough to be encouraging, these complaints stimulate the researcher to sharpen his tools and produce better research. Sometimes unhappiness also is used as a self-applied goad to so improve programming that reliable and valid significant results in favor of television may appear more frequently. As with many other problems of research, continued interest and improved research methods may cause the "NSD problem" to fade away. Another possibility is that the problem itself will be redefined in the future, like some of the problems in the mental health field, so that it will no longer loom as large.

THE LITERATURE OF ETV RESEARCH

Research, although it becomes easier with practice, is not improved by constant replication. The very word "research" implies that something "new" is going on. Although Lumsdaine (*Handbook*, p. 671) reminds us that "no major question can be answered by a single experiment," there is nothing to prevent us from trying to answer with the utmost rigor the smaller questions that the major ones comprise. As part of this effort, there should be no false pride, or laziness, to prevent us from using the existing literature of the field.

There are many excellent summaries and reviews of the research literature of educational television. Anyone who expects to do research should be ashamed to start his project before checking to see whether his question already has been answered in the literature. All ETV specialists and responsible administrators, as well as researchers, should be familiar with previous general reports and reviews, as well as with others of a more specialized nature or those published after their last search.

In the note section at the end of this chapter, I have cited a number of the more important reviews of the literature of significance for educational television research.[28] Although instructional film research, such as the review by Hoban and van Ormer, is included in these citations, most of the entries — particularly the reviews by Kumata, Schramm, Carpenter, and MacLennan and Reid — are concerned only with instructional television research.

In many instances where the answer to a specific subproblem is desired, it will be necessary to resort to examination of the research reports themselves. Many of these — reports of the instructional film and instructional television projects at Pennsylvania State University, those conducted by the University of Wisconsin Television Laboratory, and some Army studies, for example — were published and surprisingly well distributed.[29] The Research Fact Sheets published in the *NAEB Journal*, and the Research Abstracts and Title VII Abstracts in *AV Communication Review* are extremely useful to those researchers who bother to use them. These magazines, together with the *Journal of Broadcasting* and other periodical publications in broadcasting, education, and allied fields, are indexed in various standard periodical indices. Some also publish their own topical indices, such as *Journalism Quarterly*'s forty-year index, the *Journal of Broadcasting*'s seven-year index, and the *Journal of the Society of Motion Picture and Television Engineers*' five-year indices. The Center for Documentation and Communication Research of the School of Library Science at Western Reserve University has started a center for the computerized retrieval of abstracts of more than 4,700 documents of experimental studies and surveys. When in full operation, this center's holdings should be so well cross-indexed that the researcher will find his task of reviewing the literature far easier.[30] Once the uncomfortable feeling of walking into a library is overcome, the assiduous researcher should be able to find many other bibliographic aids.

KINDS OF MEANINGFUL RESEARCH

Research is not conducted solely for its own sake. It is conducted for the purpose of answering questions. In more formal terms, researches contribute to the total of organized human knowledge and understanding; they develop or improve techniques, products, or services; they assist decision-makers and permit needless waste to be reduced; and they can be used to instruct others in the values and techniques of research. The ability to *ask* questions, crucial questions that can be tested or answered, is the hallmark of that handful of researchers who stimulate much of the significant work in any field. The questions may have "practical" connotations, or they may not, but they must be questions that the researcher wants to answer. For the best researchers, these "wants" become "needs." The asking and answering of questions is essential to the well-being of a good researcher. Unhappily, when lots of "money for research" becomes available, many unthinking individuals rush in to collect all sorts of data under the false label of "research," in order to get some of the glory, prestige — and money. The answering of questions, to many of these individuals, is secondary. And, as Twyford reminds us, "to obtain telling answers, the researchers must pose searching questions."[31] Gerbner succinctly states that the "field is where the problems are."[32] Collectively, the field of communications is plowed by a large proportion of would-be researchers afflicted with omphalophobia, who are unwilling to contemplate the situation, isolate the problem, and take the time to plan the research that might answer the question or solve the problem. Fortunately, not all researchers — or readers of this polemic — are afflicted by this malady.

As in many other fields of activity, there are two types of research into educational television. Theoretical, basic, or long-range research includes the studies that are most easily generalized, and which can be used to construct theories and generate new research ideas. Operational, "how to do it," and "demonstration" research provides immediate answers to immediate or short-range questions.[33] The long-range research usually is performed by highly skilled, often full-time, professional researchers; the short-range research is often conducted by ETV practitioners themselves. Neither type is intrinsically better than the other, if conducted with the same care, thought, and standards of quality.

THE USE OF MODELS TO GENERATE RESEARCH IDEAS

The paucity of theory in the field of ETV has been noted by a number of scholars and observers. At the present stage, models to help us conceptualize or visualize the processes of communication and learning would be more useful than premature theories. Such models are a great stimulus to the generation of questions and formal hypotheses and, with the exception of "Information Theory" and some theories of human learning, largely have been neglected in ETV research. Citations to a number of the models of communication research are presented in the note section at the end of this chapter,[34] but these listings are by no means exhaustive: anyone who does enough reading, researching, and thinking, is well on the way to construction of his own model in order to facilitate more reading, researching, and thinking. For the purposes of ETV research, models and theories are most useful when used to *predict* outcomes from observable relationships and conditions. They may also be used to *explain* observable phenomena. It is up to the researcher to decide which process, relationship, event, or condition he wishes to investigate.

THE LITERATURE OF RESEARCH IDEAS IN ETV

Although every researcher is encouraged to develop his own questions for study, the unanswered questions of others should not be neglected. Several writers have suggested enough lines of research endeavor to keep a small army of researchers busy for a long time. These ideas rarely are "private property," although courtesy and efficiency dictate that an inquiry be directed to the author of a research idea before you undertake the research. Some of the more accessible and potentially fruitful "hunting grounds" for ETV research ideas are in the papers and articles cited in the note section.[35]

Researches often stimulate other researches. Not only will a senior researcher often "lay out" enough work to keep a flock of junior researchers busy, but an event or phenomenon — such as the Kennedy assassination, the "Great Debates," or the announcement of the innovation of subliminal perception techniques — will trigger many independent researches around the country and the world. A more prosaic example, closer to the field of ETV research, would be the way that Fairbanks' work on "compressed speech" led to Loper's dissertation on the compression of picture *and* sound, and the effect of this compression upon comprehension and retention.[36]

The researcher with more initiative, imagination, and experience may well find it more profitable to avoid existing areas of potential ETV research, and instead derive his research ideas from such unconventional sources as direct observation, McLuhan's writings, magazines of wide-ranging political, social, and economic opinion, and those books on philosophy that have not been looked at since undergraduate days.

RESEARCH IDEAS FOR THE BUDGET-MINDED

There are many areas of research that can be tackled by the ETV specialist or by the researcher with a limited budget of time and money. Some of these are concerned with the teacher and subject matter to be taught, some with the medium of television and the message, and some with the audience and ETV's effects on this audience and on society.

Are we sure that the traditional method of dividing subject matter into "courses" is most efficient when using TV? Would there be advantages to using TV *only* as a medium for demonstrations rather than for the presentation of lectures? Can the inherently "one-way" nature of television be overcome? What is the best way to select television teachers, and convince them that they should do television teaching? When scheduling ETV programs, should we make use of Schramm's findings that mathematics, science, and social studies apparently can be taught by television more effectively than can history, humanities, and literature (by a proportion of two to one in number of comparisons that showed a favorable significant difference).[37] How about further testing of those findings that are inconclusive and contradictory in the literature? Administratively, have there been continuing studies of cost and manpower effectiveness, as were initially presented in the Penn State studies?[38] In fact, have we conceptualized the necessary elements to construct an economic input-output model for ETV?

Why hasn't the television medium itself been more carefully explored, much as the film medium was explored in the Navy Special Devices Center–Pennsylvania State University Instructional Film Research project?[39] A number of organizations, such as the System Development Corporation, have started research in the area of "multi-media presentations." This technique uses a number of film and slide projectors, tape recorders, and other devices synchronized in order to permit the audience to perceive specific details *and* a gestalt of the entire presentation at the same time.[40] Much more research is needed to see whether use of these techniques could have a synergesic effect; the whole being greater than the sum of its parts. The technical limitations and capabilities of television have been little explored, in a systematic manner.

The audience research field is still wide open. A recent thesis concluded that television was superior to highly skilled individual instruction for certain types of mentally retarded children, because TV caused them to better focus their attention.[41] What other splinter audiences have we neglected? The experimental evidence on reading readiness and other effects of television upon preschool children is still inconclusive. The fortuitous audience to open-circuit or broadcast ETV is an important one, particularly when parents are otherwise unable to keep up with their children in subjects such as "modern math." Finally, we have the question of long-term effects of teaching by television. What happens to knowledge, attitudes, and logical thinking over a period of time? Is there a difference, over a period of time, between material absorbed from television or learned from conventional instruction? This may be the most neglected area of educational research. How can we talk about "retention" when our studies rarely extend over more than a semester or a term? The interactions between classroom TV, the "ordinary" television watched in the home more than five hours a day, and audience behavior is another area of research that *may* require a major effort and the expenditure of vast sums of money — but also *may* be investigated by the local ETV specialist on a meager budget.[42]

HOW TO PLAN A RESEARCH

No matter what the source of the research idea or topic, it is *always* necessary to plan the study carefully. Researches have been mounted in a matter of hours, in times of crisis for instance, but there is a positive correlation between the quality and quantity of planning and the quality of the finished study. A typical plan includes such matters as the reasons for the research (the importance and justification of the topic); statements of what one hopes to find or test (the questions and hypotheses); the results of a literature search to see whether anyone else previously has done research that bears on your topic; and how the data are to be collected (methodology). The finished report will, of course, also present the data themselves, analysis of the data, conclusions drawn from the analysis, and implications and suggestions for further research or application derived from the conclusions, as well as these earlier steps.

In general terms, research enables us to improve our understanding and methods of doing things through additions to or adaptations of present knowledge. Specifically, research is essentially an inductive process of observation and investigation of a problem, based (if possible) on original sources of knowledge, and resulting in the establishment of causations or probabilities of causations when *historical* method is used; the delineation of norms or standards when the *descriptive* method is used; and the construction of laws or principles when the *experimental* method is used. The usual steps in the research process include isolating and defining the problem; reviewing previous research; formulating a working hypothesis; developing or selecting appropriate methods, procedures, and techniques; collecting, recording, and classifying data; generalizing from the findings and testing the hypothesis or hypotheses; suggesting applications of the results or outlining additional research; and finally, reporting the complete research project. Almost any research, regardless of topic or technique, should be able to answer the questions explicit or implicit in each line of the following Outline Guide for Research Proposals. This guide, produced by the department of telecommunications at the University of Southern California, has proven flexible and useful. Combinations, expansions, and rearrangements of sections should be encouraged, depending upon the topic and the method selected. However, experience in a variety of graduate student and faculty researches leads one to infer that deletion of any section will usually lead to loss of the time "saved" by otherwise careful planning:

I. Title (Includes topic and method. As a general rule the *topic* may be broader in scope than the *question.*)

II. Purposes (Importance and Significance)
   A. Introduction. What do you wish to study? (This may be thought of as a brief, informal elucidation of the topic — the answer to be given to a maiden aunt when she asks you what you are studying.)
   B. Personal. Why do you wish to study this topic? (The ways in which your attention was drawn to the topic.)
   C. Social. Who is likely to benefit in which ways? ("Be ashamed to die until you have won some victory for humanity." — Horace Mann)
   D. Scholarly. How is it better than or different from other studies?

III. The Problem
   A. Question (formal statement of problem) and subquestions, if any.
   B. Definitions.
   C. Specific testable hypotheses (including alternates, tests, and criteria for acceptance or rejection).
   D. Assumptions.
   E. Limitations of scope of problem.

IV. Review of the Literature
   A. Detailed description of method of selection of sources already searched, and to be searched later.
   B. Description of pertinent articles, books, etc.
   C. Integrative summary of pertinent literature.

V. Operational Plan
   A. Method (e.g., historical, experimental, etc.) and how it applies to the study, including justification of selection of method.
   B. Procedures (steps in collecting and treating data). Must include justification of selection, and validity and reliability estimates of procedures.
   C. Specific techniques. Must include justification of selection, and validity and reliability estimates of techniques.
   D. Needed subjects (people to be studied) and materials.
   E. Feasibility of operational plan; estimates of time and cost.
   F. Special qualifications of investigator, if any. (Do not confuse with II-B.)

VI. Expectations and Recommendations
   A. Expected findings (refer to III-A and III-C).
   B. Recommendations for related studies (see II, above).

The most important standards in planning, conducting, and evaluating research are those of *validity* and *reliability*. In every research, they must be tested rigorously. "Validity" simply means that the test or other measuring instrument measured what it said it was going to measure. For example, you would not use figures on the number of television sets in a community as evidence of the number of people watching your station on a given evening. "Reliability," on the other hand, is essentially "consistency." If you repeat everything exactly in the same way (or if someone else follows your techniques), will you arrive at the same answer? An example of a technique that is *not* reliable is to guess how long a program is running, rather than look at the clock. Clocks are reliable; except in the case of a power failure, each minute should be the same length. If set to the wrong hour, however, the best or most reliable clock in the world would not be a valid measure of "what time it is." There are statistical estimates that often can be made of the reliability of a measuring instrument. Validity estimates are also possible, usually obtained by comparing your instrument to a standard. "Face validity" relies on logic for the most part.

Other research standards are also important. Many of the sampling statistics commonly used require that "random" populations be employed. This means that the selection of one member of a sample does not bias the selection of any other; all members of the universe have an equal probability of selection to the sample. Lee Alden reminds us that "it may be safely stated that medical students, college freshmen, and rats have participated as subjects [in experiments] at a rate which is inconsistent with their incidence in the general human and rodent population of our planet."[43] The term "precision" refers to the limits of error of any given measurement. Measurements that validly can be made to the nearest inch are more precise than those that can only be made lawfully to the nearest foot. A final standard is that of honesty, in all phases of the study. Common examples of dishonesty include failure to report errors of technique, and using "almost significant" findings as the basis of "significant" conclusions or implications.

THE CONDUCT OF RESEARCH ON A BUDGET

The secret of successful research on a small budget lies in the devotion of extra amounts of planning and thought to the study, rather than the "brute force" application of money. Often, as the passage quoted earlier from MacLean pointed out, "the most useful research seems to be that done by one investigator . . . on a budget of $500 to $1000. There seem to be some things about the big research team and the $50,000 or $500,000 budget that stifle common research sense." The budget restriction that prevents us from paying experimental subjects does not prevent us from obtaining volunteers, and removing a source of bias at the same time. The unavailability of assistance to program and feed a computer gives us the stimulus to learn how to do it ourselves, to our benefit and satisfaction.[44] As a matter of fact, the computer often isn't needed. Davenport has commented, "Frankly, I, for one, get rather disgusted when I see a small, inconsequential, inapplicable research project loaded down with ten times the statistical analysis and tables required or justified to make the point. This [is] pseudo-sophistication of statistical calisthenics . . . ."[45] Twyford reminds us that "in educational research we are conducting investigations of the most difficult type. Experience and training and a constant evaluation of methods are imperative. All types of research are important from the most controlled experiment to the simplest demonstration. We should, however, endeavor to use an experimental design to solve important problems, rather than just to get an answer. Likewise, statistics should be used as the tools they are rather than to obscure important results."[46] An important concept, often neglected by those inexperienced in computer use, is GIGO — translated as "Garbage in, garbage out." We are too often carried away by the opportunity to generate lots of big numbers from a few test scores. The questions of validity and reliability get lost beneath a mass of computer-generated data. This sort of operation brings us research reports that accidentally have 100-minute hours, or derive figures such as "11.77 percent" based on a sample of seventeen students.

One proposal that might lead to more efficient use of quantitative methods by those without ready access to a high-speed computer is something of a pipe dream, however attractive it might be to the author. It would require some way to supply every academic department in every college with an IBM keypunch and counter-sorter. This unlikely development would free the high-speed computers for the research that really needs equipment of this sort; it would breed familiarity rather than awe among the researchers using the less sophisticated equipment; and this unrestricted access to data-processing equipment might give researchers more incentive to do "little" studies more often. Doing the operations semimanually should give the researcher a better "feel" for the statistical manipulations he is performing. Having this simple equipment available (augmented, perhaps, by a secondhand desk calculator, and some McBee Keysort cards and a knitting needle) in every department could tend to make all researchers more problem-oriented than tool-oriented. Today we have a dichotomy of "quantitative researchers" who have access to a computer, and "old fogies" who don't. Such equipment would put all researchers on a more equal-opportunity footing, much as book publishing in multiple copies made a research library accessible to all scholars. With a variety of research tools at hand — his brain, the library, data-processing equipment — the researcher may better be able to resist the temptation to fit the research problem to the tools, and do it the correct way by selecting the proper tool to answer the question.

One stage of research at which money is of little help is in the writing of the report. For permanent reference use of the results of research, the publication of the report as an article is preferable to even the glossiest institutionally printed brochure. Similarly, wide distribution of a privately printed report is preferable to a mimeographed or duplicated report available only to those who happen to hear about it before the supply runs out. Finally, *anything* in writing is better than letting the information gained fade out, unrecorded except in the researcher's mind. Most reports and articles for submission to a scholarly periodical could be much improved by rewriting them several times, submitting each draft to a colleague or other editor and following honest criticism. Brevity is, of course, a goal of any contributor to the deficit-ridden scholarly journals. The author remembers a 58-page report that, after several tries, boiled down to an 8-page article in a journal. Although every removal of a word or phrase was painful at the time, not one essential datum or conclusion was omitted. A similar reduction in bulk, without losing any important data, would tend to reduce the academicians' constant need for additional book-cases, filing cabinets, and, most important, time to search the literature.[47]

ETV STATION RESEARCH

The ETV practitioner, particularly the open-circuit ETV broad-caster, may be called upon to do many kinds of research. Some of these may be market analysis; use of census and other demo-graphic data for describing potential audiences; coincidental tele-phone, diary, and other rating techniques (including, as ETV's audience grows, the ability to interpret data from the commercial rating services); sampling methods (random, stratified, geo-graphic, etc.); questionnaire construction; "program analyzers" and other methods of pretesting programs; attitude and forced choice measurements using tools such as the Q-Sort technique[48] and the Semantic Differential;[49] content analysis of programs and program schedules;[50] interpretation of the mail or other re-sponses received by the station; "feedback" program analysis;[51] "testing the audience" program analysis;[52] "Cloze" procedure;[53] and leisure time studies. He may conduct researches on *all* parts of the communication process (source, medium, message, audi-ence, feedback, noise, effects, etc.) using all sorts of techniques. Research is a fascinating business, leaving little time in which to produce programs, teach, or administer.

Most ETV specialists are conducting research every day, but not realizing that they are doing it. Analysis of a station's program log to see if public service time has been fairly apportioned is re-search. "Evaluation of learning" by means of quizzes, observation, term papers, etc., is research. Determining the station's coverage area is research, as is determining the number of potential listen-ers. Every department in a station conducts some research of its own.

Many questions are difficult to answer. For example, is mail response or signal-strength measurement the better way to determine the station's coverage area? How does one measure out-of-home radio listening? How can we differentiate "tuning" from "viewing" behavior? How can we economically pretest programs? How can we best schedule our station to appeal to the "splinter groups" that make up the total potential audience?

The Federal Communications Commission requires an applicant for a station license to survey the wants of the community he intends to serve, before constructing a proposed program schedule. This is an important task for the station management. Although there are various guides and reference materials available,[54] in the long run it is up to the person who wants a question answered to find a way to uncover that answer.

LEARNING TO BE A RESEARCHER

Learning how to do good research is *often* a matter of taking the proper courses in graduate school. It is *always* a matter of having your work judged by others working in the field. Graduate students are evaluated, criticized, and edited by their committees or chairmen. Editors of scholarly journals, often with the aid of referees, may devote as much time reading, evaluating, and editing a given submitted manuscript as its author spent in writing the final version. All researchers can have the benefits of evaluation and criticism. Not all, however, can conveniently take research methods courses. For them, the alternative is the reading of as much good research as can be found, coupled with the picking of colleagues' brains and the use of "cookbooks" in research methodology. There are many of these, of varying complexity. If Mildred Parten's *Surveys, Polls, and Samples: Practical Procedures* (New York: Harper and Brothers, 1950) is unavailable or too difficult to comprehend, then the researcher planning a survey should turn to Charles H. Backstrom and Gerald D. Hursh, *Survey Research* (Northwestern University Press, 1963).[55] If Pool's book on content analysis is beyond the reader's level, he should try the volume by North *et al.*[56] If all the books suggested by friends in the math department are so much Greek, one should settle for a "cookbook" such as Smith,[57] or layman's explanation such as Moroney.[58] In addition to this sort of reference, every field has a book or two on "how to do research."[59] A recently published, inexpensive, pamphlet on "how to conduct surveys" that is specifically oriented toward broadcasting is the NAB's *A Broadcast Research Primer.* This pamphlet, and its companion volume, *Standard Definitions of Broadcasting Research Terms,* is of particular value to local station personnel who must either conduct telephone, mail, or face-to-face surveys, or interpret the results of commercial research in this field.[60] Overviews of research activity are not uncommon.[61] Statistical tables and writing style-books are readily available. Remember, however, that if the "cookbook" approach is used, it is all the more necessary to have your research (both before and after the data collection phases) closely examined by a colleague or other expert in the field *before* submitting it for publication.

CONCLUSION

Educational television research for the most part has ignored the problems of ETV, has been redundant and poorly planned, and has suffered from the fact that potentially useful findings often are ignored by the administrators and specialists who must implement them. ETV research had an opportunity to take a giant step forward when Title VII money removed the most obvious obstacle to good research. Although all the results are not yet in, it seems that we may have muffed it — that there were not-so-obvious obstacles (particularly in the training of researchers, and in the organization of the researches) that prevented this money from being put to most effective use. We didn't even ask all the questions, much less find the answers.

That leaves the future squarely up to us, anybody interested in ETV research. We are going to have to rely upon our own personnel resources, the smaller research budgets, the less sophisticated data-processing — and our own intelligence. That there *are* problems and unanswered questions is undisputed. Meaningful research in ETV consists of identifying and solving these problems and questions. To do this, the ETV specialist is going to have to join the graduate students and teachers and become an ETV researcher. And, because one cannot just "become" a researcher, the learning specialist is going to have to do some learning himself if educational television is ever to live up to its promise.

NOTES

1 C. R. Carpenter, "Psychological Research Using Television," *American Psychologist*, x (Oct. 1955), 607.

2 Malcolm S. MacLean, Jr., "Critical Analysis of 12 Recent Title VII Research Reports," *AV Communication Review*, x (May-June 1962), A-103. (Prior to 1960, this publication was known as *Audio-Visual Communication Review*.)

3 A. A. Lumsdaine, "Instruments and Media of Instruction," *in* N. L. Gage, ed., *Handbook of Research on Teaching* (Chicago: Rand McNally, 1963), p. 670.

4 Charles J. McIntyre, "Applying Learning Theory to Televised Instruction," *NAEB Journal*, xxiv (Nov.-Dec. 1965), 54.

5 This is nothing new. In one of the earliest discussions of "experiments" in educational broadcasting, Armstrong Perry's *Radio in Education: The Ohio School of the Air and Other Experiments* (New York: The Payne Fund, 1929), all seventeen "Earlier Experiments in the Use of Radio in Education" were descriptive case studies.

6 With the exception of a few individuals fortunate enough to have research appointments, such as Schramm and Carpenter. Presley D. Holmes, Jr., found that eleven individuals accounted for more than 60 percent of the 542 publications produced by 129 researchers in radio and television; see "Survey of Current Research and Researchers (Research Fact Sheet)," *NAEB Journal*, xxiii (Nov.-Dec. 1964), n.p.

7 Gale R. Adkins, "Problems in Research in Educational Broadcasting," *NAEB Journal*, xix (Nov.-Dec. 1960), 30, 34.

8   Harry J. Skornia, "What We Know from New Media Research," *NAEB Journal,* xxv (Mar.-Apr. 1966), 26, 36.

9   *Ibid.,* p. 37. See also Joseph H. Kanner, "Future Trends in Television Teaching and Research," *Audio-Visual Communication Review,* v (Fall, 1957), 513–27; abstracted in NAEB Research Fact Sheet Series III, No. 10 (May 1958), 1C–4C; and C. R. Carpenter, "Approaches to Promising Areas of Research in the Field of Instructional Television," in *New Teaching Aids for the American Classroom* (Stanford University: Institute for Communication Research, 1960), p. 91.

10 Allan M. Cartter, *An Assessment of Quality in Graduate Education* (Washington: American Council on Education, 1966), p. 105.

11 A case in point is the bitter argument in California over whether or not the state colleges should be permitted to engage in research as one of their primary functions. So far, research has been the province of the state *university;* the *colleges* were supposed to devote themselves to teaching. Presently the colleges are deficient in autonomy, prestige, and financial support. Circumventions of this limitation of function are many and ingenious.

12 *NAEB Journal,* xix (Nov.-Dec. 1960), 36.

13 "Traits Revisited," *American Psychologist,* xxi (Jan. 1966), 3–4.

14 Reports are available on an interlibrary loan basis from participating libraries on a list from the U.S. Office of Education; copies of reports may be available from authors in some cases. Under contract with USOE, *AV Communication Review* has published abstracts, prepared by William H. Allen, of a number of these reports. The fourteenth installment, appearing in the Summer, 1966, issue, contained abstracts numbered through 274; the highest project number completed was 1268.

15 William H. Allen, "The Meaning of Title VII" (editorial), *AV Communication Review,* viii (May-June 1960), 84. Of the first 113 Title VII projects approved, 37 were on television and 10 others were concerned with television recordings; 19 others were on "combined media," and 8 dealt with radio and recordings. These 113 projects were distributed according to the following purposes of the media: 55 on comparative effectiveness, 29 on teacher education, 12 on classroom use, and 17 others.

16 For a discussion of how these criteria were applied, see C. Walter Stone, "Current New Media Research Title VII," in Jack V. Edling, ed., *The New Media in Education,* A Report of the Western Regional Conference on Educational Media Research, April 20–22, 1960 (Sacramento, Calif.: Sacramento State College Founda-

tion, 1961), pp. 14–15; and Lester F. Beck, "Critique of Research," *ibid.*, pp. 31–34.

17   Loren C. Twyford, "New Title VII Reports, with Proposals for Better Research," *AV Communication Review*, x (Jan.-Feb. 1962), A-63–A-72.

18   MacLean, in *AV Communication Review*, x, A-102–A-103, A-113.

19   (British) Television Research Committee, *Problems of Television Research: A Progress Report* (Leicester [England] University Press, 1966; distributed in U.S.A. by Humanities Press, New York), p. 11.

20   Kenneth Harwood, in U.S. House of Representatives, Committee on Government Operations, *Conflicts between the Federal Research Programs and the Nation's Goals for Higher Education, Responses from the Academic and Other Interested Communities to an Inquiry by the Research and Technical Programs Subcommittee of the Committee on Government Operations* (Part 2), Committee Print, 89th Congress, First Session, Aug. 1965 (Washington: U.S. Gov't Printing Office, 1965), p. 251.

21   Wilbur Schramm, "What We Know about Learning from Instructional Television," in *Educational Television: The Next Ten Years* (Stanford University: Institute for Communication Research, 1962), pp. 52–76.

22   *Ibid.*, p. 53.

23   David W. Stickell, "A Critical Review of the Methodology and Results of Research Comparing Television and Face-to-Face Instruction" (unpublished Ed.D. thesis, Pennsylvania State University, 1963).

24   Catharine M. Williams, "Reexamination of 'No Significant Differences' that ITV Studies Report," *AV Communication Review*, x (July-Aug. 1962), 263–65.

25   Wilbur Schramm, *The Research on Programed Instruction*, OE-34034 Bulletin 1964, No. 35 (Washington: U.S. Gov't Printing Office, 1964), p. 5.

26   *NAEB Journal*, xxv (Mar.-Apr. 1966), 37.

27   Richard O. Forsythe, "Radio Research," *NAEB Journal*, xxiv (Nov.-Dec. 1965), 42.

28   The following references are cited in chronological order; a few have already received full citation in earlier notes.

     Charles F. Hoban, Jr., and Edward B. van Ormer, *Instructional Film Research 1918–1950*, Technical Report No. SDC 269-7-19, NAVEXOS P-977 (Port Washington, N.Y.: [U.S. Navy] Special Devices Center, 1950). Also see Hoban, "The Usable Residue of

Educational Film Research," in *New Teaching Aids for the American Classroom,* pp. 95–115.

James D. Finn, "Television and Education: A Review of Research," *Audio-Visual Communication Review,* I (1953), 106–26.

Carpenter, in *American Psychologist,* x, 607.

Thomas E. Coffin, "Television's Impact on Society," *American Psychologist,* x (October 1955), 630–40. Strictly speaking, this review is not directly concerned with educational television, but should nevertheless be useful to open-circuit broadcasters.

Hideya Kumata, *An Inventory of Instructional Television Research* (Ann Arbor, Michigan: Educational Television and Radio Center, 1956). An earlier draft of this remarkably complete volume of abstracts was duplicated by the Institute of Communications Research, University of Illinois, in August 1956, under the title *Instructional Television: An Inventory.*

Lucinda Crile, *Educational Television Research Findings* (Washington: U.S. Department of Agriculture, Extension Service Circular No. 514, Nov. 1957).

William H. Allen, *Audio-Visual Communication Research* (Santa Monica, California: System Development Corporation, 1958). Prepared for the Third Edition of the *Encyclopedia of Educational Research.*

Hideya Kumata, "Research Results in Educational Television," in *Proceedings of the Conference on Educational Television, May 26–28, 1958* (Washington: U.S. Department of Health, Education, and Welfare, 1958), pp. 34–39.

Presley D. Holmes, Jr., *Television Research in the Teaching-Learning Process* (Detroit: Wayne State University Division of Broadcasting, 1959), also available from University Microfilms as unpublished doctoral dissertation, 1960.

C. R. Carpenter, "Approaches to Promising Areas of Research in the Field of Instructional Television," in *New Teaching Aids,* pp. 73–94.

Wilbur Schramm, "Television in the Life of the Child — Implications for the School," in *New Teaching Aids,* pp. 50–70.

Joseph T. Klapper, *The Effects of Mass Communication* (Glencoe, Illinois: The Free Press, 1960).

Hideya Kumata, "A Decade of Teaching by Television," *in* Wilbur Schramm, ed., *The Impact of Educational Television* (University of Illinois Press, 1960), pp. 176–92.

C. R. Carpenter, "A Commentary on Television Research, 1948–

1960," in *Newer Educational Media* (University Park: Pennsylvania State University, 1961), pp. 9–17.

Harold Niven, Jr., "A Glance at ITV Research," *NAEB Journal*, xx (May-June 1961), 53–57.

Schramm, in *ETV: The Next Ten Years*, pp. 52–76.

Lumsdaine, in *Handbook of Research on Teaching*, pp. 583–682.

Donald W. MacLennan and J. Christopher Reid, *A Survey of the Literature of Learning and Attitude Research in Instructional Television* (Columbia: University of Missouri Department of Speech, 1963).

Wilbur Schramm, Jack Lyle, and Ithiel de Sola Pool, *The People Look at Educational Television* (Stanford University Press, 1963).

David Manning White, "Mass Communications Research: A View in Perspective," *in* L. A. Dexter and D. M. White, eds., *People, Society, and Mass Communications* (New York: The Free Press, 1964).

Skornia, in *NAEB Journal*, xxv (Mar.-Apr. 1966), 26–37.

29 Others are not. For example, Kenneth Harwood's study of Informative Sound Broadcasting was completed, but remained unpublished when the National Project in Agricultural Communications went out of business. In many cases the mobility of academic authors, the lack of physical durability of duplicated materials, the vagaries of cataloguers in some libraries, the inefficiencies of the postal service, and the inconveniences of the interlibrary loan system combine to frustrate access to those research reports that never achieved journal publication.

30 Gordon C. Barhydt, Charles T. Schmidt, and Melanie G. Rutzler, "An Educational Media Research Information Center (EMRIC): Progress Report," *AV Communication Review*, xiii (Fall, 1965), 296–302.

31 Twyford, in *AV Communication Review*, x, A-72.

32 George Gerbner, "On Defining Communication: Still Another View," *Journal of Communication*, xvi (June 1966), 102.

33 This division is similar to that discussed in Wilbur Schramm, "The Nature of News," *Journalism Quarterly*, xxvi (Sept. 1949), 259–69.

34 Among the more interesting descriptions of models of the communication process are "A Conceptual Model for Communications Research," by Bruce H. Westley and Malcolm MacLean, Jr., *Audio-Visual Communication Review*, iii (Winter, 1955), 3–12; George Gerbner, "Toward a General Model of Communication," *Audio-Visual Communication Review*, iv (Summer, 1956), 171–99; and Gerhard Maletzke, *Psychologie der Massenkommunikation:*

Theorie und Systematik (Hamburg: Verlag Hans Bredow Institut, 1963). "Information theory" is to be found in Claude E. Shannon and Warren Weaver, *The Mathematical Theory of Communication* (University of Illinois Press, 1949) and many other writings. Charles E. Osgood's "mediation hypothesis" of learning, which is closely tied to studies of human communication, is described in his *Method and Theory in Experimental Psychology* (New York: Oxford University Press, 1953); also see Charles E. Osgood, ed., "Psycholinguistics: A Survey of Theory and Research Problems," supplement to *Journal of Abnormal and Social Psychology*, XLIX (Oct. 1954), No. 4, Part 2. An interesting volume for the ETV specialist is Wesley C. Meierhenry, "Learning Theory and AV Utilization," *AV Communication Review*, Supplement 4, IX (Sept.-Oct. 1961). Also see McIntyre, in *NAEB Journal*, XXIV (Nov.-Dec. 1965), 54–63. *The Journal of Communication* has published a number of articles dealing with models of communication; notable among them is F. Craig Johnson and George R. Klare, "General Models of Communication Research: A Survey of the Developments of a Decade," *Journal of Communication*, XI (March 1961), 13–26, 45.

35 Some of the references which follow, in chronological order, have been cited in full in earlier notes.

Donald Horton, "The University of Chicago Report on Educational Television," *in* Burton Paulu, ed., *Lincoln Lodge Seminar on Educational Television, June 1953* (Urbana, Illinois: National Association of Educational Broadcasters, 1953), pp. 17–30. Harold D. Lasswell's "The Social Role of the Educational Television Station," pp. 3–16 in the same volume, may be of interest to those concerned with the larger questions of ETV.

Carpenter, in *American Psychologist*, x, 608–9.

John J. Scanlon, "Research Needs in Educational Television," *in* Gertrude G. Broderick, ed., *Proceedings of the Conference on Educational Television*, May 26–28, 1958 (Washington: U.S. Department of Health, Education and Welfare, 1958). This is a multilithed report of a conference held under the auspices of the U.S. Office of Education in cooperation with the NAEB.

William H. Allen, "Research on New Educational Media: Summary and Problems," *Audio-Visual Communication Review*, VII (Spring, 1959), 83–96.

John W. Riley, Jr., and Matilda White Riley, "Sociological Perspectives on the Use of New Educational Media," in *New Teaching Aids*, pp. 27–49.

C. R. Carpenter, in *New Teaching Aids*, pp. 73–94.

C. R. Carpenter, "Needed New Media Research: Overview" (pp. 62–65) and "Television" (pp. 39–49) in *The New Media in Education*. Also see discussion and articles on pp. 66–76, *ibid.*, by William H. Allen, Lester Beck, Jack V. Edling, and others.

E. G. Sherburne, Jr., "ETV Research in the Decade Ahead," *AV Communication Review*, viii (July–Aug. 1960), 192–201.

Paul M. Allen, ed., "Preliminary Conference Report: National Conference on Teacher Education and New Media, University of Michigan, January 8–11, 1961" (The American Association of Colleges for Teacher Education), mimeographed, pp. 30–31.

Wesley C. Meierhenry, ed., "Needed Research in the Introduction and Use of Audiovisual Materials: A Special Report," *AV Communication Review*, x (Nov.-Dec. 1962), 307–16.

Lumsdaine, in *Handbook*; pp. 663–71 are particularly concerned with research methodology.

Leon Arons and Mark A. May, eds., *Television and Human Behavior, Tomorrow's Research in Mass Communication* (New York: Appleton-Century-Crofts, 1963).

Leslie P. Greenhill, "Research on Instructional Television Past and Future," *in* Barton Griffith and Donald W. MacLennan, eds., *Improvement of Teaching by Television* (University of Missouri Press, 1964), pp. 17–21.

Jack Culbertson, "Needed Research and Development in Mass Communication," *in* Leslie W. Kindred, ed., *Communications Research and School-Community Relations* (Philadelphia: College of Education, Temple University, 1965), pp. 215–33.

36 See Grant Fairbanks, Newmon Guttman, and Murray S. Miron, "Effects of Time Compression of Connected Speech," *Journal of Speech and Hearing Disorders*, xxii (1957), 10–19; and James L. Loper, "An Experimental Study of Some Effects of Time Compression upon the Comprehension and Retention of a Visually Augmented Televised Speech" (unpublished Ph.D. dissertation, University of Southern California, 1966).

37 Schramm, in *ETV: The Next Ten Years*, p. 54.

38 C. R. Carpenter and L. P. Greenhill, *An Investigation of Closed-Circuit Television for Teaching University Courses*, Instructional Television Research, Report No. 2 (University Park: Pennsylvania State University, 1958), pp. 101–6. Also see Marvin Laser, *Television for the California State Colleges (A Report to the Chancellor and the Trustees)* (Sacramento: California State Printing Office, 1963), pp. 59–70.

39   *Instructional Film Research Reports* (Port Washington, N.Y.: [U.S. Navy] Special Devices Center). *Volume I*, Human Engineering Report No. SDC 269-7-38, NAVEXOS P-1220, Jan. 1953. *Volume II*, Human Engineering Report NAVTRADEVCEN 269-7-61, NAVEXOS P-1543, June 1956. These researches, which are reported in some 66 documents forming a stack nearly six inches high, were conducted under Contract N6onr-269 with the Instructional Film Research Program at Pennsylvania State University. C. R. Carpenter was the project director; L. P. Greenhill, the associate director. A companion volume that should not be overlooked is *Instructional Television Research Reports*, Human Engineering Report No. NAVTRADEVCEN 20-TV-4, NAVEXOS P-1544 (Port Washington, N.Y.: U.S. Naval Training Device Center, 1956).

40   Millions were exposed to these techniques at the IBM exhibit at the New York World's Fair, 1964–65. Some early Army ETV demonstrations simultaneously fed two TV monitors in the same classroom; one showed a picture and the other a schematic diagram; or one showed a long-shot and the other a close-up. See Department of the Army Technical Manual TM 11-491, *Training by Television* (April 1959).

41   George Schardt, "A Descriptive Comparison of the Television Viewing Practices of Severely Retarded Children with Those of Normal Children in Los Angeles" (unpublished master's thesis, department of telecommunications, University of Southern California, 1964).

42   For an example of such an "interaction" study, see Edwin B. Parker, "The Impact of a Radio Book Review Program on Public Library Circulation," *Journal of Broadcasting*, viii (Fall, 1964), 353–61.

43   Lee Alden, in a thesis proposal presented to the faculty of the department of telecommunications, University of Southern California, July 1966.

44   John Hayman, of the Denver-Stanford ETV Project found the opportunity to learn to handle his own data-processing so exciting that he wrote a paper on the experience, presented at the 1960 convention of the Association for Education in Journalism.

45   John Scott Davenport, "The Functional Use of Computers in Mass Communications Research," paper presented to the Association for Education in Journalism Convention, Pennsylvania State University, Aug. 30, 1960.

46   Twyford, in *AV Communication Review*, x, A-72.

47 The pleasure that such reduction would give editors of scholarly journals is beyond measure. Editors of volumes such as this must, however, fight their own battles.

48 William Stephenson, *The Study of Behavior* (University of Chicago Press, 1953).

49 Charles E. Osgood, George J. Suci, and Percy H. Tannenbaum, *The Measurement of Meaning* (University of Illinois Press, 1957).

50 The NAEB "Monitoring Studies" conducted in the early 1950's by Dallas Smythe and others are good examples of this type of study.

51 This technique was used to poll the opinions of members of a television station's audience. "Punch out" data-processing cards were returned to the station by volunteers in the audience who were given a supply in advance. This feedback technique was started at WBBM-TV, Chicago, under the direction of Dr. Gary Steiner, author of *The People Look at Television* (New York: Knopf, 1963).

52 Programs testing audience knowledge and ability to apply knowledge of driving laws and skills, government, honesty, vision, and other topics were presented by the networks during the 1965–66 television season.

53 Wilson L. Taylor, " 'Cloze Procedure': A New Tool for Measuring Readability," *Journalism Quarterly*, xxx (1953), 415–33; also "Recent Developments in the Use of 'Cloze Procedure,'" *Journalism Quarterly*, xxxii (1955), 42–48.

54 The Television Information Office (745 Fifth Avenue, New York 10022) is always helpful to researchers. The rating services, particularly A. C. Nielsen Company, American Research Bureau, and Media Statistics, Inc., have a wealth of printed and unpublished, qualitative and quantitative, data available. The Advertising Research Foundation, the National Association of Broadcasters, and other organizations are vitally interested in broadcast ratings and other research. Frederick H. Lumley's fantastically complete book, *Measurement in Radio* (Ohio State University Press, 1934) is still valuable, despite its age. Commercial research organizations are among the many sources of data listed in the annual *Broadcasting Yearbook* and *Television Factbook*.

55 These both are excellent books. Parten is out of print, but is available at most university libraries. Backstrom and Hursh are in an excellent paperback series of "Handbooks for Research in Political Behavior," edited by James A. Robinson. Their Acknowl-

edgement that "The authors will attribute any errors to each other" is a touch of refreshing honesty.

56   Ithiel de Sola Pool, ed., *Trends in Content Analysis* (University of Illinois Press, 1959); Robert C. North, Ole R. Holsti, M. George Zaninovich, and Dina A. Zinnes, *Content Analysis* (Northwestern University Press, 1963).

57   G. Milton Smith, *A Simplified Guide to Statistics for Psychology and Education* (3d ed.; New York: Holt, Rinehart and Winston, Inc., 1962). This is *not* a textbook, and is weak in giving the rationale for each statistic that is given the "how to do it" treatment. Knowing which statistic is lawful to use is half the battle, and it is very difficult for a short pamphlet to cover these points. In the field of nonparametric statistics (particularly useful for communications research) Sidney Siegel's *Nonparametric Statistics for the Behavioral Sciences* (New York: McGraw-Hill, 1956) is the outstanding volume. There are many fine texts, and a few pamphlets and chapters, on statistics — but the choice is up to you and your advisors. Those in education and communication usually will find "psychology-oriented" statistics of more use than "economics-oriented" statistics. Of great value is Darrell Huff's *How to Lie with Statistics* (New York: W. W. Norton and Co., 1954). Both the beginning researcher and the "old pro" can benefit from this thin volume. The chapter by Allen L. Edwards on "Experiments: Their Planning and Execution" and the chapter by Frederick Mosteller and Robert R. Bush on "Selected Quantitative Techniques" in Gardner Lindzey, ed., *Handbook of Social Psychology* (Cambridge, Mass.: Addison-Wesley, 1954) have helped many researchers bridge many gaps in their knowledge of experimental methods and techniques.

58   M. J. Moroney, *Facts from Figures* (Baltimore: Penguin Books, 1956).

59   Such volumes exist in the fields of education, speech and drama, etc. The one in the field of journalism of most value is Ralph O. Nafziger and David Manning White, eds., *Introduction to Mass Communications Research*, Journalism Monographs Number Six (Louisiana State University Press, 1963). All researchers should read Milton Dickens, "Laws of Experimental Research," *Western Speech*, xxiv (Fall, 1960), 197–200.

60   Joe Belden, *A Broadcast Research Primer* (New York: National Association of Broadcasters, 1966); and *Standard Definitions of Broadcast Research Terms* (New York: National Association of Broadcasters, 1967). These items may be obtained, for 75¢ each,

from the Research Department, National Association of Broadcasters, 485 Madison Avenue, New York, N.Y. 10022.

61 For example, "A Symposium: 'Quantitative Group' Looks Back over a Decade of Research," *Journalism Quarterly*, XLII (Autumn, 1965), 591–622. This symposium contains Eugene J. Webb and Jerry R. Salancik, "Notes on the Sociology of Knowledge" (pp. 591–96); Verling C. Trodahl, "Studies of Mass Media Content" (pp. 596–606); Jack Lyle, "Attitude Measurement in Communication Research" (pp. 606–14); and Malcolm S. MacLean, Jr., "Some Multivariate Designs for Communications Research" (pp. 614–22).

Another example is Milton Dickens and Frederick Williams, "Mass Communication," Chapter IX in *Review of Educational Research*, April 1964, pp. 211–21.

Rights for Television Teachers

EMPLOYEES appearing on commercial television have been protected in the past by such unions as the American Federation of Television and Radio Artists, Screen Actors Guild, and the American Federation of Musicians. These organizations have devoted themselves to securing higher wages, liberal fringe benefits, suitable working conditions, and generous residual rights for their membership.

The television teacher, however, has not enjoyed similar protection. He experiences varying patterns of compensation, differing working conditions, and lack of formal control over his recorded lessons. It is the purpose of this chapter to examine what efforts have been made to protect the television teacher's rights, what principles apply to these rights, and what measures should be taken to protect the instructor against exploitation.

A brief review of the history of television teacher rights indicates that

In 1930 the problem was simple. Relatively few formal courses were offered, and the viable broadcasting medium was radio. Today the problem is made considerably more complex by the emergence of open- and closed-circuit television as a practicable medium for formal college instruction, and the resultant proliferation of coursework transmitted by TV. And further complicating things has been the development of steadily improving methods of mechanical reproduction, widespread educational networking facilities, and a progressively more complex body of copyright law.[1]

Although various groups have been concerned about the television teacher's rights since the 1950's, the first "action" case occurred during September 1962. The American Federation of Television and Radio Artists called a strike against New York City's new educational television station, WNDT. One of the key issues in the union's dispute with the station was whether it could represent television teachers appearing on instructional programming. On September 16, when WNDT debuted, AFTRA threw a picket line in front of the station early in the day. Since union members would not cross this barrier, management personnel was called upon that day to run the complex technical equipment. After the debut, the station was shut down, but it had resumed normal operation by September 25. Later, at an election called by the National Labor Relations Board, the union failed to win the right to represent the teachers.[2]

Also in September 1962, the American Association of University Professors published a broad statement on teacher rights.[3] Now, five years later, the Association is preparing a more detailed and formal statement on the subject. In June 1963, the National Education Association, meeting in Washington, adopted and published a formal policy statement, entitled *Professional Rights and Responsibilities of Television Teachers*, which established guidelines on what should be the role of the teacher in educational television. Traditionally the NEA is interested in the rights of elementary and secondary teachers while the AAUP represents personnel in higher education.

The most important events in the history of television teacher rights have been touched upon here as a background for a detailed review of the efforts, on behalf of the teachers, of the American Federation of Television and Radio Artists, the National Education Association, the American Council on Education, and the American Association of University Professors.

In the attempt of the American Federation of Television and Radio Artists to organize the television teacher, the union was primarily concerned with setting a national precedent by representing scholars in addition to its traditional role of protecting commercial talent. The union argued, after the fact, that WNDT should have been unionized because other stations in New York, New Jersey, and Connecticut were union shops, as were the Metropolitan Opera, Philharmonic Symphony, City Center of Music and Drama, Ballet Theater, and other important nonprofit cultural organizations. And further, to quote Mortimer Becker in *Television Quarterly*, "an 'above the crowd' dogmatic approach that a union has no standing in the face of such pronouncements as 'This is culture!' or 'We are different!' is alien to the facts of labor relations in the year 1963." The union pointed out that teachers, like other employees, have to pay rent and eat just as much as anyone else and that their personal and property rights should be guaranteed by unionism. "Scholars, doctors, lawyers, scientists, artists, literary figures and others like them have vested moral as well as legal interest in the fruits of their endeavors and are entitled to be protected against any possible exploitation." It was AFTRA's position "that collective bargaining is preferable to the law of the economic jungle and does not grant 'open season' to any employer organization, education or not." The union underlined the practical significance of its WNDT position: "Does the professor realize that if WNDT's expressed philosophy in bargaining is maintained a recorded version of his lectures may be replayed forever throughout the world on television stations and in colleges without additional compensation to him? Is it not customary that when this same professor writes a textbook he receives a royalty on each book sold?"[4]

To date the National Education Association has published several documents on teachers' rights. One is the previously cited *Professional Rights and Responsibilities of Television Teachers,*[5] while another is the research study, *Practices in Selected Public School Systems Relating to Professional Rights and Responsibilities of Television Teachers* (1963), authored by the Division of Audiovisual Instruction, and based on a study of thirty-nine selected school districts that were reported to be engaged in extensive educational television programming. The accompanying table indicates practices related to teacher compensation in thirty-eight of the schools studied.

*Teacher compensation for television performance
in 38 selected schools in 1963*

No additional compensation	5
Released time allowed	23
Higher salary paid	10[a]
Combination of above	14
Compensation for multiple use or reuse *within* school district	1
No compensation for above	35[b]
Compensation for use and reuse *outside* school district	0
No compensation for above	33[c]

[a] Two schools reported additional payment for each program.

[b] Two schools not reporting.

[c] Three schools not reporting; one school had no policy, and another reported no experience.

Source: *Practices in Selected Public School Systems Relating to Professional Rights and Responsibilities of Television Teachers* (Washington: National Education Association, 1963), p. 12.

On the subject of residual rights, the study (p. 29) revealed that a majority of the school systems (31 of 39) owned the television program. In no instance did the teacher possess ownership rights. "Fourteen school districts reported that TV teachers had certain rights in regard to revision of the content of the program after it had been produced. Sixteen districts said they had no such rights." A majority of the reporting school districts said "that from a legal standpoint the TV teacher has no right in regard to revision of the content of the program after it has been produced." These districts, however, consulted the teacher when they undertook revision of the course material. It was also reported that a majority

of the school districts had no established policy on either the
salary or time a television teacher would be allocated for the
revision, editing, or re-recording of lessons that had become out-
dated. Furthermore, "most districts continue to use recorded materials of TV teachers who are no longer employed by their district" (p. 30).

Concerning contractual arrangements, the study noted that in
nearly all cases the TV teacher is under contract to a school district, and in all but two districts the TV teacher operated under
the same contract as other teachers. "Regarding distribution,
rental and exchange of TV programs, 15 districts reported free
exchange. Nine districts reported rental agreements in effect,
ranging from 50¢ per minute to $10 per program. In one district,
a $300 rental fee is charged for a series of ninety 15-minute pro-
grams" (p. 30).

In its formal policy statement, published in 1963, the NEA suggests that all television teachers secure written agreements from
their employers indicating:

(a) compensation;
(b) teaching load;
(c) ownership of recorded and supplementary materials;
(d) other reserved rights, such as revision, editing, and withdrawal
of program materials; reuse of the materials within the institution,
agency, or system; knowledge of and approval for circulation of the
material beyond the institution, agency or system for which it was prepared; use of the material in a form other than that for which it was
originally intended; and compensation for such additional uses. (*Professional Rights and Responsibilities of Television Teachers*, n.p.)

The policy statement makes explicit the point that "any materials, including recorded programs, prepared by television
teachers as a part of their regular employment, are the property
of the employing agency." When the employer agrees "the teacher
shall retain sole rights to his original notes, literary or artistic
efforts, and inventions or discoveries developed in connection
with the program."

In summary, the National Education Association research indicates that most television teachers do not receive higher salaries for television teaching. They receive, however, either release time or some type of additional payment. There is an over-all practice of not paying teachers for the reuse of their materials either within or outside of the teacher's school district. Teachers do not own their television programs, and these programs can be repeated after an instructor has left the employing school district. Virtually all school districts use standard teacher contracts and do not treat television teaching as a special type of employment. Finally, NEA's policy statement suggests a number of general principles to protect the rights of teachers, e.g., securing a written contract before appearing on television.

Like the National Education Association, the American Council on Education commissioned a study on the problem of teacher rights involving the new media. Dean Fred S. Siebert of Michigan State University conducted the study, entitled *Copyrights, Clearances, and Rights of Teachers in the New Educational Media* (Washington: American Council on Education, Sept. 1964). One section of the study is devoted to the rights of teachers for both the lower and higher education levels. Seibert reports (pp. 37–38) that both elementary and secondary school systems have given more thought to established policies on rights than have colleges or universities. He also reports on the percentage of schools not compensating TV teachers: ". . . some 27 percent of the college and 9 percent of the elementary and secondary television-producing units replying to the survey report that the teacher receives no compensation for his services and that he does it all on his own time" (p. 42). The over-all results of the study indicate the following information on compensation for the TV teacher:

About 30 percent of all teachers reported engaged in television production receive specific payments for specific programs. The bases for determining proper compensation range from payment by the minute to payment established by the number of students enrolled or credit hours taught. The scale varies from as little as $10 an hour to $150 for the same amount of time, although in general teachers receive between

$25 and $50 per produced half hour. Wide variations occur between and even within institutions, indicating that precedent often precludes logic. Some institutions pay a higher rate if the work is done at night or if the teacher is a union member, and a number report an unspecified fee on a per-program basis. A few institutions pay according to the scale set by the American Federation of Television and Radio Artists. (p. 43)

In reference to reuse policies, Siebert indicates:

. . . even when the programs are recorded and re-used, the teacher receives very little additional reward. Only a handful of institutions give the teacher additional payment when the television program is rerun within the institution, and even more significant, there is practically no payment made to teachers when the program is licensed to, sold to, or exchanged with another institution. (p. 44)

The report indicates that most schools and institutions of higher learning have not adopted policies on teacher rights. Significantly some 70 per cent of the reporting schools "had developed no contractual agreement or policy statement" (p. 48).

Thus, the American Council on Education's report coincides with the cited findings of the National Education Association. Most teachers do not receive specific payments for their television program. Where teachers receive compensation the practices vary widely. Most teachers do not receive any money for the replay of their programs either within or outside of their institution. Finally, few schools have developed separate contracts for television teachers.

The American Association of University Professors' first official statement was the one mentioned earlier, "Report of Committee C: Policy on Educational Television" (*AAUP Bulletin*, Sept. 1962). This one-page report suggested that "drastic reduction of other duties will be necessary during the faculty member's preparation for offering a television course and during at least his first experience in teaching it." The report also emphasized the principle of giving faculty direct control over the continued use of the television teacher's material. It was felt that in order to "protect students from obsolescent teaching and teachers from damaged reputations, faculty control is necessary." The report supported the idea that any profits accruing from either the rental or sale of the television programs should be invested "for released time in grants for study and publication and in improved library and other research facilities." The statement concluded with a recommendation for institutions employing TV teachers to adopt explicit policies on the use of educational television.

Currently the AAUP is preparing a new policy statement on educational television. A draft proposal was released on March 25, 1965, emphasizing that "teacher's rights, both academic and legal . . . are not clearly understood."[6] The distinct difference between the earlier AAUP document of 1963 and this later draft is a more detailed exposition of policy. For example, on recordings the latter states:

The author of the program and its recording has proprietary rights in that portion of it which is his original creation. These rights may be transferred in whole or in part through a recognized legal device. An author may, however, grant permission for a recording in which he has a proprietary right to be used by an institution, an educational television network, or other agencies or individuals without relinquishing his copyright in the recording. Permission to use the copyrighted works of others in a program should be secured from the copyright owners.[7]

It also indicates that faculty control over programming is essential:

Provision should be made for faculty control over the future use and distribution of a recorded course of television instruction and for its periodic review by the original teacher-author, or by an appropriate faculty body to determine whether it should be revised or withdrawn from instructional use because of obsolescence.[8]

The AAUP suggests the following policy on royalties:

Should, however, royalties be charged for the loan or purchase of recordings, the funds derived therefrom should be used primarily to provide more adequate financial support for educational television within the institution. This support may take the form of an appropriate allocation of royalties to the teacher-author and to other instructional resources such as academic and clerical assistance, facilities for communicating and conferring with students, library resources, and other departmental educational television expenditures. The precise terms of this allocation should be included in the written agreement between the faculty member and the institution, and these terms should be consistent with the general provision for the making of such allocations as established by the faculty.[9]

The American Association of University Professors, then, maintains that professors have certain proprietary program rights and that faculty members should maintain control over the academic content of their programs. Finally royalties from the ETV programs should be used to support educational television activities within the separate institutions.

Before offering recommendations based on the findings which I have outlined, let me summarize briefly: The television teacher's compensation varies widely from one institution to another. Ordinarily the teacher does not receive additional pay for appearing on educational television. Working conditions vary as widely as compensation practices. Although many schools provide release time for television teaching, there is no specific standard for determining how much release time the teacher will receive. Finally, teachers are not legally protected from the improper use of their programs at another date; if a program is out of date the teacher has no legal right to stop its distribution.

The following recommendations are derived from the stated conclusions:

1. The television teacher should receive additional compensation for his unique services.

2. Residual payments should be distributed to the television teacher for *every* replay of his original presentation.

3. Release time should be granted to every television teacher.

4. Subject matter control of an ETV program should be retained by either the television teacher himself or a group of academic peers.

It can be assumed that a "chosen" television teacher is considered a good or even an excellent classroom instructor. Thus the teacher has special talents that deserve special reward: "The most able deserve more!"[10] Special reward should be additional compensation.

Residual payments are based upon the principle that if a performance is given more than once, additional pay should be given. Each year a regular classroom teacher receives a contract that stipulates teaching and other duties. The underlying premise of this document is that the instructor will repeat the teaching of previously taught courses. Thus in part he is recompensed for doing a job more than once. The same analogy applies to the reuse of television teaching experiences. Schools or television stations should realize that they cannot profit from rentals or save on expenses such as paying additional personnel, without having corresponding responsibilities toward the television teacher who has made these savings possible.

It is reported that television teaching requires more preparation ordinarily than regular classroom teaching. Such factors as the preparation of visuals, scripting, and technical considerations are some of the reasons for this difference. In order for the teacher to do a superior job it is essential that he be given release time from other duties. Moreover, release time should pay dividends in both the quality and the depth of the television lesson presentation.

In regular classroom teaching the instructor is expected to update his subject matter. The same principle should apply to educational television. If the teacher or his faculty peers are not able to retain academic control of a program, it could happen that a school administration might allow economic considerations to affect their judgment concerning the replacement of out-of-date television presentations. Students would then receive instruction not adequately representing the current state of knowledge in the field. As a result the teacher's reputation would suffer. It is essential, then, that the faculty be responsible for the academic control of the television product.

The principles and recommendations enunciated here will remain unavailing unless specific steps are taken to implement them. Methods suggested by the American Council on Education are (1) a special contract with the teacher, (2) a general policy statement by the television teacher's institution on the use of educational television, (3) collective bargaining for achieving television teaching rights. The National Education Association believes that a special contract with the teacher would be advantageous, while the American Association of University Professors advocates a general institutional policy statement. The American Federation of Television and Radio Artists, however, believes in collective bargaining.[11]

In 1965, Frank Kahn wrote that "a national central organization would do much to eliminate the 'crazy quilt' pattern of policy-making currently in effect. The faculty college administration, NEA, ACE, NAEB, JCEB, NET, AFTRA, AAUP, SAA, CBS, NBC, ABC, and the individual television stations all seem to have a large thumb in what is potentially a moderately substantial pie."[12] The centralizing which Kahn advocates seems to me essential; however, to date neither the NEA, ACE, nor AAUP has indicated a positive desire to represent and negotiate in behalf of the television teacher at either the local or the national level.

According to E. Wayne Herron, "The traditional role of the academic man has been that of a semi-independent agent. However, as institutions multiply, and increase in size, depersonalization sets in and affects the traditional teaching role. When this happens the only effective answer has to be a pressure group."[13] One of the most successful pressure groups has been the American labor union. For a pressure group to achieve its ends it must be able to enforce sanctions or exert power. A study of the history of unionism demonstrates that most labor organizations have been able to achieve both goals. Thus, it would be advantageous for a labor union to represent television teachers.

A union representing television teachers should be expected to perform the following functions: (1) to prepare demands that would guarantee adequate compensation, working conditions, and academic control for television teachers; (2) to negotiate these demands in light of the realities of the local, national, and international "market place"; (3) to research what the schools or TV stations can afford to pay the employee. Even though, as Dr.

Herron comments, "it is recognized that ETV differs from commercial broadcasting . . . the question remains why should so much of this contribution to the general social good come out of the hide of the teacher?" Thus, a union should not only examine the current market place, but determine what society should be willing to pay for the "social good." More importantly it should be aggressive in negotiating and securing protection for the television teacher against such abuses as failure to pay for residual performances.

Two unions might possibly qualify to protect the rights of television teachers — the American Federation of Television and Radio Artists and the American Federation of Teachers. Neither union is an ideal choice. The American Federation of Teachers has not been able to gain the national representation of regular classroom teachers. Furthermore it is actively opposed by both the National Education Association and the American Association of University Professors. Perhaps one of the reasons for this opposition is the feeling that this union wants all teachers treated alike. The American Federation of Television and Radio Artists, however, does not operate in this manner. Although it has established minimum pay scales, many of its famous artists make substantially above these minima because, in Dr. Herron's words "the most able get more."

AFTRA has a long history of securing noteworthy compensation and suitable working conditions for its membership. In a negative sense, however, its services have been mainly directed toward the needs of the commercial performer, not the television teacher. If it established a special educational television unit both nationally and locally, it more than likely could achieve results compatible with the principles outlined here. If it is still interested in representing the television teacher, it should not attempt to gain representation of him by "striking" at another WNDT. The union should concentrate its organizing effort on seeking out grass root support for a television teacher's union.[14] Its potential sphere of influence should include not only the educational television stations, but all those areas in which television teaching is utilized. If AFTRA or some other union does not take the initiative to protect his rights, the television teacher will continue to experience "varying practices" — primarily at his own expense!

NOTES

1   Frank Kahn, "Compensation of Faculty Engaged in ITV," *NAEB Journal*, xxiv (Jan.-Feb. 1965), 29.
2   For a review of this case, see Allen E. Koenig, "A History of AFTRA," *NAEB Journal*, xxiv (July-Aug. 1965), 56.
3   "Report of Committee C: Policy of Educational Television," *AAUP Bulletin*, Sept. 1962.
4   The information and quotations in this paragraph are from Mortimer Becker, "ETV Performance: Notes on Negotiation," *Television Quarterly*, ii (Winter, 1963), 27–29.
5   For additional background see *Proceedings of the Conference on Professional Rights and Responsibilities of Teachers in Relation to Newer Educational Media* (Washington: National Education Association, 1962).
6   "Draft Statement of Principles on Educational Television," memorandum from Winston W. Ehrmann, March 25, 1965, p. 1.
7   *Ibid.*, pp. 6–7.
8   *Ibid.*, p. 7.
9   *Ibid.*
10 I am quoting Dr. E. Wayne Herron, of the department of psychology, University of Kentucky. Dr. Herron made useful contributions in the preparation of this article and was kind enough to review the manuscript.
11 For the recommendations of the four organizations, see the following previously cited sources: Siebert, *Copyrights, Clearances, and Rights*, p. 49; NEA's *Professional Rights*; AAUP's "Report of Committee C," p. 290; and Becker, in *TV Quarterly*, ii, 27. See also Thomas F. Baldwin and Donald G. Wylie, "ITV Rights: Model Policy Statements," *NAEB Journal*, xxv (May-June, 1966), 30–36.
12 Kahn, in *NAEB Journal*, xxiv (Jan.-Feb. 1965), 37.
13 This quotation and those in the two paragraphs that follow are

derived from a personal interview with Dr. Herron on April 29, 1966.

14   A prepublication review of this article prompted the following comment from Donald F. Conaway, national executive secretary of AFTRA (letter of July 12, 1966):

"On a purely pragmatic basis, I would like to venture the opinion that a 'grass roots' drive would be an almost insurmountable technique since there are almost 1600 ET stations [including open and closed circuit operations] in the country and at least a great majority of them supply locally produced educational programs or provide so-called 'in school' teaching via closed circuit. The task of going to each of those areas on a 'grass roots' campaign would exhaust what modest moneys AFTRA has managed to accumulate in 29 years of existence and the manpower required would far outweigh the advantages of even a complete organizing of teachers. Frankly, we shall continue to protect our jurisdiction in the educational field and, hopefully, the various teachers' school board associations, or for that matter the two independent teachers' unions will arrive at some commonsense and recognize that the role of the teachers utilizing the electronic medium is a vastly different role from the usual white collar professional role which most teachers think of when anything other than teaching itself is mentioned to them. However, someone far wiser than I once said that when they become hungry enough they will unite for common protection."

Part V

EDUCATION FOR EDUCATIONAL TELEVISION PERSONNEL

Toward a Better Curriculum in Broadcasting and Film

THE curriculum in radio, television, and film is properly the subject of continuing examination, for it is the basis of training and education not only for the career student, but for the student desiring a general education. This dual purpose in communication studies must be examined in the light of several determining factors: administrative support, types of students, faculty, available facilities and equipment, and employment opportunity for career students — in all these lie the strengths and weaknesses of each school. They are the targets in efforts to improve curriculum.

ADMINISTRATIVE SUPPORT

The administration of the school and the university must be fully aware of the importance of communication as the binding force in a society. They need to understand that it is the process by which one man informs and educates another, and on the level of the mass media it is the process by which millions may be informed, educated, and entertained. The force is so pervasive that it influences our every act and is a controlling factor in every academic discipline. It is the way by which thought is transmuted into action in the whole realm of human activity.

If the administration holds this view of communication, the role of the department of radio, television, and film as guide to the mass media of communication is made viable. Recognition, opportunity for development, and appropriate budget should follow upon this view. Unhappily in many schools the exact reverse is true. Departments of radio, television, and film have been given the label of "trade schools." This charge might be set aside as only a jealous reminder from the established disciplines that upstart studies are not very welcome. A more rational approach is to re-examine the curriculum to discover what truth there is to the label. Is the department indeed a "trade school"? What courses are chiefly practical in nature? Which courses liberalize the student and thereby widen his understanding of the society he is to serve? What kind of balance exists between the liberal courses and the practical? Is it defensible to argue that a certain number of practical courses are necessary, because the broadcaster and film-maker must understand his cameras, microphones, and tape recorders as surely as the artist must know his paints and the musician his instruments?

A re-examination of the curriculum may lead the more objective observer to the conclusion that the broadcasting and film studies are not in themselves sufficiently broadly based to provide the student with a liberal education. One possibility would be to correct the balance among the courses and to improve the content in each of the courses. Perhaps a better approach would be to return to the strong base of communication on which the administrative support can fairly be enlisted.

In its more idealistic form, the establishment of a department of communication is a return to the ancient Greek idea of rhetoric as the center around which formal education is built. If one thinks of communication in oral, written, or visual form as the mold for learning and interaction among all human beings, this broad base is a happy choice.

A similar but even broader base is the establishment of a school of communication. From the point of view of a university administration committed to the value of communication on every level, such a move would be realistic. The plan may encompass the several departments of speech, journalism, radio, television, and film, along with communication research. Personal and interpersonal communication would be joined with the mass media. Communication research would point the way to new developments.

A plan for a school is sensible not only for educational values, but for administrative reasons as well. A department within a school of arts and sciences must compete with a dozen or so other departments for its share of budget. A school will have its own autonomy, its own dean, its own budget. It will enjoy a position in the university with the schools of arts and sciences, engineering, law, medicine, and the others.

The sum of the criticism of broadcasting and film education and its successful counter depends then upon the development of an imaginative curriculum whether it is offered on the level of a department or of a school.

TYPES OF STUDENTS

The kinds of students studying broadcasting and film are of wide variety; even so, they divide naturally into those who are career-bound and those wanting a general education. Curriculum emphasis from the beginning has been directed toward the career students. The core courses have been performance, production, directing, and writing. Two or three general courses have been added as though by afterthought. The assumption has been that this is the best education for careers in the media, and indeed students have gone from the universities to jobs. Seldom have educators asked what kind of education and training is most suitable.

When the question is put to commercial broadcasters, their answers are predictable in terms of their own background and education. They will suggest business training, sales, law, and almost everything but the kind of training that broadcasting and film departments have been offering. The frightening thought is that the curricula are wrong and have been from the start. The thoughtful decision-makers of the broadcast industry would prefer to hire bright young people of liberal education for positions of ultimate command. The demand for liberally educated students is reasonable enough in view of the rapidly changing aspects of the media and in view of the manifold faces of business, law, advertising, and showmanship that the broadcasting executive must be acquainted with. A liberal education is the only kind that would serve in such exigencies.

It appears that at this time most broadcasting educators are not preparing students for positions of leadership. They are preparing students to get their first jobs with very little regard for the students' long-time future. They are training students for writing, production, directing, performance, and perhaps for posts of middle-management. If the goal is, or should be, to prepare students for leadership in education and in the industry, changes must be made.

Consider now the undergraduate major who does not go into broadcasting, film, or the related areas — and it has been estimated that nearly half of them do not. This is a matter of genuine concern to curriculum planners. The corrective procedure usually followed is to reduce the number of hours in broadcasting and film that the student is allowed to take. In some universities only one-quarter of the students' total may be taken in broadcasting and film, and it is therefore possible for him to take a second major in another field. In other universities one-third to one-half of the total number of hours can be taken in the major. It is clear that the problem is one of proportion. The student who takes nearly one-half of his collegiate work in a field he does not enter may have wasted a good part of his education.

A second corrective procedure is to make sure that the courses taught in broadcasting and film are rich in content drawn from literature, art, history, psychology, politics, anthropology, and the like. This is relatively easy to do in broadcasting courses in history, criticism, law, writing, and news. It is far more difficult and sometimes nearly impossible in courses concerned with operations, methods, techniques, and performance. These skills courses should be clearly marked as those necessary for practitioners of the profession.

Should the department or school be developed from the broader base of communication, the matter of making the courses more meaningful is greatly simplified, for materials may be drawn from disciplines ranging from linguistics to learning theory. This kind of interdisciplinary approach opens the world to the student in many directions.

Much of the pertinence of the argument for a stronger curriculum rests, therefore, with the students: their quality, their number, and their goals. If for the majority the bachelor's degree is terminal, it is important that the curriculum give them both a broad education and sufficient acquaintance with the tools of broadcasting and film that they can make their way. On the other hand, if the trend continues for more and more students to take graduate study, the undergraduate curriculum must be examined in a different light. It must be made more general and more liberalizing. The student who has majored in broadcasting and film will have little reason for further specialization. Indeed, if his education is not more liberal, he may not be qualified for graduate study. Graduate schools are discovering that many applicants who have an undergraduate major in broadcasting and film cannot offer sufficiently high Graduate Record Examination scores for admission. To the extent that this is true, it means that current majors in broadcasting and film, because of the degree of their specialization, are deprived of background sufficient for graduate school and are kept from developing into communicators of genuine value to society.

THE FACULTY

Any curriculum depends upon the faculty. If a new curriculum is proposed or drastic changes recommended, the faculty are deeply affected. If the department head, the dean, and the curriculum planners can bring the entire faculty along in understanding the purpose of change in improving course content, of dropping superfluous courses, of changing the base of the curriculum, of adding new work, or of shifting emphasis to graduate study, the necessary changes may be possible. If the faculty is opposed, effective change isn't possible. Each faculty member has his own area of special interest he prefers to teach. The older the faculty and the more entrenched, the less interested they may be in change, especially in the directions they are not qualified to teach. On the other hand, faculty who are young in mind, whatever their age, may be glad to improve courses or to move into new areas with enthusiasm.

If the decision is to build the curriculum from the broader base of communication, such a change may only be possible by adding new faculty with this kind of graduate education. The matter is slightly complicated because there are only half a dozen universities offering effective graduate work in communication and this automatically places teachers with this background in short supply.

Film has been mentioned from the beginning as a corollary to broadcasting. In point of fact, most departments teach broadcasting without film or at most with a course or two having to do with film for television or news film. This position is unrealistic, for as much as three-fourths of commercial television is film. The preponderance of educational television is "live" or on tape, but over the years this too may change. Aside from television film, there is a rising interest in film-making on practically every campus. There can be no question but that film studies must be raised to the level of radio and of television.

The chief difficulty in developing a film curriculum is that of finding suitable faculty. As with television, film production must be balanced against courses in film theory, history, and criticism. There are only a few schools which teach film, and those offering graduate study in film are fewer still. Most film graduates would prefer to make film rather than to teach. At times it is possible to find a person who can teach film production, but he may lack advanced degrees important for university teaching. Academic film theorists are equally hard to find. The predicament of finding film theorists and film producers will ultimately disappear as the schools and departments begin to teach film as an integral part of the communications process.

FACILITIES

Space and equipment are not the usual considerations of curricula. In broadcasting and film, however, studios and editing rooms and the means of producing programs are necessary. Although in earlier days every department was struggling to get the necessary equipment, most of them are now well provided at least in television. Whatever the facilities, they seem never to be enough. As surely as the commercial and educational stations change to color television, so will the schools need to convert to keep the students abreast of current developments.

Even though the school is well equipped, it should work in close cooperation with both educational and commercial stations. If it does not, a kind of "educational lag" takes place. The school will be teaching practices that have since been abandoned. The faculty can only teach what they know, which will be dated by their last close association with broadcasting, which may have been two, five, or ten years ago. Faculty internships have been tried in an effort to update teaching, but a far better plan is for the school to be in continuous touch with a station. The schools which have educational stations on the campus are the envy of the others. Unfortunately, in some of these, the teaching function and the broadcast function are purposely and completely separated. The argument that the broadcast function must be completely professional has the ring of validity, but the loss of student opportunity to work daily with broadcasting is irreparably damaging to the teaching function of the department.

Film equipment and facilities present special problems. In the first place, even the space required is different from that for television. Studios may be used by both if scheduling is possible. Weather permitting, a great deal of film may be shot out of doors. For the reason of lack of sound stages and the demand for non-theatrical film, many schools prefer not to attempt feature film.

Quite properly, departments think of film in terms of cameras, lights, tripods, editing tables, viewers, splicers, and sound recorders. Over a period of time, this equipment can be accumulated. A greater cost is the raw stock and its processing. This is a recurring expense, and film-making cannot be taught without shooting film. Although enterprising film teachers can find some short cuts, including the purchase of a film processor, there is no way to eliminate the ever continuing cost. It must be budgeted at the outset.

EXPERIMENT

Most departments of broadcasting and film are preparing students for educational or commercial broadcasting and the allied fields. While this is appropriate, it is not all of the educational obligation. One of the purposes of a university is to show direction, to question principles and to test them, to find new approaches in the long search for truth. While such departments as engineering, science, and the behavioral sciences have accepted this assignment, departments of broadcasting have not. Yet nowhere is experiment more urgently needed than in broadcasting. It is the nature of the media that the daily demands are so great that there is little time for considered thought or for long-range planning. There has not been much experiment in broadcasting beyond the widely separated Columbia Radio Workshop of the 1930's and "Camera Three" on television. Both social and media criticism point to the need for improvement, but little is done to discover the ways.

Schools and departments of broadcasting and film must set about systematically and conscientiously to experiment in the media. They must be concerned with creative ideas and with content. The nature of each of the media needs to be reconsidered. What are these instruments? What can or ought they to do? The forms in which programs have been cast need to be examined and new forms discovered. The methods of operation and even the procedures of preparation, planning, and production need to be re-evaluated. The techniques of the media have not become cemented into conventions. Except in film, there has been very little innovation. Experiment is most difficult, for students cannot explore the new until they are thoroughly conversant with the old. Advanced undergraduates and graduate students should be directed by experienced faculty in special courses, in laboratory work, and in investigations in all phases of the media.

RESEARCH

Although research is a part of experiment and experiment is a part of research, they have been treated separately to focus more sharply the need for both. Communication research has been conducted in various places for more than a quarter of a century. These researches have been the work of psychologists, social psychologists, educational psychologists, sociologists, political scientists, and some anthropologists. Now a new kind of person has emerged, a communication researcher. He has drawn his background from the behavioral sciences and from communication theory and method. He is not a broadcaster, nor is he particularly oriented toward the media. The faculty and students whose lives are most closely related to broadcasting and film have had little or no stake in the communication research in progress. The new curriculum must correct this omission.

The minimum that can be expected in a broadcasting and film

curriculum would be a course or two in research that would expose the students to the literature of research and the findings which are pertinent to the media. A desirable second step would be a course in methodology in which the students would undertake to design modest research projects and carry them out. Ideally, there should be a research section or a research department or a research institute in which all of the disciplines of the university interested in communication research could gather to conduct research with the tools of the media at their disposal. The practitioners in the media should work with the researchers to provide their expert knowledge of the media. Conversely, the practitioners should engage in their own research with the behavioral scientists assisting them.

CAREERS

In the early days of television, every kind of person was needed at once. The demand was so great that there was ample opportunity for every graduate. The greater need, at the beginning, however, was for producers and directors. The direction for curriculum planners was set and curricula to this day have this emphasis. The ten year period after the 1948 to 1952 "freeze" by the Federal Communications Commission was one of great expansion; nearly five hundred stations came on the air. Now, after only a few years of relative stability, it appears that another period of expansion is upon us. The "all-channel" legislation has made the UHF band economically viable and new stations are continuing to come on the air. The direction and meaning of Community Antenna Systems have not yet been clearly determined — nor have the demands they may make for personnel. Some believe that CATV may be the first stage of pay television, which would at once create a demand for programmers and program material. National or regional synchronous television satellites are now feasible, but when they will be launched and what effect these will have on local and network television and in turn what effect on personnel needs is still a matter of conjecture. Educational stations continue to appear. In 1962 there were fifty-four, and five years later there were 140. The Carnegie Commission's 1967 report recommends one sound means of financing. If this most critical problem is solved, a period of even more rapid expansion of educational television can be expected, with a concomitant need for trained people.

A new field has appeared for students of educational television. The newly emerging countries in South America, Africa, and Asia are turning to television as a means of educating their great masses. Initially the new countries looked upon television as a status symbol, and it bore about the same relation to reality as a national air line. However, the widely separated successes of the Television Project in Colombia, the Centre for Educational Television Overseas operating from London, and educational television in such countries as Samoa and Nigeria, are leading to the possibilities of educational television in countries in the far reaches of the world. Educators knowledgeable in television should have a bright future.

In short, television is changing and will change remarkably in the next few years, and there will be tremendous opportunity for the products of the departments and schools of broadcasting and film.

Film students have a range of opportunity. Attractive as independent feature film production may be, the real film market is for nontheatrical film. Industrial firms are turning to film for product demonstration and sales, for recording processes, and for public relations. Many of the larger industrial companies have established their own film units, and the others contract with independent film producers. The large market for educational film is increasing, thanks in a great part to educational television. For some kinds of programs both educational and commercial stations find film more advantageous than videotape. News film has always been a part of news presentation. Documentary film has a market of its own as well as a market in television. Societies and organizations everywhere are discovering the advantage of using film to show their progress and their need for development. In summary, students of film have open to them jobs with independent film-makers, with industrial film units, with educational or commercial television stations, with news units or as "stringers" for the networks, with documentary units, or if they are courageous enough they may establish film companies of their own.

In addition, graduates in radio, television, and film may turn to the allied fields of advertising and public relations. Advertising agencies and advertising departments as well have need of experts in the media. Although advertising was initially oriented toward the print medium, the emergence of television as the primary information source, and with it an increase in advertising expenditures, has increased the demand for those trained in television. For much the same reason, public relations firms and public relations departments of business are now more interested in students of the electronic media. While already one-fifth to one-third of the broadcasting graduates work in these areas, it is possible that in the future there will be even more opportunity.

At the outset, it was remarked that the purpose of the curriculum was to provide the training and education both for career students and for those who want a liberal education. These two purposes which seemed so disparate at the beginning tend to come together. The range of opportunity and the wide variety of jobs are in themselves a final argument for a valid curriculum which will serve these two goals. It is now evident that the curriculum should be restructured to avoid overspecialization, to provide meaningful content in courses, to allow the student to broaden his educational background so that he is not a specialized and empty-headed communicator. Experiment and research must be made integral to the total program. If the student is bound for graduate school, it may be far better for him to take a broad, general undergraduate degree and to specialize in broadcasting or film on the graduate level.

THE PROPOSED CURRICULUM

While the requirements are now clear, the ideal curriculum is yet to be devised. This proposed structure may provide a possibility:

Introduction to Communication
Principles of Audio Production I and II
Principles of Visual Production, I, II, and III
Principles of Film I and II
Criticism I and II
Research I and II
Writing I and II
Experiment in Broadcasting and Film
Special Projects in Communication
Studies in the Mass Media

The Introduction to Communication, dealing with philosophy, theory, functions, and applications to the media, is meant to provide the broad base for students of the media and an elective course for students of other departments of the university.

The purpose of the titles "audio" and "visual" in the next several courses is to bring the students to a broader view. Audio is more than radio, for it includes acoustics and sound in recording, in television, and in film. Visual is more than television and includes the principles of graphics, composition, and matters basic to film. The third course in Principles of Visual Production places the emphasis on dramatic values of composition, movement, position, action, timing, pacing, climax, ascendant and descendant values, and the integration of the parts of production to the whole.

The courses in film, criticism, writing, and news perhaps need no further explanation. Research I deals with the kinds of research, research methodology, the contributions of the behavioral sciences to mass communication research, the findings of research, an examination of current research, and the development of a simple research project. Research II has to do with methodology, design, and completion of communications studies in the laboratory and in the field and will include the control of variables, sampling, data processing, and reporting research. This course might be offered on the graduate level only.

The course Experiment in Broadcasting and Film should explore and develop new ideas, new forms, new methods, and new content through research, writing, and laboratory practice.

Studies in the Mass Media is an "umbrella" type of course, the topics being changed each semester, and it could therefore be repeated by the student. Some of the topics to be covered in this fashion would be history, regulation, power structure, cultural effects, the uses of radio, television, and film in education, and mass media in national policy and international development.

Where appropriate, the courses would have laboratory sessions and ideally would be geared to the productions of an educational television station. The Introduction to Communication, the first course in Audio Production and the first course in Visual Production would be the only requirements. Beyond these the student with the help of his advisor would select the courses most appropriate to his goals. He would be allowed to take 30 hours, one-fourth of the 120 hours required for graduation. This would permit further study in two minor areas or in a second major.

A college or a university with a less ambitious program might keep only the core courses of this curriculum. If a Master of Arts were to be added, the experiment course, the second research course, and the Studies in the Mass Media might be shifted to the graduate level. In addition to the thesis or creative project, the remaining work of the graduate year would include criticism, seminars in each of the media, and a special problems course.

How well this plan meets the requirements of a good curriculum depends, as do all curricula, on the variables suggested at the beginning. Assuming the attitudes of the university toward broadcasting and film to be favorable, the students of high quality and of a reasonable number, the faculty enthusiastic, and the space facilities adequate for classrooms, laboratories, experiment and research, the proposed curriculum could provide what is needed.

Its base resting firmly on the broad concepts of communication and the new concepts of audio and visual principles will shake both the faculty and the students out of the old ways of thinking and will provide a wider approach to each medium. Two-thirds of the courses are broad, theoretical, and liberal. The remaining courses should be structured to admit more than the usual practical approach. The content of each of the courses can be made rich, and high standards of achievement rest with the faculty.

The important matter is not this particular curriculum with its own special weaknesses and strengths. The important thing is to bring curriculum planners to examine once again the programs they are offering in broadcasting and film. These are the powerful means of communication in modern society. The students today who study the media may control them in the future. These must be bright, well-educated men and women conscious of the effects of the power they wield.

A Curriculum for Educational Television

ADVOCATES of curricula in educational television are likely to find themselves fighting an academic battle on two fronts. In the face of the historical controversy between the liberal arts orientation and the skills-techniques approach, it still may be difficult at some colleges and universities even to justify broadcasting as a curriculum, although many have solved that problem long ago by compromise or adaptation. An additional conflict may develop between the ETV specialists and those insisting upon a communication or mass media orientation. The dangers of overspecialization are indeed present if, in the process of training ETV administrators, production personnel, and television teachers, at least some of the basic foundations in communication and broadcasting are not included in a curriculum for educational television. These difficulties, together with the desire of educators that graduates be well educated and the demand of employers that graduates be well trained, make the problem of curriculum design almost insurmountable.

Although employment opportunities in the field of educational television are not overwhelmingly great in terms of numbers of positions available, there is a definite and immediate need for professionally trained personnel. Maloney and Donner have pointed out that "in general, the personnel needs of ETV in the next decade are not to be reckoned in great numbers, and we are not — with one exception — concerned to set up large-scale training programs. We shall need, at most, a relatively small number of extremely well-trained and educated key personnel, a few thousand in all."[1]

The exception noted is an important one and refers to classroom teachers who, according to the authors, must be trained in new skills in order to make the most effective use of instructional television. The number of people included in this category is, of course, enormous. Even though the quantitative need in other positions appears to be relatively small, there is an increasing use of television in school systems, colleges, and universities. Personnel are needed for administrative and production positions in these institutions as well as in educational television stations. In addition, on-the-job training of television teachers should be replaced with formalized education in curriculum planning, course and lesson preparation, and presentation techniques.

There is a great deal of concern about the quality of people seeking employment in educational television, not only that they should be creative, imaginative, and have the skills for the job, but also that they should be able to translate the academic discipline with which they are concerned into an effective instructional presentation. Costello and Gordon maintain that "the man or woman who directs educational television lessons is an educator first, an expert in the arts and crafts of television second."[2] It is possible that many observations about the inconsistent quality of much instructional television can be traced to the employment of inadequately educated and trained personnel in ETV operations.

Personnel needs in educational television have been described in terms of six different types of positions: engineers, production personnel, television teacher-performers, classroom teachers, television consultants, and communication experts.[3] More specifically, the needs are for television engineers and technicians, television equipment operators (cameramen, video switchers and shaders, lighting personnel, and so forth), producers and directors, researchers and writers, ETV administrators (directors of educational television, television coordinators, project directors, and so forth), television teachers, and classroom teachers trained in use of instructional television. Educational television stations have positions in additional areas that are particularly related to station operation, but are not usually found in ETV systems in schools, colleges, or universities: publicity and community relations, accounting, and programming personnel. It would be an unmanageable task for any one educational television curriculum to prepare students for all of these positions. However, specialized training in ETV is not usually necessary for engineers and station personnel listed above. Maloney and Donner point out that training of television engineers and technicians is accomplished in already established specialized schools,[4] and if those positions peculiar to station operation alone are also deleted from consideration, the task is at least within the realm of possibility.

The decision to offer an undergraduate degree in educational television, then, is based upon the determination that such a course of action is feasible and desirable: that it is possible to design a curriculum that will prepare students to be ETV administrators, production personnel, qualified television teachers, and classroom teachers with knowledge and skills in utilization of educational television programs. At this point, the process of building a curriculum may be initiated. Influencing the development of such a curriculum are a number of factors that may be grouped according to policy matters, characteristics of the institution, and industry needs.

The existence of any official policy concerning broadcasting is certain to influence the structure of a proposed curriculum, whether it be a policy of the institution itself or a system-wide policy of which the institution is a part. The educational television policy of the California State Colleges, for example, encourages the development of professional broadcasting curricula, but "this alternative is one which should be made available to the colleges which have substantiated a basis for providing such instruction."[5] It is possible that, under this policy, approval of a major program in educational television would be difficult unless a significant amount of radio and television activity already existed on a given campus. The Television Committee of California State College at Los Angeles, established as a standing subcommittee of the College Instructional Affairs Committee, is empowered "to recommend new policies and review existing policies governing the use of all television facilities of the college."[6] Careful adherence to official policy is mandatory in order to avoid time-consuming revisions or even possible disapproval as the curriculum proposal proceeds through proper channels.

Consultation with authorized curricular committees, administrators, and individuals is also an important and sensitive area in curriculum development. Curricula are neither planned nor established in a vacuum, and the legality of any actions can be seriously questioned unless safeguards are taken to insure that all voices concerned with the proposed curriculum are heard. If, for example, the curriculum is to include sequences of courses in the humanities or social sciences, the academic departments involved must be consulted so that the correct courses are chosen. Catalog descriptions are often misleading.

It is important to investigate the relationship between the proposed curriculum and any existing broadcasting activities on the campus. There might be an instructional television service in operation whose facilities and objectives would be related to the ETV curriculum; the college might operate a radio or television broadcast station, or a carrier-current station; other kinds of broadcasting curricula or broadcasting course sequences might be located in academic departments other than the one proposing the ETV degree program; the college's student body association might be involved in broadcasting activities that would be related to the proposed curriculum. The extent to which the spheres of influence — particularly in the areas of finances, personnel, and facilities — of these various activities are related to the proposed curriculum in educational television could well determine its scope.

Characteristics of the institution at which the proposed degree is to be offered will affect the form and content of the curriculum. The college which is a part of a system of colleges is likely to have certain specialized functions that may or may not be favorable to the development of an educational television curriculum. If an institution already has professional schools within its academic framework, a highly specialized educational television degree program may be approved without difficulty. If an institution is characterized by a heavy orientation toward the liberal arts, the curriculum might have to reflect that orientation. Teacher-training institutions are natural locations for curricula emphasizing the preparation of television teachers and classroom teachers in educational television. Universities may demand one kind of curriculum, colleges another; differences between the private and the public institution may be reflected in the curriculum that is developed. The size of the institution may also have some effect upon an ETV curriculum.

In most cases proposals for curricula in educational television will originate with an administrative unit of the college already involved in some kind of broadcasting activity; however, it should not be assumed that the originating unit is the appropriate administrative location for the curriculum. Although placement of the curriculum will depend to a great extent upon the curricular pattern that is developed, any degree program in the field of broadcasting has some relationship to many disciplines. Faculties in speech, drama, and education will have opinions about where an ETV curriculum should be located; and the advocates of a separate department, union with other media-oriented departments, formation of a communications area, or association with an instructional television service will also influence the final decision.

The financial support that is available will influence an ETV curriculum. Fiscal affairs committees and administrators demand extensive justification when high-cost/low-enrollment programs are under consideration. Such matters as financial feasibility, faculty staffing needs, operating expense costs, and physical plant and equipment problems are of concern to those involved in the fiscal approval of curricula.

Needs of the local industry and community which the curriculum will serve must be taken into consideration. It must be determined whether there is a demand in the geographical area for graduates of the proposed program; consultation with appropriate people in local school systems using television, educational television stations, and other ETV operations can yield valuable information about not only employment opportunities, but the kind of training desired in prospective employees.

An investigation should be made into other broadcasting programs in neighboring institutions. Degree programs vary widely. Although a unique program would be desirable, it will probably contain features that are common to many broadcasting curricula. It is very difficult to design an educational television curriculum that is unique in all aspects; most faculties of such programs try to strike a balance between offering something unusual in order to attract students and offering a program that is broad enough to incorporate a number of the specialized areas within the field of educational television.

An undergraduate degree program in educational television could be based upon a variety of curricular patterns, all of which have certain advantages and limitations. The comprehensive approach in which liberal arts, communication, broadcasting, and educational television courses are all included certainly exposes the student to the subject areas usually thought to be necessary in such a curriculum, but is likely to be too broad, and deficient in enough specialized courses. A curriculum designed for educational television generally, and only providing for other subject areas within the student's General Education and elective courses, would guarantee a graduate who is highly skilled and trained in ETV, but who lacks a background in other related disciplines. The liberal arts approach, with educational television subjects restricted to elective courses, workshops, and extracurricular activities, would prepare the student in the humanities, sciences, and social sciences, thereby giving him background in content materials; however, such a curriculum would tend to be too diverse and amorphous in structure. Providing a series of elective courses within a more general broadcasting curriculum would be an alternative allowing a certain amount of specialization. Building an ETV curriculum around a group of core courses with options in various areas of educational television suffers from the disadvantages of the more comprehensive approaches described and yet offers the advantages of specialization.

Three of these curricular patterns are selected for presentation in greater detail, not because they are thought to be superior, but in order to provide some insight into three different curricular approaches.

ELECTIVE COURSES IN ETV

In an already existing broadcasting department assume that the decision is made to offer a sequence of courses in educational television. The objectives of its present program are to prepare students generally for the field of broadcasting and to provide a basis for graduate studies. The following courses are proposed to form an elective sequence in educational television:

Survey of Educational Television. — Development, potentials, and limitations of educational television systems in schools, colleges, and communities. The instructional television process: developing, producing, teaching, and evaluating television lessons.

ETV Programming and Program Development. — Analysis of educational television programs. Elements and problems in creating and producing cultural, instructional, and public affairs programs: research techniques, program content and format, visualization of ideas, and production facilities.

Producing and Directing ETV Programs. — Special problems in producing and directing cultural, instructional, and public affairs programs. Application of basic broadcast production techniques to unique situations in programs on the elementary, secondary, and college levels.

Television Teaching and Course Preparation. — Study and preparation of televised lessons; development of course guides, syllabi, and lesson plans. Presentation techniques and preparation of visual materials. Demonstration teaching of selected instructional television programs.

Utilization of Television in the Classroom. — Methods of evaluating the quality of learning and effectiveness of instructional television programs. Techniques of preparation and follow-up; relationship between classroom and television teacher.

CORE-OPTION PATTERN

The concept of a core-option curricular pattern provides an opportunity for foundations in communication, broadcasting, and educational television generally; it also allows the student to specialize in one of the three main subject areas of ETV: administration, production, or teaching and utilization. In addition, liberal arts sequences are suggested as series of courses which the student may choose according to individual interest and need.

Core courses

Foreign Language. — Although courses vary from institution to institution, basic language courses as opposed to General Education language courses would seem to be preferable.

History and Philosophy of the Mass Media. — Introduction to mass media of communication, showing relationships to social, political, and economic forces.

Survey of Broadcasting. — Consideration of various domestic broadcasting systems, with emphasis on structure of American radio and television. Current status of broadcasting: programming, stations, law and regulation, advertising and commercials.

Social Role and Responsibility of Broadcasting. — Unique position of radio and television among the media in operating "in the public interest." Effects of broadcast programs on learning, children, taste, public opinion; role of various groups, such as broadcasters, advertisers, networks, advertising agencies, educators, and critics.

Broadcast Law and Regulation. — Consideration of the FCC in its historical and philosophical role in broadcast regulation. Consideration of other government agencies affecting broadcasting as well as agencies of self-regulation.

Educational and Instructional Broadcasting. — Similar to course listed under elective sequence as Survey of Educational Television, but with a more equal distribution of course content in the two areas.

Introduction to Broadcast Production. — Radio and television production techniques and an introduction to basic production facilities. Aesthetics of picture composition, principles of camera movement, lighting, control room operations, basic sound patterns, and direction of various program types.

Criticism of ETV Programs. — Analysis of educational television programs in relation to role of ETV stations and systems. Could be offered as an elective.

Independent Study. — Projects should not only reflect the interest and ability of the student, but also should be a contribution to the field of educational or instructional television. Probably should be offered as an elective.

Option A: ETV Administration

ETV Station Operation. — Operations of educational television stations. Analysis of station structure with consideration of selected United States educational television stations.

Administrative Problems in ETV. — Organization of school and educational station broadcasting; regulatory practices, residuals, released time policies. Analysis of current uses of television for educational purposes: direct instruction, image magnification, enrichment; integration of audiovisual activities.

Financing Educational Television. — The financial problems of open and closed-circuit ETV systems; costs of operation, regulations; federal grants and funding, outside support; state and local resources, including direct appropriations, tax funds, and funding available from Average Daily Attendance resources. Special problems in cost analysis of ETV operations.

ETV Personnel, Buildings, and Equipment. — Staffing problems; personnel organization for school operations, educational television stations. Planning, design, procurement, and installation of ETV and ITV facilities; resources available including consulting engineers, manufacturers, federal, state, and local agencies.

Evaluating ITV Programs. — Survey of television teaching reports and studies; variations of techniques used with regard to subject matter and grade level. Evaluations of controlled research.

Option B: ETV Production

ETV Programming and Program Development. — See description under elective course sequence.

Producing and Directing Cultural Programs. — Perfecting production-direction skills with special emphasis on cultural television programs, such as drama, opera, music performances, ballet.

Producing and Directing Instructional Programs. — Special problems in producing and directing programs for direct instruction and enrichment. Differences in grade level and subject matter; ITV in elementary, secondary, and college level situations; televising the humanities, sciences, and social sciences.

Producing and Directing Public Affairs Programs. — Special problems of news, documentary, and special events. Survey of community resources for program materials.

Option C: ETV Teaching and Utilization

Television Teaching and Presentation Techniques. — Design and use of visual materials; analysis of television lessons; on-camera presentation techniques, blocking, movement. Demonstration teaching of selected instructional television programs.

Course, Syllabus, and Lesson Development. — Analysis of curricular needs in various ITV situations. Development of course guides and syllabi. Writing of ITV lessons and scripts; planning content and methodology.

Television in the Classroom. — Preparation and use of evaluation materials. Methods of evaluation of quality of learning and effectiveness of ITV programs. Role of classroom teacher and television teacher.

Related courses: — It is also recommended that the student be required to take courses in the humanities, social sciences, and sciences. Courses may be placed in those three categories and the student required to take one or two courses in each sequence in order that a background in the liberal arts will be insured. Courses in literature, ancient and modern art, music history, sociological theory, social psychology, and mathematics might be included.

GENERAL ETV PATTERN

A general curriculum in educational television would include many of the same courses as the core-option curriculum. However, the courses would be rearranged into a different structure so that the student would be prepared in all areas of ETV, not merely as a specialist in ETV production, administration, or teaching.

Lower Division (or Premajor)

Analysis of ETV Programs. — Similar to core course in the core-option pattern, Criticism of ETV Programs. Would be on a more fundamental level and designed to develop an awareness of form and content of ETV programs.

Facilities and Personnel of ETV. — Unique needs of ETV in terms of personnel and equipment; familiarization with the basic facilities of broadcast production. Role and duties of broadcast personnel.

Required Courses

Foreign Language. Educational and Instructional Broadcasting. ETV Station Operation. ETV Programming and Program Development. Producing and Directing ETV Programs. ETV Personnel, Buildings, and Equipment. Course, Syllabus, and Lesson Development. Television in the Classroom. Broadcast Law and Regulation.

Elective Courses

History and Philosophy of the Mass Media. Survey of Broadcasting. Television Writing (although this course should include the basic techniques of writing for television, it should emphasize special problems encountered in educational television). Advanced Production Problems (producing and directing cultural, informational, and instructional television programs; emphasis on solving unique problems of ETV and ITV program production). Administrative Problems in ETV. Evaluating ETV Programs. Independent Study.

Related Courses

Additional elective courses might be required in the humanities, social sciences, and sciences.

The sequences described in detail and those only mentioned do not by any means exhaust the possibilities of curricular patterns that might be developed for educational television. Given a situation in which opposition to an undergraduate curriculum in ETV cannot be overcome, for example, consideration might be given to the establishment of a specialized graduate program in educational television, with the support of a more general undergraduate degree in broadcasting. Whatever the structure of a curriculum in educational television and the extent to which that structure is composed of courses that reflect real academic needs, professional broadcasting educators venturing into the field of ETV will not only encounter the usual problems of curriculum development, but will also have to face the task of justifying such a specialized degree program within the college or university curricular framework.

NOTES

1 Martin J. Maloney and Stanley T. Donner, "Personnel and Training Needs in Educational Television, 1961–1971," in *Educational Television: The Next Ten Years* (Stanford University: Institute for Communication Research, 1962), pp. 210–11.

2 Lawrence F. Costello and George N. Gordon, *Teach with Television* (2d ed.; New York: Hastings House, 1965), p. 90.

3 Maloney and Donner, in *ETV: The Next Ten Years*, pp. 206–10.

4 *Ibid.*, p. 206.

5 "Educational Television in the California State Colleges" (multilith document distributed by the Board of Trustees of the California State Colleges, Jan. 21, 1965), p. 14.

6 "Television Policy" (multilith; California State College at Los Angeles, June 14, 1965), p. 1.

Internship in ETV Management

THE management of an educational television station, especially the community station, is perhaps the most difficult job in ETV today.

The ideal station manager should have the attributes of a college president, especially in the area of fund-raising and community development. He must have a solid grounding in business management and broadcast law and regulation. He should know the problems faced by program and production personnel, and he must have the creative and critical ability to distinguish good programming from bad, at least as it relates to the community served by his station. In effect, he is the architect for the grand design of the station's programming.

The manager must be the type of person who offers leadership and inspiration to his staff, and who, looking outward from the station, can work closely with a board of directors, usually composed of civic leaders and distinguished educators. His education must be broad enough to allow him to move comfortably in many circles, ranging from the local universities to the various service and professional organizations. The manager should be equally at home in his city's best private club or at a neighborhood street dance.

Today's ETV station manager must have a working knowledge of media research and be able to prepare and defend funding proposals submitted to foundations and governmental agencies. If his is a college or university station, he probably must possess appropriate advanced degrees, and if it is a school-operated station, the manager must be able to meet certain credential requirements.

While all of the attributes mentioned are not necessary for all management positions, the effective ETV executive must at least be aware of those qualities which will help make his station a successful operation.

Where are the people who will fill management positions, not only at existing stations, but in the many new operations that will begin as educational broadcasting expands? Personnel studies by the National Association of Educational Broadcasters, the Association for Professional Broadcasting Education, and other organizations interested in the field have indicated that too few persons are being trained specifically for careers in educational broadcasting. No academic program seems to have been specifically developed to train management personnel.

Perhaps this is as it should be. For as indicated, the ideal manager should have a broad general education and background with experience in a wide variety of activities. It is at this point that the internship program in ETV management becomes a necessity.

If management people are not now being formally trained, it devolves upon the educational stations themselves to institute a program which will lead people in this direction. Several stations, notably WTTW, Chicago, and WGBH-TV, Boston, have operated internships for a number of years.

The WGBH-TV program is designed to train producers for the station, with further explanation that the training will lead to production and management positions in educational television. Some six months are spent learning the station operation and becoming familiar with the studios and functions of various departments. If appropriate, some actual experience in directing is included. The remaining six months are spent working directly with producers as a production assistant or associate producer. In addition, the trainee works independently on one or several projects to show what he has learned and to prove his competence. A mimeographed statement by Michael Ambrosino, assistant program manager of WGBH-TV, describes the program thus:

We are looking for individuals who have broad interests, mature judgement and well-developed tastes. At WGBH the television producer is responsible for the content, casting, script, budget and general style of programs. He should have a talent for organization, and the ability to write clear expository English is a great asset. He needs to become familiar with all aspects of television and be able to cope with a whole range of problems from the technical to the intellectual. He is more of a generalist than a specialist.

We feel that graduates of liberal arts institutions are the best potential producers. We are not looking for any technical training or experience — a liberal education with the right attitudes and talents are the only requisites.

The nature of his job enables the producer to experience a real sense of creative accomplishment. It often requires long hours of intense work. It is therefore not a job for anyone desiring regular working hours five days a week, nor will it appeal to those who want or need very high salaries.

The salary for television trainees will be generally commensurate with current employee training program rates.

The WGBH-TV program has produced a number of people now working in ETV, including several managers. The WTTW internship, offered primarily in cooperation with Northwestern University, has largely concentrated on producing skilled production personnel.

While there will never be enough creative producers and directors involved in educational television, perhaps it is now time to re-evaluate existing internship programs and establish new projects which will directly train station managers and other upper level personnel. Such a program must necessarily not be provincial in scope but rather expand beyond the traditional station boundaries. The WGBH-TV training schedule includes one week of observing other stations and working at NET. This is a good base, but with the expanding dimensions of educational television, considerably more time should be devoted to off-premises training.

The following is a proposed plan for a broad-gauge internship program in ETV management:

First, a national organization such as the Educational Television Stations Division of the National Association of Educational Broadcasters, or National Educational Television should agree to establish and administer such a program. Funding should be located to provide a financial base for the training.

Second, stations and agencies which would be useful in the program and willing to cooperate should be identified. Station types, in particular, should cover a wide range in licensees, size of operation, and degree of success. It is clear that large and small community ETV operations must play a principal role in the program. In addition, the college and university and school operations should be represented.

Agencies cooperating with the program should be both the New York and Ann Arbor operations of NET, the ETS office in Washington, and the ETS Program Service headquarters in Bloomington, Indiana. Also while in Bloomington, the intern should become familiar with the National Center for School and College Television.

Especially important to the intern would be a working knowledge of the various federal offices and bureaus connected with ETV funding. The main offices of the Federal Communications Commission would be a required stop for the intern, as would the Department of Health, Education, and Welfare.

The internship program should include a regional network, like the Eastern Educational Network, for example, and perhaps a state organization such as the Alabama ETV Authority.

Third, the program should be no less than one year in duration and possibly longer. While considerable time should be spent with the above-mentioned agencies, the intern should be based at a station of the type which most nearly coincides with his main interests. At the station, the trainee should work directly under the supervision of the general manager while rotating through various departments. He should be paid on a scale equal to that for management trainees in other industries and should, in addition, be given a living stipend depending upon his family situation.

Fourth, the intern himself should be carefully selected according to his background and his dedication to ETV as an alternative type of television. He should be a mature individual with at least a B.A. degree. The field of undergraduate study is not as important as the breadth of education and the individual attitude toward the profession.

The interns should begin their program with a concentrated training session based primarily on seminars with leading authorities in the ETV world. These sessions would extend over a one to two week period and should be held at NET, NAEB, or one of the major educational stations. During this indoctrination period the prospective intern would be assigned an advisor with background and experience similar to his own. This advisor would be responsible for the intern's schedule and assignments during the training year and would be available for consultation during the period.

What has been described is a high-level training program similar to several now in operation which are specifically created to produce potential university presidents. Such a program is feasible, and is necessary if the educational television movement is to continue at a high professional level.

Training Teachers for Television Utilization

THE need for additional training on the part of teachers in the area of instructional television is becoming widely apparent. Not only are some teachers using televised instruction in their classrooms with little knowledge of its educational potential but school districts are themselves proceeding to equip their buildings with television facilities of various kinds with less knowledge of the planning and utilization procedures than is necessary to insure the optimum educational value of such ventures.

When a teacher in a Chicago school recently remarked as she turned on the television set in her classroom, "Everybody sit tall and listen to the program," and, when the program was over, admonished, "Let's turn the set off and get back to work," she was defeating the very purpose for which the instructional television had been designed. All of the electronic genius which had gone into the invention of television originally and all of the knowledge and effort which had gone into the preparation of the program particularly could well have been wasted by this lamentable teaching procedure.

While it is true occasionally there may be a program so moving, so inspirational, so impactful on student minds that any utiliza-

tion procedure would be anticlimactic, the bulk of classroom television programs will need considerable reinforcement from the
competent classroom teacher. Indeed, the attitude of the teacher
toward the program is one of the crucial elements in its acceptance
by the group. The problem facing us is how to train teachers to
accept and use best the magnificent tool which has been placed
in their hands.

Teacher resistance to new tools and techniques is not unknown
in the past. There are those, for instance, who claim that even after
many years of existence, visual aids still remain the stepchild of
education. Why should the acceptance of television follow any
different pattern? Educational radio, with a few splendid excep-
tions, never impinged upon the main stream of education in this
country.

Any training program in television utilization by teachers must
include full discussion of the advantages of television as an educational tool. Television, basically, is a multiple medium device.
It is radio, it is the film strip, it is the phonograph, the museum,
the exhibit, the blackboard, the field trip, the demonstration, the
lecture. It is all of these things singly, and, more importantly, it
is all of these things combined in an integrated way and presented by a warm, communicative personality. The multiplicity
enhances its advantages. Among other things, it can enable pupils
to observe the use of materials and to visit places of interest and
significance to which they would not otherwise have access. Mu-
seums, for instance, lend such items as a teapot by Paul Revere,
George Washington's Diary, priceless paintings and manuscripts.
The walls of the classroom fall away.

With televised instruction, the classroom teacher can see other
good teachers at work. How many teachers today ever get out
of the splendid isolation of their own classroom and see how other
teachers, in their own building no less, teach? The stimulus of
observing the televised instruction can only result in better classroom instruction.

Weak spots in the curricula can be strengthened by supplying specialists in foreign language, science, mathematics, social science, and even cursive writing. Further, in whatever subject area, television can bring to the classroom a high quality of instruction by carefully selected and prepared teachers, while the availability of teacher guides and study aids can be of considerable value to the teacher in the design of a particular course. Good teachers' manuals tend to ease the lesson planning load and thus provide more time for attention to individual differences within the class group.

These are only a few of the sizable advantages of television to the American classroom, but they always need reiteration to skeptical and reluctant teachers. Additionally, early in our training programs there must be the opportunity for allaying of suspicions and fallacies which continue to plague the acceptance of television in the classroom.

No one we know has any intention of replacing the teacher in the classroom with a television set. No one has any plans for reducing the number of teachers, or reducing their incomes, or regimenting the classrooms, or replacing books, which are getting better all the time, or shelving good educational films. The television set is another teaching tool, perhaps more glamorous than some, which, because of its potential in upgrading American education, deserves a fair place in the classroom. A *fair* place: one might well question, for instance, whether its use for more than forty-five to sixty minutes per class day is justified.

Closely allied with the attitude toward television itself in the classroom is the attitude of the teacher toward the on-camera teacher. Obviously, a new role is required of the classroom teacher when he consents to let someone else, via television, do his instruction. The on-camera teacher is not a usurper; he is a new member added to the teaching team. He is a successful, experienced teacher in his own right and is well aware of the problems of the classroom. He is neither an actor nor a performer nor the final authority on any subject matter. He is simply a good teacher, perhaps a little better communicator, but not necessarily so, than the teacher in the receiving classroom. He has been given extra time and help in the preparation of his television lesson and he is trying to do a creditable job. Further, in his preparation he has had to adhere to certain time limits more closely than most teachers, limits which pose an additional challenge. His efforts are to minor avail, however, if the classroom teacher chooses to deprecate them or fails to respond to them.

Much of this attitude of mistrust can be alleviated by providing the classroom teacher with some knowledge of studio procedures. The training program must accept the responsibility for such provisions. While few teachers plan to become television directors, familiarity with program production procedures and the kind of behavior which is required of the on-camera teacher will develop not only understanding but in many cases respect for the studio teacher. There is nothing particularly formidable about the operation of electronic equipment in a television studio, and the planning and producing of individual programs can be a superb broadening experience for potential users of classroom television.

No program designed to train teachers in the use of television could ignore the results of research studies which have now become legion in the field. In comparison, it is remarkable how little research was completed in the area of educational radio and how prolific such research has become in educational television, even at this date. The results of comparisons between pupils taught by use of television and those taught conventionally, the effects of televised teaching on retention, comparison of large versus small class reception, kinds of subject matter best taught with television, and attitudinal studies of both teachers and students — these and other research areas must needs be included in the teacher training program.

It is reasonable to assume that all teachers in preparation for their profession have had courses in educational psychology. Such courses traditionally include an examination of the various theories of learning as they apply to the classroom situation. A training program in the utilization of television should include, where possible, the application of such theories as they may possibly relate to television.

The depressing fact is that after years of thought and millions of words nobody knows for certain the nature of the learning process. Theories follow theories — sometimes contradicting, replacing, modifying, supplementing, or even reverbalizing their predecessors. An examination of some of the literature in the field[1] forces us to the conclusion there are virtually no laws of learning which can be taught with confidence. Small wonder that because of the confusion and conflicts in learning theories teachers complain of finding little help in organizing a teaching-learning situation; as a result much of the classroom method is based upon a trial and error technique.

In utilizing television in the classroom, therefore, teachers are neither better nor worse off than those using conventional methods as far as application of learning theories is concerned. Clearly, teaching involves far more than presenting information or making demonstrations, and the complete teaching function is beyond the capability of any electronic device. Teaching involves the arousal of the student's desire to learn, assessing his readiness to study the subject, creating opportunities to utilize learning, evaluating his accomplishments, adapting the matter at hand to queries, facilitating that kind of discussion which leads to clarification of the subject, and rewarding the final accomplishment.

"If television is to be used to facilitate learning," Robert D. Smith has written, "then obviously those who design the television material should have a sound understanding of human learning processes. . . . We suggest that the Stimulus-Response-Reinforcement school seems to provide principles useful to program design."[2] In addition to its value in program design, there are those who feel the application of the concepts of motivation, stimulus, response, and reinforcement to the full continuum of utilization (i.e., prebroadcast, program, postbroadcast, and the follow-up) can only enhance the entire learning procedure.[3]

Even if learning theory in its present state could not be adequately translated for television utilization, a review of it and an examination of its possible applications should be included in our teacher training program. Since most of the learning theories within academic psychology have a stimulus-response orientation (and this appears true whether one is considering conditioning, animal learning, verbal learning, or thinking),[4] their inclusion is warranted.

Emphasis must be given in the training program for the need of creativity and imagination on the part of the teacher in the utilization process. Study guides and program outlines are merely suggestive of how a given program can be made more meaningful to a class. When one considers, for instance, the multiple ideas for postprogram and follow-up activities, one recognizes that the imagination of the teacher is the only limitation. Art projects, various types of experimentation, use of maps and charts, writing assignments, panels and symposia, music, dramatizations, and word games, to say nothing of conventional reports, reading assignments, and observations, represent only the beginning of the possibilities of reinforcing the contents of a program. Teachers need to recognize in their utilization procedures that they can be as creative as the program itself and that variety and change of pace in their activities are as important in the classroom as they were in the planning of the program originally.[5]

In training teachers some attention must be given to the physical aspects involved in using television in the classroom.[6] The design of the viewing room, the placement of the set or sets, height from the floor, size of picture tube, seating patterns, number of viewers per set, prevention of glare, lighting adjustments, sound reception, safety measures in set installation, optimum tuning procedures, and responsibility for care and maintenance are matters which require provisional knowledge by the classroom teacher.

Finally, any teacher training program for television utilization must include time for examination of and possible solution for those nagging, ever continuing problems which seem to plague the medium in its educational application. There is the matter of blind, obstinate opposition to the use of television in the classroom on the part of, unfortunately, some very able teachers. The set is an invasion of classroom privacy and the on-camera teacher is a charlatan. One superintendent estimated approximately 15 percent of his teachers were in this category. There is probably no better way of handling this hardcore resistance than to ignore it. Certainly, no teacher with such an attitude should be forced to cooperate in a television venture. The results would be self-defeating.

What about the problems of equipment breakdown? Tubes burn out, electrical power expires, and transmitting operations cease. The cliché is that since we live in a mechanical age, we must learn to adjust accordingly. There has been faulty reception in the classrooms before and assuredly there will be again. The trained teacher, knowing this, will not permit it to be catastrophic to her instructional environment; she will have stand-by material available which she will use with poise and direction.

And the matter of scheduling? Fifth grade science may be telecast at 11:00 A.M., when a certain teacher would prefer it at 9:00 A.M. Multiple channel broadcasting in the 2500 megacycle band will make possible far more rebroadcasts of programs in the future than has been true in the past. Videotaping of certain programs off the air for later school use is also a possibility. And libraries of instructional program materials will become more inclusive. Even so, no schedule of programs will be ideal for every classroom in every school. A homely comparison might be with the bus which does not stop at every house along the street. To use its services, the good citizens must be at a certain place at a certain time. Schools wishing to use telecast materials may have to make similar adjustments.

With no communication between the studio teacher and the receiving student, does not television strike a blow at the discussion method of teaching? Very often the televised lesson can serve as a springboard for a lively discussion in the classroom after the program. It is also possible to install — as is done at the Skokie Junior High School, Winnetka, Illinois — telephone lines which permit questions from the receiving classrooms to the on-camera teacher at the conclusion of the program. Further, review programs featuring questions collected over a period of days or introductory segments devoted to answering questions from the previous day's telecast can be inserted. The problem would not seem to be insurmountable where teachers feel the feed-back is necessary.

How are on-camera teachers to be selected and rewarded? Obviously, refinements in both of these procedures will come in the future. Selection by reputation, by volunteer, by audition, and even by seniority have all been tried. Until we know more about what makes the best television teacher, it is difficult to chart an exclusive path. Remuneration, to date, seems to have been either a reduced instructional load for the on-camera teacher or some additional stipend, but there are cases of sheer gratuitous service by the teacher. Guidelines for the future are needed.

Whether the classroom teacher has any responsibility for out-of-school viewing, who has final determination of content, how much rehearsal time is desirable, and how significant is the absence of color are additional matters which should be discussed by teachers interested in using the medium.

Fortunately, there are institutions which include the program we have described, or similar ones, in their current colleges or departments of education. In addition, there is some indication of the crossing of traditional disciplines between existing departments of education, radio, television, film, and audiovisual instruction for the purpose of combining instructional talents and creating such a program. Also, the United States Office of Education, through the provisions of Title XI of the National Defense Education Act (1963), has funded over thirty "educational media institutes" in various institutions for each of the past three summers, which concern themselves in varying degrees with instructional television. Presumably, there will be more in the future. Teachers wishing the training program here described would be well advised to investigate the NDEA institute programs.

The danger in such a training course as we have described is that a near-messianic attitude results. Villains become those who do not share this fervor. While this attitude is essentially constructive, it must be tempered with reality. Electronic hardware is not cheaply come by and some administrators will not be able to afford it no matter how much their teachers wish. Further, it should be recognized that televised education will not solve all the problems of American education. It is not going to solve the teacher shortage, and there are not clear indications it will save very much money or make teaching any easier. There is also some research which indicates instructional limitations,[7] and it may be reinforced or supplemented in the future.

Again, it should be clearly emphasized that instructional television is basically a new tool for instruction. It requires training on the part of teachers and adjustments on the part of schools to reach its fullest potential, but since electronic education gives every promise of teaching more people better than they have ever been taught before, we have no choice but to give it our full support. Training teachers for television utilization is a major element in this support.

NOTES

1 The following are particularly recommended: W. A. Fullager, Hal G. Lewis, and Carroll F. Cumbee, *Readings for Educational Psychology* (2d ed.; New York: Thomas Y. Crowell Co., 1964); N. L. Gage, ed., *Handbook of Research on Teaching* (Chicago: Rand McNally, 1963); H. T. Klausmeier and Wm. Goodwin, *Learning and Human Abilities* (2d ed.; New York: Harper and Row, 1966); Clark L. Hull, *A Behavior System* (Yale University Press, 1952), a treatment of the behavioral learning theory.

2 Robert D. Smith, "Needed: A New Approach to Structuring In-

structional Television Programs," *Programmed Instruction* (Columbia University), IV (March 1965), 3–6.

3 Charles J. McIntyre has discussed this subject in an unpublished paper, "Some suggestions for the application of a theory of learning to televised instruction" (University of Illinois, 1964).

4 Winfred F. Hill, "Contemporary Developments Within Stimulus-Response Learning Theory," *Theories of Learning and Instruction*, 63d Yearbook of the National Society for the Study of Education (University of Chicago Press, 1964), pp. 27–53.

5 See Mary Howard Smith, ed., *Using Television in the Classroom* (New York: McGraw-Hill, 1961) pp. 62–78. This contains many specifics for utilization.

6 *Design for ETV-Planning for Schools with Television*, prepared for Educational Facilities Laboratories, Inc. (New York, 1960). This is one of the best sources for examination of physical aspects of ETV in the classroom.

7 See W. F. Seibert, *An Evaluation of Televised Instruction in College English Composition*, TVPR Report No. 5 (Lafayette, Ind., 1958); Earl C. Herminghouse, *An Investigation of Television Teaching* (St. Louis Public Schools, Feb. 1957).

Part VJ

THE FUTURE OF EDUCATIONAL TELEVISION

The Role of Space Communications in ETV

ALBERT EINSTEIN once commented that the unleashed power of the atom had changed everything except man's way of thinking. The relevancy of this statement is especially clear in any investigation of space communications. In brief, technology has provided us with the capacity for global instantaneous communication, but our inability to modify traditional modes of thinking and to adjust established social, economic, political, and legal institutions is seriously hampering effective use of this wondrous new communications extension.

Perhaps at the heart of this "institutional lag" is the dogged refusal to accept a concept championed long ago by Marshall McLuhan. It is his contention that every new communications medium introduces new environmental relationships which ultimately require new ways of thinking and modified social institutions and conventions.[1] Consider, for example, the impact on society of the printing press (quite apart from what it prints), of the railroad (quite apart from what it transports), or of radio and television (quite apart from what they broadcast). These, and other technological developments like them, have radically changed man's way of living, but his adjustment has always been

311

difficult and late. In spite of repeated exposure to this problem of the technology/institution gap, man has seldom been able to prepare the way for easy assimilation of scientific inventions and innovations.

In space communications we are again precisely at this juncture. We have at this moment the technological capacity to link by communications satellites two or more points on earth for instantaneous transfer of information. However elementary our system is today, the technological possibilities for the not-too-distant future are staggering in their sophistication. But even more impressive are the speculations on the marvelous uses to which this new communications extension can be put to improve the human condition. The eradication of illiteracy with the aid of educational television by satellite (ETVS) is just one of these speculations. And while all the evidence seems to indicate that ETVS will be possible, practical, and providentially beneficial, existing restrictive and limiting policies, vested interests, inadequate decision-making machinery, and sluggish and conservative enabling legislation seem clearly to suggest that educational television by satellite will not soon fulfill its potential. The nature of this potential and the obstacles to its early fulfilment are the subject of this chapter.

A first step in such an investigation is to isolate and define certain variables which are central to an understanding of the problem. To begin with, it is necessary to consider the potential of ETVS in terms of a technologically more developed stage than the formative state of the space communications art in which we now find ourselves. Let us assume, therefore, a sophisticated enough technology to make possible the kind of space communications service our conclusions will necessarily imply. It seems safe to suggest that any limitations in future technological developments will derive from social, economic, legal, or political shortcomings rather than from scientific inadequacies.

Next, it is important to distinguish between informal (cultural) educational television (ETV) and formalized instructional (school) television (ITV). Communications satellites offer opportunities to both these arms of educational television, but, considering the massive instructional needs of the world's developing nations, it would appear that the potential may be greater for the latter, requiring ITV to be considered separately.

In a recent report, the Brookings Institution suggested another important variable.[2] Educational television by satellite has one potential for underdeveloped or developing countries and quite another for those which are highly developed and characterized by oversaturation of communications media. For example, while ETVS might have greater educational impact on an emerging nation where the illiteracy rate and the unskilled worker rate are high, the advanced nation already possessing communications facilities could more readily receive and distribute satellite transmissions, having, therefore, earlier benefit from an ETVS system.

Finally, the importance and uniqueness of American cooperation in an educational-television-by-satellite project cannot be overlooked. American technological expertise would, of course, be vital to the establishment of any ETVS system, be it national, regional, or global. American experience in pedagogical research and in national educational television also would be invaluable. But, while the United States would surely be influential in any international project to use communications satellites for educational purposes, it seems likely that the American approach to an ETVS system would be cautious and conservative. The commercial broadcasters have been generous in their support of educational television. The Columbia Broadcasting System and the National Broadcasting Company have both contributed equipment and hundreds of thousands of dollars to various ETV stations in the United States. But the responsibilities and objectives of commercial broadcasting management do not permit a *multimillion dollar* commitment of funds and facilities such as would be required in an ETVS project. The evolving and formative status of American educational broadcasters, especially bearing in mind the uncertainty of adequate financing of the noncommercial stations in the United States, likewise makes this group an unlikely source of unified, strong support for a satellite project. The magnitude of an ETVS undertaking suggests the possibility of a cooperative venture involving government support and financing, or a funding arrangement along the lines of the Ford Foundation or the Carnegie Commission proposals, to be discussed later in this chapter. In any case, the indefiniteness of the final direction to be taken implies extremely cautious support of any ETVS system which will commit American resources.

From a technical point of view, before space broadcasting of any kind can become common, three problem areas must be successfully attacked: (1) the provision of high quality broadcast service from space; (2) the provision of compatible broadcast services; and (3) the assurance of equitable operation.[3]

At this point high quality broadcast service from space is a *fait accompli*. Numerous satellite and launch systems have been developed, each new system improving on earlier ones. At the moment the favored communications vehicle is the synchronous active satellite, in which category Early Bird is a prime example.[4] Synchronous satellites have orbital altitudes of approximately 22,300 miles and attain revolution speeds which approximate the relative speed of the earth's rotation on its axis, resulting in the satellites' apparent stationary positioning above the same point on Earth twenty-four hours a day. In the first eight years of the space age, improved launch systems have permitted the insertion into orbit of heavier, ever more complex communications satellites. This kind of progression can be expected to continue. From the early days of the 150 pound, fifty-telephone circuit Syncom satellite launched by a Delta-Tad rocket in 1963, one can look forward to a soon to be completed global multiple access satellite such as the Hughes Aircraft Company's P307 model weighing 1,500 pounds, to be launched by an Atlas-Agena rocket in 1968, carrying between 2,000 and 10,000 telephone circuits or corresponding television relay capacities.[5] Early Bird carries 240 voice channels or one television channel and is powered by solar cells. Future satellites can be expected to use nuclear power sources. It seems safe to assume that advanced technology can provide the necessary refinements in satellite vehicles to meet immediate and projected high quality broadcast service needs.

In linking together the various existing television systems of the world, attention must be turned to compatibility of services. Presently there are four major systems in use, characterized by the number of lines used to scan the picture on the screen: 405 (England); 525 (the Americas, Japan, Asia in general); 625 (most of Europe); and 819 (France). The 405 and 819 line systems will eventually be phased out, reducing the problem of scansion conversion. But there are other variations to be considered, such as frame rate, image detail structure, direction of modulation (polarity), use of AM or FM sound, and frequency spacing between picture and sound channels.[6] Currently, the internationally accepted list of variations totals thirteen different systems, and the introduction of color telecasting may increase this number. Technically speaking, all of the foreseeable standards divergencies can be successfully accommodated. Eurovision, for example, has been converting scansion standards since 1954. It goes without saying, however, that the more standardization that can be planned for and achieved in the various world television systems, the greater will be the ease in the establishing of an international educational television by satellite system.

The assurance of equitable operation presupposes a degree of international control. How far this control should go, and what its precise nature should be are still very much moot questions. But its seems irrefutable that some kind of international administration must exist if the chaos of the early radio days is to be avoided. A step in this direction was taken in 1963 when the Extraordinary Administrative Radio Conference of the International Telecommunication Union allocated various radio frequencies for the exclusive use of space communications. A strong preference for the use of the UHF band in space transmission has been evidenced since technological advances have made possible the sharing without interference of the same ultra high frequency by satellite transmitters and terrestrial stations.[7] Future developments along the lines of international control for equitable operation will be developed as needs are determined and a willingness to cooperate in international legislation manifests itself.

At a recent UNESCO conference on space communications, Wilbur Schramm suggested three developmental stages for communications satellites.[8] We are presently engaged in the first stage, which provides for point-to-point transmissions, from earth station to low power synchronous satellites to earth station. In this phase the ground-based sending and receiving stations are elaborate relay points (such as Andover, Maine; Goonhilly Downs; or Plumeur-Bodou), capable of feeding a satellite signal into existing national broadcasting facilities. The second or intermediary stage provides for the distribution of a satellite signal to various local area reception points. These community receiving stations would be more numerous and less elaborate than the relay points in stage one. An example of this phase would be the recent American Broadcasting Company proposal to operate a satellite to feed ABC programs to its affiliated stations, instead of using the conventional long lines system. The third stage, variously estimated at from five to twenty years distant, would involve the transmission of a satellite signal directly into individual homes, bypassing for relay purposes the traditional local broadcast station.

The development of communications satellites suggests some incredible changes in the social order. For example, seen from space, Earth is a planet, not a collection of countries. The ability of satellites to transcend man-made or natural barriers with instantaneous multipurpose communications implies a new relationship to our spatial environment, providing for the possibility of making all points on earth equidistant.[9] Satellite transmissions should be able, for example, to alter fundamentally the present concept of charging telephone calls by distance, reducing long distance charges to the point where a ten cent call to anywhere would be feasible and profitable.

Any change in spatial relationships suggests as well a change in man's relation to time. Equidistance in space means simultaneity in time. Satellite communications will encourage man to live in *real time* rather than in *clock time*. His living habits will be modified and governed in large measure by the necessity of his communicating with other parts of the world. There is virtually no overlapping of daylight hours, for example, in New Delhi and San Francisco. But if common interests and an efficient and inexpensive communications satellite system make a business conference by closed-circuit television between these cities imperative, the fact that it will be noon in San Francisco and 12:30 A.M. a day later in New Delhi will not stand in the way of the *real time* conference. It has been seriously suggested that satellite communications may require man to learn how to get along with less sleep, or at least to organize his living habits so that they accommodate the time schedules in those other parts of the world which most concern him.[10]

Communications satellites are far more flexible than existing technical communications facilities. Not only can they provide a greater volume of traffic, such as giving access to several different users at the same time, but they have also a multipurpose capacity allowing for many different kinds of communications. In addition, for example, to telephony, telegraphy, and radio and television signals, satellites will permit facsimile and data transmissions. The day may come when facsimile by satellite will be used for long distance postal mail or for "publication" of a facsimile newspaper in a subscriber's home. The effects of long distance data exchange are even more startling. Satellites could link together computers all over the world. The sum total of man's knowledge could be stored and readily retrievable on instantaneous recall by any scholar anywhere on earth. Libraries for browsing as we know them are likely to be replaced by research information centers where a computer can store, search, and retrieve data electronically with incredible speeds. Decision making will become faster and more centralized, and there will be vastly more information available on which to make a decision. This in turn will require new and much more complex governmental, industrial, and educational organizations to absorb and act upon the increased flow of information.

II

When the usefulness to man of communications by satellite is discussed, the example most frequently cited is the role of spacecasting in the service of world education. The possibilities are indeed attractive, and the problems the communications satellite potential suggests are no less formidable.

One of the first judgments to be made is the economic feasibility of an educational television by satellite system. A cost/benefit decision must be made by every potential user. The nature of existing educational facilities, available financial and technical resources, and existing and projected educational requirements will all be a part of this analysis.

The great need facing most of the world's nations is the rapid expansion of an effective educational system capable of training huge masses of people. Hundreds of experiments in the last decade have clearly shown that television is a valuable teaching tool. Its usefulness augurs particularly well in underdeveloped countries where its educational impact has for the most part only been speculated on, not tested. A major advantage of an ETVS system seems to be significantly lower distribution costs for reaching very large audiences. A recent study has favorably compared satellite communication costs against costs of reaching large audiences by more conventional means.[11] Film distribution was shown advisable for small total audiences and in areas where rapid and inexpensive mail or freight delivery systems exist. Land microwave or cable distribution systems are useful in reaching local urban areas but not suitable for inexpensively linking geographically widespread audiences. Airborne television, such as the Midwest

Program for Airborne Television Instruction (MPATI), is effective in reaching between 1 and 10 million people in areas approaching 200,000 square miles. For audiences of 5 million or more with average population density, an ETVS system is least expensive and most efficient. At current costs, per capita distribution charges for educational television by satellite are calculated at one dollar per student per year in most areas of the world. An operational program calculated for all of Mexico and all of India resulted in a cost per student, including charges for operation and maintenance, of forty-four cents and twenty-two cents, respectively.[12]

A pilot program has been suggested by the Hughes Aircraft Company based on a dual mode concept. This involves a ground station transmitting six television channels to a synchronous equatorial satellite which rebroadcasts these signals in two modes: two channels at relatively high power transmitted primarily for rural reception in individual schools or homes, and four channels at lower power for ground reception and rebroadcast by urban television stations directly to conventional home or school receivers. Life of the satellite itself is predicted at five years, and the scope of the pilot project includes use of 2,000 direct reception "rural" receivers and 5,000 conventional "urban" receivers. The total estimated cost of this proposed demonstration program, based on United States dollars and manufacture and including booster capacity, is $37,430,000 or $4.50 per American student per year.[13] From an economic point of view, therefore, the feasibility of developing and establishing an ETVS system seems readily assured.

Some of the uses to which satellites might be put in the service of world education were outlined at the recent UNESCO conference on space communications.[14] It was suggested there that an ETVS system could free educators from restrictive traditional educational philosophy and methodology. In developing countries, for example, education no longer would have to be extended in terms of land expansion, i.e., duplication of the centralized school system in outlying districts as funds and teachers become available. Space communications could reach all of a nation's hinterlands with a minimum of effort and cost in one spectacular effort. This would make possible salvaging an entire generation of potential students who might otherwise be missed in the slower extension of the educational system district by district. It would also be a far less discriminatory method of instruction, providing for the education of all citizens rather than for those fortunate few who happen to live in a district blessed with a local school.

The establishment of an ETVS system by a developing nation would be a dramatic move and would require careful planning, coordination, and investment. Not only would high quality reception equipment in outlying districts be needed, but a coordinated staff of "monitors" or local teacher-supervisors would also be essential. The role of this corps of intermediaries is at the moment unclear. How much assistance students will require in assimilating televised information, and therefore how sophisticated the local teacher will have to be, are yet to be determined. But it is agreed that a local intermediary who will encourage television students and help them apply television instruction to meet their personal needs is indispensable. The cost and effort in providing both the equipment and personnel would be, however, a fraction of the cost incurred if the educational system were developed by a conventional land extension.

Another important consideration of mass education by satellite deals with the quality of instruction. To what extent is education likely to decrease in value as it gains in coverage? It was suggested at the UNESCO conference that even if television instruction were 20 percent less effective than a local teacher could be, this reduction in efficiency would be compensated for by the far greater number of students exposed. Space communications add new importance to this method of evaluating educational efficacy in terms of student population.

Perhaps the best way to prophesy what can be expected for world education as communications satellites are perfected is to investigate the three stages of development mentioned earlier as they might apply to an ETVS system. Each stage has particular significance for both developed and developing countries in terms of informal educational television and formalized instructional television.

As noted before we are currrently in the first stage of space communications, where point-to-point signals transmitted via low power synchronous active satellites can occur. For educational television in developed countries, this period is characterized by broadcast dissemination through existing conventional facilities, such as community or university educational television stations to schools, television clubs, and home receiving sets.

The first intercontinental ETVS program for general public consumption took place by this means in the United States and France on May 31, 1965.[15] On that date, through the facilities of the University of Wisconsin educational station, WHA-TV, and Radio-diffusion Télévision Française in Paris, a French class at West Bend (Wisconsin) High School and a similar class at the Lycée Henri IV were linked by Early Bird satellite. During the broadcast, American students spoke to Paris in French, and the French students replied in English. Conversation between the two schools ranged from the curricula of the institutions to the Beatles. The transmission is important more because of its form than its content. Nothing startling from an educational point of view happened during the hour-long broadcast, but the fact that two schools were interconnected by communications satellite for the open exchange of ideas has great significance for educators concerned with the exposure of foreign cultures and extension of instruction in both advanced and emerging nations.

The future may well provide a *pedagovision* system, providing for regular international exchanges of educational broadcasts modeled on the program exchanges of the Eurovision or Inter-vision projects. *Telepedagogical corporations* could be established to specialize in the production of broadcast materials for international instruction on a regional basis. Certainly, not every subject could be offered internationally with the same ease since local cultural differences would probably require different emphases in areas such as the humanities. But courses in the sciences, languages, and other universal subjects surely could be produced jointly and shared internationally. The success of the Modern Mathematics series currently being offered through Eurovision is important evidence in support of this idea. It is also conceivable that universities around the world could be linked by communications satellites for specific, specialized academic investigation or scientific research or for general scholarly pursuits such as the sharing of lectures by outstanding faculty members.

Regarding informal educational television, the first stage may see reallocation of frequencies so that an increased number of cultural broadcasts from international sources can be made available to existing broadcasting networks in developed countries. This presupposes both a willingness and an ability to produce and rebroadcast such programs. Countries which have only commercial broadcast systems would probably carry few international cultural programs unless the transmissions could be legally and realistically exploited for commercial purposes.

Redistribution of educational materials by satellite will probably begin modestly in the first stage. Large countries or continental areas will doubtless be the first to invest in an ETVS system. Studies have indicated that communications satellite coverage of India, Australia, Africa, and the Americas would be highly efficient.[16] North and South America would be ideal starting points because of limited time zone involvement and linguistic homogeneity.

The problem of language diversity is not as great as it might first seem. Dubbing and subtitling are used in film a great deal today to overcome language barriers and have come to be accepted generally by world audiences. Eurovision has exchanged television programs among diverse language groups for years. One method is to have separate sound channels for different language commentaries. The home viewer receives the picture and "international sound" (i.e., nonlingual sound inherent in the broadcast), which every member of the international audience gets, combined with a commentary in his native tongue furnished by a special channel. Future communications satellites will have multilingual capacities, whereby separate language channels can be rebroadcast in the appropriate receiving nation.

The first stage will have less immediate benefit for the developing nations, since communications satellites are not a substitution for an adequate technical infrastructure. A local redistribution system must exist if a country is to rebroadcast the satellite signal. When satellite communications are exchanged between those countries which can make regular use of them, developing nations will be encouraged to give priority to the establishment of a similar accommodating infrastructure. As the technical capacity for reception spreads, developing nations will be able to plan and organize a massive concerted effort at national education. One of the earliest benefits will be improved teacher-training for those local teachers already in the field. This aspect of instruction might well be modified for training of health workers, farmers, and government administrators as well.

On the informal educational level in developing countries, programs might be developed, free from commercial or political vested interests, which would produce visual reinforcement for national unification, raising professional standards, and providing for adult literacy. Since receiving sets would presumably not be generally available to the public, community reception centers would have to be developed and monitor-supervisors trained so that maximum effect could be derived from the group reception. The necessity of training local intermediaries would prove a serious obstacle to early benefit from informal educational television by satellite in emerging nations.

The second or intermediary stage, where the satellite signal is redistributed by various local reception points, will see the proliferation and perfection of the community reception center concept. In developed countries, these local redistribution points may be regional television stations serving local schools which incorporate the rebroadcast satellite transmission into their local curricula. A forerunner of this concept is the MPATI experiment noted earlier. Another local reception point may be centers for adult education where workers can receive in-service training courses requested by their firms.

In developing countries this stage of group reception should furnish an unparalleled opportunity to reconsider traditional educational methods. New "television schools" could be developed in outland districts which would receive a majority of their curriculum via satellite from the centralized education authority. International transmissions could enrich this educational experience by exposing foreign culture and instruction to students who would not otherwise be so benefited. There would have to be heavy emphasis placed on the training of monitors or local "television teachers" to supervise the integration of the local curriculum with the television curriculum.

At the informal educational level, postschool adult education through the auspices of television clubs would likely develop in advanced nations. In emerging nations vocational training and adult literacy courses would be offered at community centers and through home receivers as they existed. In short, the second stage would be characterized for both developed and developing states by regular use of television and communications satellites for educational purposes and by the educational saturation of given geocultural regions.

The third stage of satellite development involves reception of educational material directly in individual homes without the supervision of intermediaries. This stage represents a shift from providing educational benefits through group reception to universalization of educational communications with their direct accessibility to any citizen possessing the technical equipment for reception. There is, therefore, no longer control of the message on arrival as in the previous stages; the viewer is completely free in his decision to receive any communication offered. This stage suggests far-reaching political and legal questions since it implies that a local government would no longer be able to control what international messages might be made available to its citizens by satellite.

Educational transmissions by satellite in this stage could be entirely free of the national educational system. The positive aspects of this include providing material supplementary to that offered via conventional educational means, relieving pressures on traditional educational systems for reaching outland districts, and even replacing traditional methods with a more effective educational system. The negative aspects involve the possible encroachment on local educational programs by national authorities, and similarly the possible reception by citizens of unauthorized transmissions such as "educational propaganda" from foreign sources with vested political or economic interests.

In developed countries, in addition to giving individual homes maximum opportunity to receive directly cultural programs from any transmitting source in the world, the third stage would particularly benefit home instruction. Various courses in specialized training, such as mechanical engineering, nursing, and mathematics, could be received at home. Reorientation and retraining instruction of workers could be conducted at home in cooperation with training centers or adult education institutes responsible for final accreditation. Another possibility could be the establishment of regional university systems offering sophisticated urban instruction to frontier areas.

The developing countries will expand the number of schools equipped for television instruction. Students who have access to universalized communications through home receivers will have increased information with which to prepare lessons. In adult education, the potential of reaching illiterates everywhere will be realized. New methods of simplified electronic transmission will make possible the facsimile representation of basic texts for study and reflection. As more program channels are provided, more diversified programming can be furnished, such as supplying educational broadcasts especially suited to the training needs of minority group workers. The eventual result will be a rise in the general level of public education. This in turn will favorably affect the economies of developing nations, allowing them to compete more successfully in the world's market places.

It is fairly obvious that if the potential of educational television by satellite is ever to be reached, there must be an international accord to guarantee permanent intercommunication among nations, free from commercial or educational competition, overlapping or duplication of effort, pointless and costly production, and wasted research. The arrival at such an accord will not be an easy task. National educational systems are largely based on national interests. International educational planning will suffer, therefore, from conservative and nationalistic influences. But the difficulties need not be insurmountable given enough time and the proper approach. A starting point might be the creation of nonbroadcast educational materials for distribution to the various national authorities to be adapted and used under their own responsibility.

Whatever the problems, present-day limitations should not hinder planning and experimentation for the future. Every developing nation should recognize the important role educational television by satellite can play in its economic and social growth and should plan a national infrastructure which will accommodate such a system. In a recent survey, UNESCO recommended that adequate communications facilities in a developing country would include ten radio receivers and two television receivers for every one hundred inhabitants.[17] While introduction of new techniques involves substantial investment, costs should not be a decisive factor. The paramount importance of public education in developing countries makes this imperative.

Nor must we forget the fact that literacy is interrelated with the supporting culture.[18] Public education cannot be achieved to any significant degree unless the cultural environment makes literacy skills necessary for earning a living, winning social recognition, functioning as a citizen, and obtaining basic human satisfactions. A viable educational system, therefore, cannot exist in a vacuum, but must furnish information which can and will be used.

III

The role the United States of America will play in the eventual establishment of an ETVS system is difficult to foresee. Myriad vested interests and a unique broadcasting industry make the American position ambiguous and ambivalent.

The United States government took an early interest both in educational television and in satellites. For example, in 1952 the *Sixth Report and Order* of the Federal Communications Commission set aside the original 242 frequencies reserved for exclusive educational television use. American scientists and governmental administrators took quiet note of Arthur C. Clark's *Wireless Age* article, October 3, 1945, entitled "Extra-terrestrial Relays," which first proposed use of artificial satellites for broadcasting twelve years before Sputnik I was launched by the Soviet Union. National legislators, such as Senator Warren G. Magnuson, have often reminded the Congress of communications satellite potential.[19] In 1962, Congress took unprecedented action in establishing the Communications Satellite Corporation, better known as Comsat, to develop a system of satellites for relay of communications between the United States and foreign countries. Comsat is unique in that it is the first profit-making corporation authorized by the United States Congress to be both publicly and privately owned.

While it has been American technology and legislation which so far are primarily responsible for the present state of the communications satellite art, it is also interesting to note that some of the satellites' most severe criticism has come from American quarters. Commercial broadcasters, for example, have been particularly critical of the predicted tertiary direct-transmission stage of satellite development. They quite naturally foresee a danger to the established American system of local broadcast stations if satellite transmissions direct to home receivers are permitted. Given a powerful broadcast lobby, it is doubtful that a system making obsolete local broadcast stations will ever be legislated into existence in the United States. It is difficult to predict how this might affect satellite development in other parts of the world.

Another criticism has been the high costs of renting Comsat facilities, which run in the neighborhood of $5,000–$7,500 for a ten-minute transmission. The tariffs depend on such variables as peak and nonpeak telephone usage hours, one or two-way transmission, black and white or color facilities, weekday or weekend use, and destination charges levied by the Comité Européen de Poste et Télégraphe (CEPT) based on the transmission receiving points. At this writing, Comsat is engaged in a reappraisal of its rate structure for global services,[20] which broadcasters hope will result in a downward adjustment. At the present time there is no rate differentiation between educational and commercial users.

Legal questions have also created problems. Satellite broadcast transmission, contrary to what may be the general impression, is from the legal point of view more than the mere extension of broadcasting, governed by the same rules applying to conventional radio and television. Broadcasting via satellite requires a whole new legal approach.[21] By way of example, in connection with present limited satellite transmissions, European Post-Telephone-Telegraph (PTT) administrations reserve the right to decide if a requested television transmission is important enough to displace telephone traffic. Prior to April 1, 1966, CEPT rules permitted the PTT's to require advance knowledge of broadcast content in order to exercise this special form of "censorship." In April new language was adopted which lessens the implication of prior restraint censorship. But the fact remains that, insofar as the experimental Early Bird is concerned, both the CEPT and AT&T, the licensed common carriers, must agree to the displacement of telephone traffic by a television program before the television transmission can take place. What arrangements are to be made for television transmissions via future Comsat satellites remains to be seen.

Looking forward to the day when facilities and rates permit regular transmissions of artistic programs, there must be modification of copyright legislation, of contracts with authors' societies, and of collective conventions with the various performers' unions, writers' guilds, and other affected labor organizations. In the area of copyright, for example, the United states is not a party to the Berne Convention, with the result that there are many European musical works (especially symphonies and operas) which are not protected by United States law. If an American satellite transmission, received in Europe, included an artistic work unprotected in the United States but enjoying protection in Europe, the relaying broadcast organization would be committing a copyright infringement, assuming no prior authorization from the copyright owner. In addition, no talent remuneration agreement exists presently with appropriate performers' unions for payment of performers seen by satellite relay outside the Eurovision and Intervision countries.

When and if satellite transmission involves the broadcasting of a program from a satellite-borne transmitter directly to home sets, all prior level agreements will not pertain, and new documents will have to be written. A global system of television will require agreements far broader in scope than now at hand, allowing, for example, for the payment of large sums to authors, performers, and entrepreneurs to compensate them for their vast loss in earning resulting from the fact that their productions and performances will rarely if ever be purchased directly by relaying broadcast organizations.

A clue to the extent of the American commitment in an ETVS system can be found in the current interest being shown for a domestic satellite which would transmit space signals to numerous relay stations around the nation. The beginning of this idea was the ABC request to launch its own satellite for feeding its affiliated stations.[22] Comsat took the position that only *it* was authorized to operate a space communications relay system, but offered to place in service a domestic satellite which could be used by all three

American networks and educational broadcasters as well. This vehicle would transmit the space signal to ground stations, which in turn would pass the signal along to existing local broadcast stations. The advantages are at once obvious. In the first place, the networks foresee a possible reduction in the $50 million they spend each year renting long-line service from the American Telephone and Telegraph Company to link their affiliates. Secondly, all broadcasters recognize that such a system would protect the local broadcast station since it would still be used for final dissemination of the satellite signal. Educational broadcasters are hopeful that special transit rates would apply to them, making possible the satellite's frequent use for educational fare by the 140 American educational television stations expected to be in operation by the end of 1967.[23] Comsat President Joseph V. Charyk noted in April 1966 that the major limitation to the idea is not in the satellite but in establishing the necessary 225 ground stations to serve some 600 American television stations.[24]

Another suggestion along these lines was offered by the Ford Foundation, August 1, 1966. In a letter to the Federal Communications Commission, Foundation President McGeorge Bundy urged the establishment of a nonprofit nationwide television distribution system by satellite. The Ford plan would place four synchronous active satellites, each carrying eleven channels, over the four North American time zones. Besides providing national educational television network services (such as uninterrupted coverage of significant hearings or debates; musical, dramatic, and literary events from anywhere in the country; and live instructional programs for an aggregate of 60 million students at all educational levels) the satellites would also be used by commercial broadcasters. The networks, for example, would distribute programs to their affiliated stations by satellite at cost rather than by AT&T long-lines at considerable expense. A major portion of the resulting savings, estimated at the outset to be some $45 million annually, could then be used to support ETV programming in the United States.

ABC, CBS, and NBC agreed in principle to the proposal, but with certain reservations. The networks quite naturally resisted any implication that legislation should be passed which would restrict their freedom in selecting a common carrier for dissemination of their programs, or which would earmark themselves as the sole financial support of ETV in America. Comsat and the American Telephone and Telegraph Company disapproved of the Ford proposal. The Comsat objection is based on its contention that Congress has given it sole authority to operate a communications satellite system; AT&T quite naturally wants to avoid any loss of revenue. The Ford Foundation point of view is, however, that Comsat should turn its full energies to the Gargantuan problem of providing international space communications, leaving domestic relays to the proposed nonprofit agency, and that the loss of income which would be experienced by the common carriers represents less than 1 percent of their gross. According to the Foundation, the purpose of its proposal was more to urge the FCC to make no precipitous decisions which might foreclose the future development of ETV in America rather than to gain adoption of its suggested model. To this end it pleaded that definitive deliberations concerning domestic use of communications satellites and the role of ETV await the report of the Carnegie Commission on Educational Television. The Commission, which has the endorsement of President Johnson, conceded in a preliminary report to the FCC that a national ETV distribution system may be advantageous, but warned that such a system presented problems of educational monopoly and centralized instead of local control of instructional material.[25]

In a later development recorded in the *New York Times* (August 29, 1966, pp. 1, 59), Comsat was reported working on a proposal which would support educational television on a far broader scope than the Ford Foundation plan. Comsat would assess a "user levy" for all domestic communications carriers and major users of satellite service, including telephone and telegraph companies and the commercial television networks, to underwrite ETV. Presumably, this levy would accrue from savings earned by commercial users of a domestic communications satellite system to be proposed soon by Comsat. This system would be similar to the Ford plan in that (1) four satellites would hover in fixed positions over the different time zones in the United States and (2) reduced transit rates would be offered to ETV; it would differ in that the system would not be reserved wholly for television transmissions, but would also carry long-distance telephone and other commercial communications traffic. A key provision of the Comsat proposal may well prove controversial. It calls for television networks to deal directly with Comsat in arranging for transmission of their programs by satellite rather than with AT&T as the accepted retailer of television relay circuits.

When the Carnegie Commission on Educational Television released its report, *Public Television: A Program for Action* (New York: Bantam Books), on January 25, 1967, it, like the Ford Foundation, called for a nonprofit corporation to support American educational television. (See Appendix 1 for a summary of the Carnegie Commission's findings.) In its report, the Commission coined the new term "public television," a phrase it hopes will replace the less succinct terms "noncommercial television" and "educational television." While most of the report was concerned with informal (cultural) educational television, the commissioners stressed the importance of instructional television as well. The purpose of Public Television was characterized as stressing local and regional diversities in the arts, education, and opinion. With the announcement of the Commission's findings, Dr. Frank Stanton, president of the Columbia Broadcasting System, Inc., wired Dr. James R. Killian, Jr., chairman of the Carnegie Commission, congratulating the Commission on its work and pledging $1 million toward the $25 million enabling endowment for the proposed Corporation.

The precise role to be taken by the United States government in any American communications satellite system is as uncertain as the system itself. Will public funds be used to finance educational television by satellite? Will the satellite system be strictly national for domestic use? or national for international use? or internationally administered? Will there be more than one satellite system, each one independently administered? If only one, will it be owned and/or operated by an existing organization such as Comsat, or the State Department, or UNESCO? Or will the system be turned over to a newly created organization, such as a consortium of participating nations or a nonprofit agency as proposed by the Ford Foundation and the Carnegie Commission? Will the system be commercial, noncommercial, or quasicommercial? Unanswered questions such as these make speculation on the future of ETVS in the United States extremely difficult if not impossible.

Whatever route is finally taken, it seems safe to assume that only a satellite system which will accommodate the existing educational and commercial stations and networks will be acceptable to broadcasters in the United States. How this system will be used for educational purposes will depend largely on what costs will be incurred and what legal latitude will exist. Educators and educational broadcasters in the United States are anxious to see communications satellites fulfill their potential. They have demanded, consequently, that they be represented in any deliberations to determine American involvement and have insisted that the cause of education is at least as great as that of commerce, industry, and government and should be given equal consideration in any system predominantly developed and financed by the American government.[26] While this is the official line, unofficially educators are frank to admit that there are manifold problems to be solved and that there is no real assurance that educational interests will be successful in winning their objective. In fact, there is a considerable divergence of opinion in the educational community itself on how best to use the communications satellites. A recent National Association of Educational Broadcasters report indicated, for example, general agreement among a large number of educators that there was more opportunity in the foreseeable future for use of satellites for educational symposia, international conferences, and the sharing of clinical material than for general educational broadcasting.[27]

There is hope that a workable pattern will emerge from all these pieces — that American educators will be in accord on how best to use satellites for educational purposes; that Congress will write and pass legislation guaranteeing an adequate ETVS system in the United States; that broadcasters will cooperate so that the system will grow in effectiveness and prestige; and that the American government will provide the necessary leadership and assistance to assure educational television by satellite for the rest of the world. These are ambitious hopes, but so they must be, for the need is great and the time is short. Unless the various nations can manage soon to actuate permissive policy, the great potential which satellite technology has promised mankind may forever fall short of its goal. As Shakespeare observed in *Julius Caesar*:

> ". . . we must take the current when it serves,
> Or lose our ventures."

NOTES

1 See in particular *Understanding Media: The Extensions of Man* (New York: McGraw-Hill, 1965).

2 Donald N. Michael, *Proposed Studies on the Implications of Peaceful Activities for Human Affairs* (Washington: U.S. Gov't Printing Office, March 24, 1961, No. 66831). Prepared for NASA by the Brookings Institution.

3 R. P. Haviland, *Selected Studies of Space Broadcasting* (Philadelphia: General Electric Company, n.d.), pp. 253–54. Reprinted from the *Proceedings of the XVth International Astronautical Congress*, Warsaw, 1964, Vol. II.

4 Satellite systems are classified into five categories: (1) nonsynchronous passive, such as the Echo Series; (2) nonsynchronous active, such as Telstar; (3) synchronous passive, of which there is no example; (4) synchronous active, such as the Syncom, Relay, and Early Bird series; and (5) any combination of the above. The

synchronization of a satellite is determined by the altitude of its orbit; its passivity or activeness refers respectively to its ability merely to *reflect* radio signals or to *retransmit* them.

5 John W. Ludwig, "Distribution of Educational Television by Satellite" (mimeographed; El Segundo, California: Hughes Aircraft Company, n.d.), p. 3. Wilbur Schramm has reported that the Hughes satellite P307 may carry as many as 50,000 voice channels.

6 R. P. Haviland, "Choices in Space Broadcasting" (mimeographed; Philadelphia: General Electric Company, n.d.), p. 7.

7 *Ibid.*, pp. 11, 13–21.

8 Wilbur Schramm, "Communication Satellites: Some Social Implications," a paper presented at the UNESCO Meeting of Experts on the Use of Space Communications by the Mass Media, Paris, Dec. 6–10, 1965, paragraphs 23–33.

9 Edward W. Ploman, "Some Observations on Space Communications," *EBU Review*, 96B (March 1966), pp. 33–36.

10 Schramm, "Communication Satellites," paragraph 28.

11 Ludwig, "Distribution of ETV by Satellite," pp. 14–24.

12 "Multiple Channel Educational Television Satellite System" (multilith; Hughes Aircraft Company, Space Systems Division, Jan. 1966 [SSD 60003B], pp. 18–19.

13 *Ibid.*, pp. 16, 21–24.

14 Henri Dieuzeide, "Education," a paper presented at the UNESCO Meeting of Experts on the Use of Space Communications by the Mass Media, Paris, Dec. 6–10, 1965, paragraphs 105–57. Mr. Dieuzeide is director of research and head of the department of educational radio and television, National Pedagogical Institute, Paris. Many of the following comments on the potential of an ETVS system are based on the UNESCO report.

15 Dr. Lee S. Dreyfus, professor of speech and radio-TV education, University of Wisconsin, Madison, conceived and executed this exchange project, overcoming considerable obstacles and many months' delay to see its completion. His files were made available to me for research purposes.

16 Haviland, *Selected Studies*, and Ludwig, "Distribution of ETV by Satellite."

17 V. K. Narayana Menon, "Space Communication and the Developing Countries," a paper presented at the UNESCO Meeting of Experts on the Use of Space Communications by the Mass Media, Paris, Dec. 6–10, 1965, paragraph 12. Mr. Menon is director-general, All India Radio.

18 I. Keith Tyler, "Combating Illiteracy with Television," *AV Com-*

munication Review (*World Communications*) (Fall, 1965), pp. 309–24.

19 For example, see Senator Magnuson's speeches before the 87th Congress in 1961, "Programming Planning for Space Communications" and "The Potential of Satellite Communications."

20 Letter from Joseph V. Charyk, president, Communications Satellite Corporation, March 21, 1966.

21 Georges Straschnov, "Some Legal Aspects of Television Transmissions by Satellite," a paper presented at the UNESCO Meeting of Experts on the Use of Space Communications by the Mass Media, Paris, Dec. 6–10, 1965, paragraphs 1–21.

22 Morris Gelman, "The Invisible Shield," *Television Magazine*, Feb. 1966, pp. 45–60.

23 This aspect of satellite transmission was discussed by Senator Magnuson, "Educational Television Facilities Act, Extension of Remarks," *Congressional Record*, Vol. III, No. 199, Oct. 27, 1965.

24 "Possible Approaches to Domestic TV Distribution Via Satellite Presented," *Industrial Communications* (multilith weekly newsletter; Washington, April 22, 1966), p. 13.

25 See *New York Times*, Aug. 2, 1966, pp. 1 and 18.

26 National Association of Educational Broadcasters, *The Needs of Education for Utilization of Space Transmission Techniques* (May 1962), p. 32.

27 *Ibid.*, p. 26.

Summary and a Look Ahead at ETV

THE twenty writers who have contributed to this publication share the conviction that educational television is a major international resource. Industry, government, education are all fascinated by the potential of this electronic phenomenon which combines sight and sound and emotion within its capabilities and which transcends national bounds. ETV planners are working with a medium capable of providing instantaneous information exchange among all of the peoples of the planet and extending educational and cultural opportunities to all within access of a television receiver. The year 1967 will be, in the words of Fred Friendly, the year in which distance dies for television. The next decade will determine the dimensions and scope of ETV's contributions.

But why ETV? The educational establishment recognized as early as 1927 that this new medium had potentials in the adaptation of an audio and visual medium to the process of learning. But, as Maloney points out, the problem has been to determine the most effective uses for television, whether educational or commercial. We have now discovered that television does not provide a panacea. It is merely a form of communication, perhaps a lens, perhaps a language, perhaps a mosaic with the filling-in accomplished by the viewer. Television as a teaching tool must acknowledge the unidirectional flow of information, lacking the face-to-face exchange of reaction and interaction. But perhaps these lacks in themselves are linked with an exciting revolution in educational thinking. Undeniably, television has the power to indicate that something is happening *now*; its simultaneity vivifies the present instant in the educational process.

Is there a philosophy for educational television? Is there a discernible direction for ETV, beyond the shared and apparent interest on the part of industry, government, and education? What is ETV trying to do? What part of ETV should be for classrooms, what for other audiences? The Breitenfeld chapter analyzes the relationships of instructional television to educational television, and in four imaginary case histories examines the philosophies of the school station, the state station, the university station, and the community station. The state station, says the writer, by the nature of its source of support, tends to shy away from the controversial. The university station tends to think of its service as an extension of liberal education for an elite. The community station, soliciting support from schools, power groups, industry, and community organizations, shares concern for the answer to the same question: "Whom are we educating, and why?" Breitenfeld characterizes ETV as the only broadcast service in the world without defined means of support, only a set of restrictions to steer by: no commercials and no profit. What price philosophy?

The university educational television stations in this country, Dreyfus points out, reflect their academic environments, and such stations tend to program in accord with the traditional view of the function of the university: to acquire, preserve, and transmit human knowledge through teaching and scholarship and continuing education for those beyond the limits of the campus. Without guidelines, the university station may tend to be a university wholly unto itself. For its function, by dicta set down by the Federal Communications Commission, is to meet the needs of the entire educational community. Therefore the university station must provide formal and informal education, educational and media research, community relations and community service, a public forum, a training laboratory, a recreational service, and an alternate program service for minority audiences. With such a load of responsibility, it is small wonder that most university stations cannot mobilize strength in serving the vital needs of community relations or educational and media research. Quite uniquely, by its mere location on campus, the university station is obligated to meet the goals of a universally available education for all.

The community station, that ETV station held in trust for a community by a board of trustees, is a resource of the same character as a symphony orchestra, museum, art gallery, or daily newspaper. Author Collins takes the position that there is an inevitable and predictable gap between promise and performance for the community ETV station, based largely upon the problems involved. Too infrequently are mass audiences appealed to. The difficulty for any ETV station, admittedly, is to provide competitive program quality, competitive promotion budgets, competitive talent to stimulate the interest of mass audiences. Too, matters of program balance are often apparently areas of academic interest rather than focused planning. The community station manager may take comfort in the Schramm view that ETV's audience is comfortably above average in education, but Collins suggests that ETV's efforts might well be addressed to the blue-collar worker as well as the white-collar worker. Because the community station is so dependent upon the public for support and financial aid, its bond to its public should be commensurately strong. Collins realistically acknowledges that TV viewing is a leisure time activity; and yet, the hopeful response of audiences to "involvement programming" (the bridge lesson, planning a summer trip, gourmet cooking) suggests the role of ETV outside the controlled classroom environment. Why not plan consumer education programs for the disadvantaged — programs teaching basic literary skills, offering aid to the alcoholic or the drug addict? The problem — and its answer — is money!

The problems peculiar to the community station are detailed in the Schwarzwalder chapter, in which the station manager is likened to the medieval cathedral builder, whose products are monuments to flexibility and invention. The ETV manager for the community station must be a builder, or he is replaced. He must establish and maintain relationships with all local educational institutions; he must belong to voluntary and civic and community organizations (as well as the business community and commercial broadcast stations). He must build a solid base of financial and fund-raising support, and, having built it, sustain it. Schwarzwalder disclaims the popular view that all ETV is in deplorable financial straits, saying rather that those stations now on the air are operating with better facilities and equipment and are serving audiences better than ever before. The role of the community station, Collins and Schwarzwalder agree, must be that of an absolutely indispensable institution within its community.

A bulwark and a strength for the ETV station is National Educational Television, begun in 1954 as a weekly noncommercial television program service supplying four stations. There are now about 112 NET-affiliated stations reaching approximately 130 million people. In the beginning, according to NET President White, affiliate stations produced programs for the network under contract for subsequent distribution to the balance of the affiliate membership. Now, most of the 260 hours available yearly are produced by NET, both here and abroad. Program service support, making this programming possible, has come from the annual $6 million contributed by the Ford Foundation. White details six principal guidelines for the public affairs programming which absorbs more than half of NET's resources and program schedule: (1) to seek out the "submerged" issue; (2) to focus attention on otherwise neglected issues; (3) to anticipate issues and prepare programs to build understanding for future problem areas; (4) to bring historical perspective to contemporary concerns; (5) to suggest the interrelation of present and future problems; and (6) to take on controversial areas solely on strength of the issues involved. The balance of NET programming is devoted to general cultural programs and to children's series. NET does not seek to replace books or theater or concerts: its programs must and do provide an alternate service, fill the need for experimentation for all of television, and finally enhance the programming of affiliate stations.

The "marriage" of NET and its affiliates, now in its thirteenth year, has not been free of matrimonial differences and tensions. But the union has been bonded by a shared concern that the network and its affiliates must serve the total society as well as the formal educational establishment. Although the early days of NET required the bulk of programs to be produced by affiliate stations, Appy indicates that the trend was toward network control over program content in order to insist on maximum quality. An affiliates' committee and a field services department have been responsible over the years for urging member stations toward increasingly higher standards of technical proficiency, weekend program service, color, etc., as well as toward the proper climate of corporate agreement allowing revolutions of the future to take place (i.e., regular live interconnection, international program services via satellite, etc.). The network's basic difficulty is understandable. It must provide a common service to each of the four kinds of ETV stations discussed. Understanding the difficulties of the first thirteen years of marriage and the successful solution to the myriad problems faced, there seems every reason to believe that this marriage of interest, convenience, and necessity may flower into an even more fruitful union.

In many ways comparable to the growth of NET is the development of regional networks, as several authors point out. The rationale for regional network growth is simply explained by Quayle. There is no one ETV station in the country with financial, personnel, or program resources sufficient to supply the meaningful and superior programming by which noncommercial broadcasting will be judged. The Eastern Educational Network (EEN) serves as an example of what the present function and potential services of regional cooperation are and may be.

Originating in 1959, following a meeting of personnel from two New England ETV stations together with representatives of the New Hampshire and Massachusetts departments of education and of the Ford Foundation, EEN now comprises twenty-one ETV stations, two production centers, four "developing areas," seven state departments of education, three networks, and four program service subscribers.

Like all regional television consortiums, EEN provides both general and instructional services (i.e., programming for out-of-school and in-classroom audiences), with most of the programming contributed by member stations. Having consistently noted the need for high-quality programs, EEN's ability to provide live interconnected program services suggests a paradigm for regional study and emulation. NET is acknowledged as the primary general program source, and care is taken not to produce duplicated programs. Instructional programs develop out of critical curricular areas in which television can play a major role.

The availability of regional ETV networks augurs well for continuing interinstitutional cooperation necessary to the development of an Educational Communications System. Physical interconnection throughout an entire region is possible through leased long-lines or independent microwave or satellite systems which are presently available. Time-sharing concepts or multichannel capabilities will be required as national interconnections receive more serious consideration. No less serious must be considerations of regional characteristics and needs, regional control over programs, and technical capabilities of individual stations serving such a national Educational Communications System. Implicit in all considerations are matters fiscal. As supported by contributors Schwarzwalder, Taylor, Gumpert, McBride, and Barber, Quayle cites the expansion and improvement in regional and state networks as providing a most significant element in the total national

ETV complex. These networks must be strengthened if the optimum expectation of noncommercial broadcasting is to be achieved.

Any history of educational television must also take into account the development of instructional television as an integral service function of ETV. Educators, as we have seen, early perceived the values of a multifunction medium to the instructional process, and have sought the most effective means of adapting television and the educational technology to the learning process.

The Joint Council on Educational Television, an amalgam representing the shared educational interests of the total educational establishment, was instrumental in leading education to reserve spectrum space with the FCC, which in 1952 assigned 242 channels for noncommercial telecasting. As the Taylor article details, the Fund for the Advancement of Education supported much early examination of television's teaching strengths, and as early as 1954 findings were available recording "no significant difference" in resultant achievement or attitude between televised instruction and traditional classroom teaching. ETV projects multiplied to the extent that by the 1960's the spectrum squeeze was easily apparent: there were too few channels reserved for education's needs. In-school programming had virtually doubled in the period from 1961 to 1964. Closed-circuit television was an answer, and the Instructional Television Fixed Service was authorized in 1963 by the FCC. At publication, twenty systems are in operation.

As Miss Taylor remarks, any discussion of instructional television would be incomplete without pointing out the possible future roles of translator stations and community antenna television systems, by which instructional service from other areas, or improved technical service, might be provided. As we approach the last of the decade, we see ITV absorbed in a highly necessary revolution in education. The development of the Educational Communications System envisages the combination of the media to extend the values of the instructional process: the relating of conference circuits, slow-scan television, radio and television program service circuits, data exchange channels, and computer-assisted instruction to an eventual nationally interconnected multiservice educational network.

Closed-circuit television, with its fascinating variety of applications to the educational process, is described by Gumpert as one most important form of instructional television. CCTV allows multichannel utilization, permits lessons to be shaped to the needs of individual classrooms, provides service to segmented and sub-group student populations, protects the privacy of the classroom through the nature of the closed system, enriches the teaching-learning process through the flexible functions of television, and allows freedom from time and control imposed upon the open-circuit operation. Perhaps the most avid acceptance of CCTV was by the medical teaching profession, which by 1962 was making regular use of CCTV in forty-two medical schools and thirty-one dental schools. Concomitant growth was seen in the military, with service utilization dating from CCTV maneuver observation in 1944. Extensive use is made of CCTV throughout all of the services' instructional programs; and it is worth noting that the innovation of videotape recording has appeared to be of much greater significance to the military than has color television.

In education itself, direct instruction via CCTV was adopted more slowly, with the first experimentation at an institution of higher learning occurring in 1950. In elementary and secondary education the earliest notable use of CCTV was undertaken in 1956, in Maryland. In the late 1950's education discovered the utility of videotape recording as an instructional storage device.

The future of CCTV, says Gumpert, will lead to a systems approach to teaching and learning, with dial access retrieval of instructional materials, computer-assisted programmed instruction, as well as the Educational Communications System multiservice national network capability. Gumpert admonishes that the goal must be to narrow the gap between "technical virtuosity and effective teaching and training."

Returning to the fiscal problems of ETV, Harwood assays the

improbable area of earning nonprofits, early establishing ETV and the Church as corollaries. Both institutions have the responsibility of operating on a nonprofit basis, and share a surprising collection of potential sources for nonprofits: private subscription, corporate or foundation support, every-member canvasses, trust funds, auctions, fairs, bazaars, thrift shops, lotteries, sale of stock, "bootstrap" operation of private property, and, of course, government. The concept of the "glebe" as a means of ETV support — operation of a commercial radio station run by the university as interim owner-operator — has already proved to be successful to the Los Angeles ETV station. In the matters of revenue and incentive, Harwood warns that fiscal ossification will ensue if there is an inability to change with changing human wants and needs. Compensation, therefore, becomes a factor in providing incentive. "The long-run result of the single benefit-cost ratio in fund raising is to have a very good plant for the production of inconsequential broadcasts which attract declining interest to the station from potential donors." The ETV station, as with any respectable nonprofit earning corporation, needs three or four main sources of revenue, and there must be a balance of revenue over cost for the purpose of providing an investment fund from which capital may be drawn on a rainy day. With assiduous attention, then, the nonprofit may well be the means of putting substantial gains or assets to the community good, instead of to individual use.

Author McBride cites two principal trends in ETV station programming: librarying, and the increased use of nonlocally produced programs and the pooling of resources for cooperative program production. In the 1950's, local production was the only answer, both for ETV stations and for instructional television. Local insistence upon local origination tended to emphasize quantity rather than quality. By the 1960's the recording of programs on kinescope and videotape for delayed and repeated programs brought recognition of shared instructional approaches and the potentials of program exchange. Activation of television libraries served the growing interest in systemized program exchange and distribution. Concurrently, ETV station interconnection began to take place, and the Eastern Educational Network, the Midwest Program for Airborne Television Instruction, and Midwestern Educational Television developed. Systematically, "acquisition programming" began to fill increasingly more ETV schedule time, and the quality of instructional programs began to improve. New ETV stations taking the air did so largely by virtue of the recorded materials available to them. ETV, through NET and the Educational Television Stations division of the National Association of Educational Broadcasters, has an increased quantity of high quality recorded programs available.

McBride cites the importance of higher quality, mentioning the unconscious quality-comparison made by viewers of commercial TV and ETV. Insistence upon high quality programs has been increasingly possible through the combination of individual production budgets and cooperative program planning. There is a welcome upsurge of cooperative productions under way, both regionally and nationally. Another factor in improving quality has been the growth of educational broadcasting "compacts" or television councils, unique to American education, serving elementary and secondary educational needs but with exemplars in higher education as well. There is clearly awareness at every educational level of the need for cooperative program planning. McBride concludes with a prediction of ETV broadcast station operations' growth in least populated areas, since metropolitan areas are now virtually blanketed by ETV coverage. Smaller stations will require nonlocal program sources. Growth of state-wide networks and interstate ETV interconnections will be stepped up, and there will be increased stockpiling and use of instructional materials. Undoubtedly, too, we will view combinations of live broadcast feeds, locally originated production, and widely sophisticated high quality outside "program providers," offering the ETV programmer maximized flexibility.

To be well founded, predictions for the future should take into account the research that has been done in the past. The Kittross chapter surveys the spate of ETV research and concludes that there have been few practical results from so much inquiry. To conceive, mount, and interpret significant research, well-prepared researchers must be developed and trained, with some standardization and centralization of research programs. However, Kittross is wary of the possible drain on teacher potential in lesser institutions that might result from a concentration of major research in a few universities. An answer might be mandatory enrollment by ETV specialists in research-oriented courses outside the professional schools — courses teaching the techniques and the proper subject matter of research (in this connection, the "shotgun" approach, data collection for its own sake, is cited for its fallibility).

Penury, an early rationale for inadequate research standards, ceased to be good and sufficient excuse after 1959 when the Rockefeller and Ford Foundations began to support research in the communications media. With the passage of Public Law 85-864 and Title VII, several millions were expended by the United States Office of Education in support of research, experimentation, and dissemination of information about the media. Several hundred reports from more than a thousand projects are available to educational agencies and institutions. Kittross counters the "So what?" comment by one critic of Title VII with an array of advantages deriving from this windfall to the ETV researcher. In the main, Title VII studies investigated the relative effectiveness of television teaching and conventional instruction. Time and again, "no significant differences" were discovered. Kittross suggests three answers to the "NSD" findings: (1) variable factors affecting the learning situations studied; (2) wrong questions asked and wrong factors analyzed; and (3) imprecise measuring instruments and techniques. The fact that no single experiment can answer a major research question suggests to the author that the literature of research in the field be the starting point for any investigator; the note section contains an excellent compendium of the literature of significance for educational television research. Of value to those who do conduct, have conducted, should or will conduct research are Kittross' analyses of "meaningful research": the use of models to stimulate research, the literature of research ideas in ETV, budgetary considerations, planning the study, the conduct of research on a budget, ETV station research, and learning how to do research. Kittross concludes with the charge to the ETV specialist to be a learner and a researcher, so that ETV may measure up to its promise.

The television teacher, unprotected by unions such as the American Federation of Television and Radio Artists, meets complications like those facing the professional performer: growing networks of broadcast distribution, a complex copyright law, the proprietary rights of the television teacher as originator of the material, ownership questions, residual payments due him for recorded and repeated use, etc. By the 1950's (and even more following an AFTRA strike against station WNDT in 1952), the National Education Association, American Association of University Professors, and American Council on Education had seen the handwriting on the studio wall: the television teacher had vested moral and legal interests in his television efforts: and policies regarding the right to revision, the matter of compensation (in his planning, production, and subsequent reuse of televised instructional materials), the question of ownership – all desperately required clarification.

The NEA in 1963 adopted a formal policy on ETV and the teacher; the AAUP made a 1962 general statement of position and is in the process of handing down a more formal comment. Studies have been conducted across the country providing indexes of practices relating to teacher compensation, release time, residual rights, contractual rights, and determination of ownership. A 1964 study commissioned by the American Council on Education reviewed teacher rights involving all of the instructional media. The study clearly revealed that greater attention had been given to the problem at elementary and secondary levels. Indeed, some 70 percent of the colleges and universities polled at that time had developed no contractual agreement nor a prepared policy statement. Too, roughly one-third of the college teachers involved in the study received no compensation for TV instruction, and of all TV teachers at all levels, slightly less than one-third received specific payments for specific programs. For recorded courses, few institutions made payment to the faculty members for additional utilization even though the course was licensed to, sold to, or exchanged with another institution.

Koenig recommends four directions for the television teacher and his administration, based on analysis of policies and practices: (1) the teacher should be additionally compensated for television teaching; (2) the television teacher should be compensated for each replay of his telecourse; (3) the television teacher should be granted release time for preparation and production; and (4) the teacher should retain subject matter control. Others have recommended special contracts, institutional firm policy on ETV use, and collective bargaining for achieving the teacher's rights. Koenig's view is that a national organization, a teachers' labor union, should be inaugurated in order to centralize and standardize the answering of nationally shared problems relating to teacher rights and compensation. The author concludes that lacking union assistance and support, practices will continue to vary widely, normally at the TV teacher's expense.

The starting gate to improved curricula in broadcasting is said to be the door to any institution's administration building. For, says Donner, the study of the mass media becomes viable only if central administration knows and appreciates the role of communication — the educative potential of the ubiquitous mass media. Unfortunately such understanding is not guaranteed; the label of trade school persists on some campuses, still. Donner suggests the wisdom of the establishment of a department or a school of communication as broadly based curricula normally attractive to administrators. A second consideration must be the student for whom the curriculum is fashioned. Traditionally, the career student has been the primary curricular target despite the industry's preference for liberally educated graduates who can be professionally groomed for broadcast administration. Changes in curriculum must be made to accommodate the needs of the field, to prepare students for leadership roles beyond the narrow requirement of a first job. Interdisciplinary study should be encouraged in courses involving law, criticism, writing, news preparation and analysis, while the skills courses should be clearly labeled as precareer preparation. As clearly, curricular roles at the graduate and undergraduate levels must be carefully appraised: the undergraduate student who majored in broadcasting will find little reason to specialize at the graduate level and in most cases may not be prepared to cope with advanced training.

Curricular changes will inevitably be conditioned by the attitudes as well as the competence of the faculty; and, particularly in broadcasting, curriculum improvement is tied to the adequacy of the physical plant and technical equipment. A healthy curriculum can develop only under conditions which also foster research and experimentation. Donner agrees with Kittross that a new curriculum should expose students to the literature of research and should be thoroughly conversant with methodology and techniques of inquiry.

At a time when the need for trained people in the broadcast media is greater than ever before, campuses must face the need for curricular reflection of the changing career picture. Graduates in film, as well as career-prepared specialists in advertising and public relations, share the bright prospects of the broadcasters. The range in opportunities, therefore, tends to bring together the seemingly disparate curricular functions serving both the specialist and the generalist. Donner's proposed curriculum would serve both types of student through core courses and specialized areas applicable at graduate and undergraduate levels. In appropriate circumstances, the courses would have laboratory applications and could be geared to ETV station operation.

Following upon Donner's proposals for curricula in broadcasting and film, Price discusses a specific curriculum for educational television. An undergraduate degree program could be based upon a variety of curricular patterns, and in order to provide insight into three different curricular approaches, Price outlines courses of study (1) forming an elective sequence, (2) following a core-option pattern, and (3) providing a nonspecialist major in ETV.

The ideal ETV station manager, says Loper, is the kind of paragon Schwarzwalder earlier described. He should be the electronic equivalent of a college president, a fund-raiser, a community development expert, knowledgeable in business management and broadcast law and regulation. He must be cognizant of program and production problems and be willing to accept the role of grand vizier in the station's master program design. He must lead his staff, work intimately with a board of directors. The list of qualifications is virtually endless, for the ETV station manager serves many masters, and must be master of many divergent skills.

Thus, the training of this renaissance man, increasingly in demand as new ETV stations are activated, is of paramount concern. To date, no academic program has been specifically developed to train ETV management. In the absence of academic provision, internship programs have been in operation for several years in Chicago and Boston. WGBH-TV, Boston, seeks the liberally educated college graduate with broad and well-developed tastes and with skills in organization, in writing, and in coping with station problems ranging from technical to intellectual. WTTW, in Chicago, makes its main objective the preparation of skilled production personnel.

Loper suggests that neither of these two internship programs is far-ranging enough for ETV's needs, and proposes a rather more extensive plan: (1) a national organization should establish and administer the program; (2) cooperative stations and agencies of varying sizes and functions should be identified; (3) the program should be of no less than one year's duration; and (4) the candidate should be most carefully selected, on the basis of his breadth of education and his attitude toward the profession. Interns would be exposed to extensive training seminars conducted by national leaders; an advisor would be assigned for periodic consultation; and a thorough familiarity with stations, NET, FCC, administrative and distribution centers would be required. Such a program, concludes Loper, is both feasible and necessary if there is to be a high level of professionalism in educational television.

In many cases, the classroom teacher has been lamentably unprepared to accept and effectively utilize ITV. Although this is unfortunate, there is little reason to be surprised, says Hunter, particularly after noting the less-than-optimum acceptance of educational radio or of the audiovisual media during their longer histories.

Television is a multiple medium device, combining radio, film strip, phonograph, museum, exhibit blackboard, field trip, demonstration, and the lecture. The classroom teacher can use television to see good teachers at work. Weak spots in the curriculum can be bolstered, and lesson loads can be eased by the introduction of well-prepared TV lesson plans. These are but a few of television's many flexible capabilities, all of which need to be made clear and upon occasion re-emphasized for those who use the medium in the classroom. The attitude of the teacher toward television is vital to its acceptance by the pupils, for if the teacher on the TV monitor is depreciated by his colleague in the classroom, the value of televised instruction may well be correspondingly minimized. It is essential for the classroom teacher to be aware of the true role of the television teacher, to have some knowledge of studio procedure and of research results in the field, and to have a basic familiarity with the various learning theories.

"Clearly," says Hunter, "teaching involves far more than presenting information or making demonstrations, and the complete teaching function is beyond the capacity of any electronic device." Discussion between the television teacher and the students being impossible, television should become a springboard for eager classroom discussion led by the classroom teacher. To make television an effective instructional tool, training in its utilization is as necessary for the classroom teacher as for the studio teacher; and school administrations must give wise attention to problems of scheduling and physical planning.

Man and his institutions have always resisted and distrusted technological change. Author Barber remarks upon the "institutional lag" between our present capacity for instantaneous global communication and its useful application to the universal problems of our time, and he devotes his chapter to an examination of potentials and obstacles foreseen for educational television by satellite. ETVS is now both possible and practical. However, the chances are that it will not soon fulfill its potential. Financial support is crucial and as yet uncertain. The multimillion dollar commitment of funds that ETVS will require suggests the necessity of government involvement, and Barber discusses various current proposals for the financing of ETVS.

Certain other problems which ETVS faces are likely to endure longer in their present forms. It will be desirable to standardize world television systems to ease the establishment of international television by satellite; this will presuppose some form of international control. The change in spatial relationships which communication by satellite will bring to our planet will make itself felt in the social order and in governmental, industrial, and educational organizations of all countries. However, the potential of ETVS is quite different for the underdeveloped countries from what it is for highly developed, media-saturated countries. Barber analyzes the economic feasibility of ETVS and concludes that the system would have distinct advantages in speeding up universal education in emerging nations.

Speculation on the role the United States will play in the establishment of an ETVS system is difficult. Barber discusses the areas where policy must be established and notes some recent developments that will help shape the future of ETVS in America. He ends by expressing his hope that the American government will provide the necessary leadership and assistance to assure educational television by satellite for the rest of the world.

During the two years in which this book has been in progress, we have seen major interest expressed in ETV by the Carnegie Commission and the Ford Foundation, and innovative legislation presented to Congress by the President of the United States. It is very likely that before the publication date of this book, a Public Broadcasting law will have been enacted. To the editors, this dramatic activity exceeds in quantity and concern anything in ETV's history since the first channels were made available through the FCC's *Sixth Report and Order* in 1952. Our purpose has been to seize upon this transitional moment to examine the problems, performance, and promise of educational television. The problems are by now painfully clear: program quality, financing, distribution, research and experimentation, training of personnel, utilization — all in relation to a rapidly changing image. In performance, ETV is evolving toward an ever more sophisticated programming cooperatively produced by state, regional, and national organizations. The promise of ETV is most excitingly manifest in the medium's international role. Distance dies, with satellite communication, and dreams of universal education and world-wide understanding seem attainable.

More immediately, the promise of ETV is implicit in what has been written here regarding the problems and issues and the achievements of the medium. However, it may be profitable to speculate briefly about the future. We can see the probabilities of a truly international ETV system, realizing television's potentials in serving educational needs throughout the world. Live interconnected national programs will be possible among the eventual 250 NET stations foreseen. Rather than dominant use of open-circuit instructional television there will be increased use of closed-circuit systems serving campuses and communities, and also wider acceptance for the use of the 2500 megacycle band through Instructional Television Fixed Service. Continued technical innovation such as miniaturized cameras, transmitters, receivers, etc., will make ETV ever more ubiquitous. As these systems become more flexible and versatile, information retrieval via satellite activation of computer-based "libraries" will be possible, and even computer-assisted instruction via ETVS will one day be a viable educational tool. With so much information available from so many sources, it can be presumed that educational stations will one day share their commercial confreres' problems of network option times and of program acceptance or rejection.

The question of ETV financing may be satisfied in large part by funds assigned under the Public Broadcasting Act. Increasingly, ETV's problems will center on the preparation of personnel for the medium, and colleges and universities will accept their responsibilities as major providers of such specialists.

Although ETV may have been characterized, until this point in time, as having more problems than promise, the future of ETV as a dominant electronic medium affecting many millions of people throughout the world seems bright enough for the editors to close on a note of supreme optimism.

REFERENCE MATTER

The Findings of the Carnegie Commission on Educational Television

IN January 1967, the Carnegie Commission on Educational Television issued twelve recommendations for "public television," based on a yearlong study financed by the Carnegie Corporation. The general objectives of the study were endorsed by the President of the United States; its principal focus was on programming of a community type. The Commission recommended that a "public television" corporation be established as a national educational television service. "Public Television . . . includes all that is of human interest and importance which is not at the moment appropriate or available for support by advertising, and which is not arranged for formal instruction." Such a proposed system is unique; it does not emulate either the commercial, or the British, or the Japanese systems of broadcasting.

The Carnegie Commission on Educational Television's report has been published by Bantam Books, Inc., and is entitled *Public Television: A Program for Action*. With permission from the Carnegie Corporation the study's twelve recommendations are reprinted:

1. We recommend concerted efforts at the federal, state, and local levels to improve the facilities and to provide for the adequate

support of the individual educational television stations and to increase their number.

2. We recommend that Congress act promptly to authorize and to establish a federally chartered, nonprofit, nongovernmental corporation, to be known as the "Corporation for Public Television." The Corporation should be empowered to receive and disburse governmental and private funds in order to extend and improve Public Television programming. The Commission considers the creation of the Corporation fundamental to its proposal and would be most reluctant to recommend the other parts of its plan unless the corporate entity is brought into being.

3. We recommend that the Corporation support at least two national production centers, and that it be free to contract with independent producers to prepare Public Television programs for educational television stations.

4. We recommend that the Corporation support, by appropriate grants and contracts, the production of Public Television programs, by local stations for more-than-local use.

5. We recommend that the Corporation on appropriate occasions help support local programming by local stations.

6. We recommend that the Corporation provide the educational television system as expeditiously as possible with facilities for live interconnection by conventional means, and that it be enabled to benefit from advances in technology as domestic communications satellites are brought into being. The Commission further recommends that Congress act to permit the granting of preferential rates for educational television for the use of interconnection facilities, or to permit their free use, to the extent that this may not be possible under existing law.

7. We recommend that the Corporation encourage and support research and development leading to the improvement of programming and program production.

8. We recommend that the Corporation support technical experimentation designed to improve the present television technology.

9. We recommend that the Corporation undertake to provide means by which technical, artistic, and specialized personnel may be recruited and trained.

10. We recommend that Congress provide the federal funds required by the Corporation through a manufacturer's excise tax on television sets (beginning at 2 percent and rising to a ceiling of 5 percent). The revenues should be made available to the Corporation through a trust fund.

11. We recommend new legislation to enable the Department of Health, Education, and Welfare to provide adequate facilities for stations now in existence, to assist in increasing the number of stations to achieve nationwide coverage, to help support the basic operations of all stations, and to enlarge the support of instructional television programming.

12. We recommend that federal, state, local, and private educational agencies sponsor extensive and innovative studies intended to develop better insights into the use of television in formal and informal education.

The Public Broadcasting Act Of 1967*

IN general, the Public Broadcasting Act of 1967 has three purposes: (1) to extend the program of grants for construction of noncommercial educational television broadcasting facilities and authorize a program of grants for construction of noncommercial educational radio broadcasting facilities, (2) to establish and finance a nonprofit corporation to assist program operations in noncommercial educational television and radio, and (3) to authorize a study of instructional broadcasting and its relationship to the total educational broadcasting system.

CONSTRUCTION OF FACILITIES

(Title I)

Title IV, Part III of the Communications Act of 1934 (47 U.S.C. 391-397) would be amended by title I of the bill:

1. To extend its provisions through fiscal year 1972, with $10,500,000 authorized for fiscal year 1968 and such sums as may be necessary authorized for the next four fiscal years.

*Based on a document supplied by the Department of Health, Education, and Welfare; revised by the editors to conform with the approved U.S. Senate Bill 1160 of May 1967.

2. To replace the $1,000,000 per State limit with a State limit annually of 12½ percent of the total appropriation for grants in that fiscal year.

3. To authorize grants for construction of noncommercial educational radio as well as television facilities.

4. To increase the maximum allowable Federal share in project costs from 50 percent to 75 percent and to eliminate the additional 25 percent credit for the cost of broadcasting facilities owned by the applicant before the date of filing his application.

5. To extend the territorial coverage to the Virgin Islands, Guam, American Samoa, and the Trust Territory of the Pacific Islands.

6. To extend the scope of eligible project costs to include planning of the acquisition and installation of transmission apparatus as well as the costs of actual acquisition and installation itself.

ESTABLISHMENT OF NONPROFIT EDUCATIONAL BROADCASTING CORPORATION

(Title II)

1. Title II of the Public Broadcasting Act of 1967 amends part III of title IV of the Communications Act of 1934 to authorize the establishment of a nonprofit private corporation (the Corporation for Public Broadcasting).

2. The Corporation would have a Board of Directors of 15 members: 9 appointed by the President with the advice and consent of the Senate, 6 elected by the appointed board. The members must be citizens of the United States selected from fields such as education, cultural and civic affairs, or the arts, including radio and television (3 members must come from educational broadcasting); and must be representative of various regions of the country, professions, and occupations, and kinds of experience and talent, appropriate to the Corporation's functions and responsibilities. The members of the Board would serve six-year staggered terms. Each year (except the first year) one of the members would be

elected by the Board to serve as Chairman and one or more would be elected to serve as vice chairmen.

3. In addition to the Board of Directors, the Corporation would have a president and other necessary officers; and no political test or qualification could be used in selecting, promoting, or taking other personnel actions with respect to the Corporation's officers, employees, or agents.

4. The Corporation would be nonprofit and it would have no power to engage in any political activity.

5. The Corporation may assist in the establishment and development of a system of intercommunication for distribution of public and instructional programs among noncommercial educational television and radio stations.

6. In carrying out the above purposes, the Corporation would have the usual powers conferred on District of Columbia nonprofit corporations and could:

(a) Accept grants and enter into contracts with other agencies and institutions;

(b) Contract for production or procurement of educational television and radio programs for distribution to educational television and radio stations;

(c) Make payments to noncommercial educational television and radio stations for programming and other operating costs;

(d) Establish and maintain libraries and archives for noncommercial educational television and radio programs;

(e) Publicize and disseminate information on educational television and radio;

(f) Support interconnection facilities for distributing and transmitting instructional and public television or radio programs;

(g) Encourage the creation of new noncommercial educational television or radio stations.

7. The Corporation could not own or operate any television or radio broadcast stations, system, or network, or CATV system, interconnection, or program production facility.

8. Nothing in the Communications Act of 1934 could be construed to prohibit U.S. communications common carriers from rendering free or reduced rate interconnection services for noncommercial educational television and radio services, in accordance with FCC rules and regulations.

9. Annual reports of its operations and on its condition would be made to Congress by the Corporation.

10. For fiscal year 1968, $9,000,000 would be authorized to be appropriated and for fiscal year 1969, such sums as may be necessary, to assist the Corporation in carrying out its activities. These appropriations would remain available until expended.

STUDY OF EDUCATIONAL AND INSTRUCTIONAL TV BROADCASTING

(Title III)

Title III of the Public Broadcasting Act of 1967 authorizes the Secretary of Health, Education, and Welfare to conduct or contract for a study of instructional radio and television and their relationship to one another and their role with other educational media. This report shall be submitted to the Congress on or before June 30, 1969. An appropriation of such sums as may be necessary (but not exceeding $500,000) is authorized for this purpose.

Index

AAUP. *See* American Association of University Professors

ABC. *See* American Broadcasting Company

Adelphi College, 143

Adler Electronics, 145

Affiliates of NET, 97–105

AFTRA. *See* American Federation of Television and Radio Artists

Alabama ETV Authority, 296

American Association of University Professors, 248, 249, 253, 254, 255, 257, 258, 348

American Broadcasting Company, 137, 316, 329, 331

American Council on Education, 5, 139, 140, 213, 249, 252, 253, 256, 257, 348

American Federation of Teachers, 258

American Federation of Television and Radio Artists, 247, 248, 249, 257, 258, 259, 348

American Telephone and Telegraph, 103, 119, 206, 328, 330, 331, 332

American university system, philosophy of, 52–55

Arnheim, Rudolph, 18, 19, 21

Association for Education by Radio-TV, 139

Association for Professional Broadcasting Education, 294

Association of Land Grant Colleges and Universities, 139

AT&T. *See* American Telephone and Telegraph

Audience of ETV, 44, 45, 71

British Broadcasting Company, 3

British Television Research Committee, 217

Broadcasting stations: KCET, Los Angeles, 77, 110; KCTS, Seattle, 51, 77; KOMU, Columbia, Mo., 64, 65; KQED, San Francisco, 110; KUAT, Tucson, 77; KUHT, Houston, 6, 169; W9XAK, Kansas State, 134; W9XG, Purdue, 134; W9XK, Iowa City, 5, 134, 160; WBKB, Chicago, 137; WCAU, Philadelphia, 137; WCBB, Augusta, Me., 109; WCBW, New York, 136; WEDH, Hartford, 109; WENH, Durham, N.H., 108; WETA, Washington, 77, 118; WEWS, Cleveland, 137; WFIL, Philadelphia, 137; WGBH, Boston, 108, 109, 294, 295, 351; WHA, Madison, Wis., 169, 321; WHBQ, Memphis, 64; WHCU, Ithaca, 64; WHYY, Wilmington, 109, 137; WJCT, Jacksonville, 77; WKAR, Michigan State, 169; WMEB, Orono, Me., 109; WMHT, Schenectady, 109; WMSB, East Lansing, 77; WNDT, New York, 77; WNED, Buffalo, 77; WNYE, New York, 136; WOI, Ames, 64, 136; WOW, Omaha, 138; WPTZ, Philadelphia, 137; WQED, Pittsburgh, 109; WSUI, Iowa City, 134, 160; WTTW, Chicago, 77, 110, 142,

294, 351; WUHY, Philadelphia, 137; WWJ, Detroit, 138; WXBU, Kansas State, 136
Brookings Institute, 313
Bundy, McGeorge, 330
Burke, Kenneth, 27

Carnegie Commission on Educational Television, 8, 73, 74–75, 76, 95, 103, 112, 148, 204, 273, 314, 331, 332, 333, 354, 359–61
CATV. See Community antenna television
CBS. See Columbia Broadcasting System
CCTV. See Closed-circuit television
Centre for Educational Television Overseas, 273
Charyk, Joseph V., 330
Chelsea Closed-Circuit Television Project, 172–73
Chicago City TV College, 202
"Chicago style," 18
Closed-circuit television, 4, 142, 143, 145, 155–79, 344
Cohen, Edwin G., 178
"College of the Air," 138
Colombia television project, 146, 273
Color television, 95–96, 122–23, 165, 166
Columbia Broadcasting System, 136, 137, 138, 174, 313, 331, 332
Comité Européen de Poste et Télégraphe, 328
Committee on Institutional Cooperation of the Big Ten and University of Chicago, 203–4
Communications Satellite Corporation, 206, 327, 328, 329, 330, 331, 332, 333
Communist nations, and ETV, 3
Community antenna television, 119, 148, 272
Community stations, 45–48, 69–78, 79–86, 338, 339, 340

Comsat. See Communications Satellite Corporation
"Continental Classroom," 138–39
Corporation for Public Television, 95, 103, 360–61
Cortland County Closed-Circuit Television Project, 174
Council on Higher Educational Institutions, 204
Council on Medical Television, 143

Delayed programming, 7, 174
Dial-access retrieval, 178
Disney, Walt, 28–29
Dumont Laboratories, 141, 165, 171

Early Bird Satellite, 177, 314, 321, 328
Eastern Educational Network, 8, 107–29, 200, 203, 296, 342
Educational Television and Radio Center, 87, 88, 94, 98. See also National Educational Television
Educational television by satellite, 312–34, 353
Educational Television Facilities Act, 35, 111, 119, 148, 205
Educational Television Stations (of NAEB), 115, 120, 124, 201, 206, 296, 346
EEN. See Eastern Educational Network
Einstein, Albert, 17, 311
Elementary and Secondary Education Act, 35, 76, 118, 147
Emerging nations, ETV in, 4, 146–47, 273, 319–20, 323–25, 353
ETS. See Educatioinal Television Stations
ETVS. See Educational television by satellite
Eurovision, 315, 321, 322

FAE. See Fund for the Advancement of Education

FCC. *See* Federal Communications Commission

Federal Communications Act, 64

Federal Communications Commission: application to, for channels, 4; "freeze," 5, 12, 139, 163, 167, 169, 272; *Sixth Report and Order*, 5–6, 163, 327, 354; licensing, 38, 51, 52, 100, 134, 144, 159, 161, 190, 233; noncommercial channel reservation, 55, 87, 140, 343; 1944 hearings, 135; establishes ITFS, 145, 343; mentioned, 296, 330, 331, 352

Federal Radio Commission, 134

Feedback: lack of, in ETV, 22–24

Film, misuse of, 27, 28, 29

Financing of ETV, 6, 8, 41, 48, 49, 51, 52, 127, 128, 185–95, 345

Ford Foundation, 8, 87, 88, 95, 100, 103, 108, 141, 144, 146, 199, 204, 206, 214, 314, 330, 331, 333, 340, 347, 354

Fourth network, 89, 90

Friendly, Fred, 8, 337

Fund for the Advancement of Education, 87, 141, 142, 170, 171, 214, 343

"GIGO," "garbage in–garbage out" concept, 178, 320

Great Plains Regional ITV Library, 8, 125, 145, 146, 175, 200, 201, 202, 203

Harding College, 64

Hawthorne effect, 219

Hennock, Freida, 140

Higher Education Act, 35, 147

Hughes Aircraft Company, dual mode proposal, 319

Institute for Advancement of Medical Education, 143

Instructional television, 11, 38, 49, 117, 119, 133–49, 155, 197, 198, 201, 203, 204, 211, 312–13, 343–44, 354

Instructional Television Fixed Service, 4, 6, 117, 145, 148, 343, 354

Intermedical TV Network, 142

International Business Machines, 149

International Institute for Educational Planning, 147

International Telecommunication Union 1963 Conference, 315

ITFS. *See* Instructional Television Fixed Service

Ithaca College, 137

ITV. *See* Instructional television

JCET. *See* Joint Council on Educational Television

Johnson, President Lyndon B., 8, 95, 148, 331

Joint Council on Educational Television, 139, 140, 343

Junior College of Chicago, 142

Kennedy, President John F., 29, 224

Killian, James R., Jr., 332

Kinescope recording systems in ETV, 198

Labor unions, and TV teachers, 249, 255, 257–58

Learning process, nature of, 303

Lincoln Center for the Performing Arts, 94

Lippmann, Walter, 149

McLuhan, Marshall, 18, 19, 20, 21, 27, 28, 224, 311

Magnuson, Senator Warren G., 327

Management of ETV stations, 79–86, 294–97

Metromedia, 113

Metropolitan Museum of Art, 136

Midwestern Educational Television network, 125, 203, 346

Midwest Program for Airborne Television Instruction, 144, 200, 203, 318–19, 324, 246
Montclair State Teachers College, 141
MPATI. *See* Midwest Program for Airborne Television Instruction

NAEB. *See* National Association of Educational Broadcasters
National Association of Educational Broadcasters, 5, 115, 139, 146, 147, 204, 294, 297, 333, 334, 346
National Association of State Universities, 139
National Broadcasting Company, 113, 138, 139, 162, 313, 331
National Center for School and College Television, 8, 111, 118, 124, 146, 175, 178, 201, 296
National Council of Chief State School Officers, 139
National Defense Education Act (1958), 111, 147, 199, 214, 215 — (1963), 306
National Educational Television: mode of operation, 7; financial support, 8; as the fourth network, 87–96; affiliates, 87, 88, 89, 97–106, 341; and EEN, 115, 124; interconnection tests, 206; summary of goals and achievements, 340–41; mentioned, 58, 59, 297, 346, 352, 354
National Educational Television and Radio Center, 88, 198. *See also* National Educational Television
National Education Association, 138, 139, 248–49, 250, 252, 257, 258, 348
National Information Center for Educational Media, 149
National Instructional Television Library, 115, 146, 200, 201
National Program Foundation, 140, 146

National Project for the Improvement of Televised Instruction, 146
NBC. *See* National Broadcasting Company
NCSCT. *See* National Center for School and College Television
NDEA. *See* National Defense Education Act
NEA. *See* National Education Association
NET. *See* National Educational Television
Noncommercial television, 187, 189, 191–95
Nonprofit television, 185–88
Northeastern Regional Instructional Television Library Project, 111, 115, 146, 200, 203
"No significant difference," findings, 13, 217–20, 347
NRITLP. *See* Northeastern Regional Instructional Television Library Project
NSD. *See* "No significant difference"

Peace Corps, 4, 146
Pedagovision system, 321
Program Service of Educational Television Stations, 115, 124
Public Broadcasting Act, 8, 354, 355, 363–66
Public Broadcast Laboratory, 103, 206
Public television, 103, 112, 148, 332, 359, 360
Public Television, Corporation for, 95, 103, 360–61

Radio, educational, 11, 12
Radio Corporation of America, 134, 149
Radiodiffusion Télévision Française, 3
"Radio House," 138
Ratings for commercial TV and ETV, 23, 63, 65

RCA. *See* Radio Corporation of America
Redundancy, 24, 25
Regional networks, 107–29
Research in ETV, 15, 209–45, 271–72, 302, 346–47
Rockefeller Foundation, 214, 347

Samoa, American, 147, 273
Sarnoff, David, 134
Satellites, communication, 8, 103, 123, 126, 177, 178, 312–34, 353, 360
School stations, 36–38, 338
Schramm, Wilbur, 37, 71, 139, 218, 219, 221, 225, 316
Screen Actors Guild, role in commercial TV, 247
Screen size, effect on ETV, 26, 27
Seldes, Gilbert, 63
Simultaneity of television, 29, 30
Skornia, Harry, 212
State stations, 39–42, 338
State-wide ETV networks, 36, 39, 40, 41, 42
Subliminal perception techniques, 224
"Sunrise Semester," 138–39
System Development Corporation, multimedia research, 225

Telescuola, 3
TEMP. *See* Texas Educational Microwave Project
Texas Educational Microwave Project, 143, 176, 204
Time, Inc., 149
TV Programs Institute, 140

UHF (ultra high frequency), 6, 12, 87, 163, 171, 272, 315

Underdeveloped countries, ETV in, 146–47, 273, 319–20, 323–25, 353
UNESCO: conference on space communications, 316, 319, 320, 326; role in ETVS, 333
United States Department of Health, Education, and Welfare, 296, 361
United States Office of Education, 5, 111, 115, 118, 139, 145, 199, 203, 215, 306, 347
Universities: American, 5; Boston, 212; Brandeis, 145; California, 135; Columbia, 214 Connecticut, 144; Cornell, 64; Creighton, 138; Houston, 6; Illinois, 212; Indiana, 201; Iowa, 5, 133; Iowa State, 5, 64, 136; Kansas, 143; Kansas State, 5, 134, 136; Michigan, 5, 138; Michigan State, 169, 212, 215, 252; Missouri, 64, 65; Nebraska, 145, 199, 200; North Carolina, 135; Ohio, 135; Pennsylvania State, 140, 221; Purdue, 34, 114; Southern California, 149, 227, 228; Stanford, 212; Texas, 138; Washington, 51; Wayne State, 64; Western Reserve, 137, 221; Wisconsin, 53, 169, 212, 221, 321
University stations, 42–44, 51–67, 338–39

Van Hise, Charles, 53
VHF (very high frequency), 6, 12, 87, 157, 163, 171
Videotape, 29, 164, 165, 174–76, 199, 201
Video-tutorial laboratories, 178

Washington County Closed-Circuit Television Project, 172

Xerox Corporation, 149